1997
AN EXTRAORDINARY YEAR
JUST WAITING FOR YOU!

Chart your very own star-studded course to love, adventure, good health, or good fortune with Sydney Omarr's amazingly accurate forecast for every aspect of your life. Offering 18 full months of on-target predictions from July 1996 to December 1997, this remarkable guide shows you:

—How to make your love connections strong and sexy
—Astrology's first-aid kit for patching up a broken heart
—How the power of eclipses affects your life
—How to fine-tune your life by coordinating your activities with the rhythms of the universe
—How to use the moon and planets for prosperity
—How to relieve stress and live a healthier life

Enter Sydney Omarr's fascinating world of astrology and discover what this world-renowned expert is dicting for your life—for today and for every da 1997!

SYDNEY OMARR'S DAY-BY-DAY ASTROLOGICAL GUIDE FOR

ARIES—March 21–April 19
TAURUS—April 20–May 20
GEMINI—May 21–June 20
CANCER—June 21–July 22
LEO—July 23–August 22
VIRGO—August 23–September 22
LIBRA—September 23–October 22
SCORPIO—October 23–November 21
SAGITTARIUS—November 22–December 21
CAPRICORN—December 22–January 19
AQUARIUS—January 20–February 18
PISCES—February 19–March 20

IN 1997

S0-AFT-776

SYDNEY OMARR'S 1996 DAY-BY-DAY ASTROLOGICAL GUIDES
18 Months of Daily Horoscopes From
July 1996 to December 1997

Let America's most accurate astrologer show you what the signs of the zodiac and Pluto's welcome transit into Sagittarius will mean for you in 1996! Sydney Omarr gives you invaluable tips on your love life, your career, your health—and your all-round good fortune.

☐ **Aquarius**—January 20–February 18   (188292—$4.99)

☐ **Pisces**—February 19–March 20   (188365—$4.99)

☐ **Aries**—March 21–April 19   (188284—$4.99)

☐ **Taurus**—April 20–May 20   (188381—$4.99)

☐ **Gemini**—May 21–June 20   (188322—$4.99)

☐ **Cancer**—June 21–July 22   (188314—$4.99)

☐ **Leo**—July 23–August 22   (188349—$4.99)

☐ **Virgo**—August 23–September 22   (188403—$4.99)

☐ **Libra**—September 23–October 22   (188330—$4.99)

☐ **Scorpio**—October 23–November 21   (188373—$4.99)

☐ **Sagittarius**—November 22–December 21   (188357—$4.99)

☐ **Capricorn**—December 22–January 19   (188306—$4.99)

Buy them at your local bookstore or use this convenient coupon for ordering.

PENGUIN USA
P.O. Box 999 — Dept. #17109
Bergenfield, New Jersey 07621

Please send me the books I have checked above.
I am enclosing $_____ (please add $2.00 to cover postage and handling). Send check or money order (no cash or C.O.D.'s) or charge by Mastercard or VISA (with a $15.00 minimum). Prices and numbers are subject to change without notice.

Card #_____ Exp. Date _____
Signature_____
Name_____
Address_____
City _____ State _____ Zip Code _____

For faster service when ordering by credit card call **1-800-253-6476**

Allow a minimum of 4-6 weeks for delivery. This offer is subject to change without notice.

SYDNEY OMARR'S

DAY-BY-DAY ASTROLOGICAL GUIDE FOR

CAPRICORN

December 22–January 19

1997

A SIGNET BOOK

SIGNET
Published by the Penguin Group
Penguin Books USA Inc., 375 Hudson Street,
New York, New York 10014, U.S.A.
Penguin Books Ltd, 27 Wrights Lane,
London W8 5TZ, England
Penguin Books Australia Ltd, Ringwood,
Victoria, Australia
Penguin Books Canada Ltd, 10 Alcorn Avenue,
Toronto, Ontario, Canada M4V 3B2
Penguin Books (N.Z.) Ltd, 182–190 Wairau Road,
Auckland 10, New Zealand

Penguin Books Ltd, Registered Offices:
Harmondsworth, Middlesex, England

First published by Signet, an imprint of Dutton Signet,
a division of Penguin Books USA Inc.

First Printing, July, 1996
10 9 8 7 6 5 4 3 2 1

Copyright © Sydney Omarr, 1996
All rights reserved

Sydney Omarr is syndicated worldwide by
Los Angeles Times Syndicate.
Cover art by Faranak

 REGISTERED TRADEMARK—MARCA REGISTRADA

Printed in the United States of America

Without limiting the rights under copyright reserved above, no part of this
publication may be reproduced, stored in or introduced into a retrieval system, or transmitted, in any form, or by any means (electronic, mechanical,
photocopying, recording, or otherwise), without the prior written permission
of both the copyright owner and the above publisher of this book.

BOOKS ARE AVAILABLE AT QUANTITY DISCOUNTS WHEN USED TO PROMOTE
PRODUCTS OR SERVICES. FOR INFORMATION PLEASE WRITE TO PREMIUM MAR-
KETING DIVISION, PENGUIN BOOKS USA INC., 375 HUDSON STREET, NEW YORK,
NEW YORK 10014.

If you purchased this book without a cover you should be aware that this
book is stolen property. It was reported as "unsold and destroyed" to the
publisher and neither the author nor the publisher has received any payment
for this "stripped book."

Contents

INTRODUCTION

Getting Interactive with Astrology

Astrology is becoming more interactive than ever in '97, as the global community of astrology fans are connecting via E-mail, the Internet, online classes, and conferences all over the world. And the good news is you don't have to be a professional astrologer to jump into the action. Just use this book as your user-friendly guide. It gives you the language, the symbols, and the basic knowledge and resources (including computer resources) to put astrology into your life every day. Plus, you'll also find fun information to help you find and understand a lover, make the most of your sun sign potential, and boost your career prospects.

Like millions of Americans who turn to astrology for fun, curiosity, or guidance, you're in for a fascinating experiences as you explore the cosmos in this unique way. Unlike other arts or sciences, astrology can give you specific details on who you are and where you're going and immediate practical advice on how to deal with the whole range of problems and situations that crop up in daily life. It's no wonder that the lure of discovering a real human connection with the universe has kept people in all walks of life, from tycoons to the man on the street, intrigued with astrology.

As you discover astrology for yourself, you'll learn that, far from being a vague, intuitive art shrouded in mystery, it is quite a precise language that communicates in a very orderly and specific way. Yet it retains a sense of wonder and mystery. We marvel at how those faraway planets can tell us so much about ourselves with such uncanny accuracy! But haven't there been times when

7

you've felt an unexplained pull in a certain direction, or when everything seems to be going haywire and nobody seems to understand you, or yet other times when you seem to have hit a lucky roll? Astrology offers explanations to these baffling conditions, points out trends and cycles, and suggests solutions to difficulties or alternative courses to take. It brings the happenings in the universe down to human terms, though it never dictates a moral code or involves the worship of deities.

Though it is a precise and demanding study, no one can deny that there is a mysterious spiritual quality about astrology. And, because it is often used for prediction, it has been the subject of much misunderstanding through the ages, especially when fortune tellers and unscrupulous practitioners masqueraded under its banner. Today, astrology has become recognized as a respectable endeavor practiced by qualified professionals who don't gaze into crystal balls, tell fortunes, or operate out of gypsy caravans. Most of the ten thousand or more astrologers in the United States are serious consultants accredited by one of several reputable astrological associations.

Working with precise scientific calculations, usually done by computer, today's professional astrologer adds interpretive insight that goes beyond the scientific dimension. This requires great skill and knowledge of human behavior, relationships, and planetary happenings—which is why leaders of government and corporations, bankers, and dictators often consider astrological conditions before making major decisions.

When forecasts and predictions are involved, some inevitable questions arise, such as: Where do I fit in? How much free will do I have? Can I do anything about an unfavorable forecast? Or, on a supposedly critical day, why did everything go smoothly?

The responsible astrologer will answer: you make the difference and the decisions. Astrology can point the directions, give you clues about the kind of energy prevailing on a specific day, put events in a grand perspective, so they seem easier to handle. But what you do with this knowledge is up to you.

Can you study and use astrology on your own? Why not? This book will give you basic tools for taking your own personal voyage through the zodiac. You'll be amazed how even a basic knowledge of astrology gives you valuable insights about others. Your most important tool is your own horoscope, a map of the heavens based on the happenings at the moment you were born. This tells you about your potential in every area of life, what talents to develop, where to look for a profitable career, even what kind of partner to choose for business and love. It can target your trouble spots in relationships, giving you clues about why you have difficulty communicating with someone and how to improve the situation. It can help you improve the quality of your life by giving you hints about health and how to make the most of your strengths to protect yourself from stress, to make the most of your physical appearance.

Then there is the matter of timing. Astrology helps you pick the perfect moment to initiate a plan, sign a contract, go to a party, meet someone special or close a deal. It's all based on an understanding of the way the energies of the planets are acting and interacting at a given time. This book will explain what forces are harmonizing or conflicting. It reveals which planet affects your communications for better or worse and what the 1997 outlook will be. You'll learn which phase of the moon is best for starting new ventures, and when to expect a major transition in your life. Starting with the groundwork of astrology, you can learn to speak its language and discover what those baffling signs and symbols really mean. Then we'll explore the horoscope—how each planetary force affects you and the events in your life. The fun part comes next, as you learn what you really want to know about picking a partner, as well your chances for being rich and famous, by simply playing up the strengths of your sign and playing down its weaknesses. We'll even show you how to set up a success timetable for 1997 to benefit from positive planetary influences.

For your day-to-day living, there are fifteen months of personal predictions. Each day there are highlights of the planetary, lunar, and numerical cycles, as they relate to your sign with custom-blended interpretations. What's more, you'll find the daily moon sign and lucky numbers for significant days.

So, whether you're new to astrology or a regular reader, let this guide help you discover the many ways astrology can help you get ahead this year. May the stars light your way to the happiest, healthiest year ever!

CHAPTER 1

Breaking In to Astrology: The Rules of the Road

Astrology is like a fascinating foreign country, with a language all its own, territory that's easy to get lost in, and natives with unique personalities. For hundreds of years, astrology was secret and even dangerous territory. It began as a priestly art, practiced by scholar-priests entrusted with timing sacred ceremonies. Early man noticed that certain heavenly bodies moved, and that events seemed to coincide with these movements, mainly the changing of the seasons. As observation continued over the centuries, other events in our personal and collective life were observed to correlate as well, and astrology was born. From the beginning, astrology was studied for its relationship to our daily life, as summed up by the ancient maxim "As above, so below." Later, the study of the stars were undertaken for its own sake, and astrology became what we now know as astronomy. Throughout history, it has cycled between periods of favor and disfavor, banned by churches and dismissed by scientists, yet astrology has survived the ages, continuing to confound its critics and fascinate everyone. Why? Very simply, because so many have found that it works!

Now, astrology is open to anyone who has the interest. Clubs, computer programs, study groups in every major city and shelves full of astrology books have brought this ancient art into the mainstream. While it takes years of study and practice reading thousands of charts to become an expert, you can derive much pleasure, as well as self-knowledge, from learning the basic way astrology works.

It's not difficult to break into astrology. Whether

you're planning a brief visit or a lengthy, intensive study, this guide can provide you with the rules of the road, a get-acquainted tour that will help you set off on exciting adventures on your own.

The Highway: Signs and Signposts

The Zodiac, which comes from the Greek word meaning "circle of animals," is an imaginary 360–degree highway circling around the earth, divided into twelve equal 30–degree signs. The signs begin at zero degrees Aries, at the point where the sun crosses the equator at the vernal equinox, and end with the last degree of Pisces.

The signs got their names from the constellations of stars, mostly named after mythological animals or sea creatures, which originally marked off each sign's territory. However, over the centuries, the earth's orbit has shifted so that the constellations are no longer true signposts.

A sun sign is the 30–degree segment that the sun is passing through (from our point of view on Earth) at any given moment. Most people think of themselves astrologically in terms of their sun sign. For instance, "I'm an Aries" means that the sun was in Aries when that person was born. However, there are nine other planets that also form our total astrological personality, and some or many of these will be located in other signs. No one is completely Aries, with all ten planets in one sign! Note here that in astrology, the sun and moon are called planets, even though the sun is a star and the moon is a satellite.

How We Define a Sign: The Raw Materials of Our Vehicle

There is a wonderful math-magic in astrology based on the number twelve. This number has been significant in mystical lore throughout history. Think of the twelve tribes of Israel or the twelve apostles. Astrologers have even given each of the twelve apostles a sign of the zodiac—impulsive St. Peter is supposed to be Aries, for instance.

The way each sign is defined is based on the numbers that can divide into twelve: four, three, and two. There are four building blocks, or elements, which describe the physical concept of the sign (therefore three signs of each element). Its quality describes the way each sign acts, and there are three qualities (four signs of each quality). Finally, polarity describes the electrical charge of each sign, also known as masculine/feminine, yin/yang, positive/negative. And since there are two polarities, there are six signs of each.

Each element, quality, and polarity alternates around the zodiac, and, as it ends up, no combination is repeated. The zodiac is perfectly balanced, so every kind of energy can be fully expressed. Nothing predominates—despite what some astrologers may say, there are no good or bad or extreme signs. Each sign is vitally necessary for the whole circle to function. There is a place for each sign that fits perfectly into the total scheme of the zodiac.

Astrological territory is made up of the elements of our planet: earth, water, fire, and air. These are the very same elements that make up our physical bodies and that we need to survive. But in astrology, the elements are used symbolically to describe concepts that link our body and psyche to the rhythms of the planets and the phases of the moon.

Each sign is assigned one of the four elements, starting with Aries, which becomes the first fire sign, then following with earth, air, and water signs repeating in that sequence around the zodiac.

How Your Element Fuels Your Sign

Fire is the raw material of Aries, Leo, and Sagittarius. Like their element, fire signs spread warmth and enthusiasm. They are able to fire up or motivate others. They have hot, explosive tempers. These are people of action who make ideas or people come to life.

Earth is the fuel of Taurus, Virgo, and Capricorn. Earth signs are the builders of the zodiac. These are the signs that follow through after the initiative of fire signs to make things happen. These signs are solid, practical realists. They enjoy material things and sensual pleasures.

Air is the fuel of Gemini, Libra, and Aquarius. Air signs are idea people, great communicators, mental and sociable. These are the signs that reach out after the consolidation of earth signs to inspire others with mental concepts, through the use of words, colors, pictures. They thrive on social contact, discussion, debate.

Water is the fuel of Cancer, Scorpio, and Pisces. Water completes each four-sign cycle with the element of emotions, compassion, sensitive feelings, and imagination. Water signs are nonverbal communicators, poets, and artists.

A Quality Shows How A Sign Operates

Is the sign a reckless driver, given to speeding tickets, one who stays in the slow lane and keeps within speed limits, or one who switches lanes constantly? It's quality (or modality) will tell.

Cardinal Signs—Aries, Cancer, Libra, Capricorn—like life in the fast lane. These are start-up signs that signal the beginning of each of the four seasons. They are initiators, anxious to get things underway, often impatient.

Fixed Signs—Taurus, Leo, Scorpio, Aquarius—are steady, stable, always in control. They happen in the middle of the season, when the character is established. Fixed signs are naturally centered.

Mutable Signs—Gemini, Virgo, Sagittarius, Pisces—embody the principle of distribution. These signs prepare the way for change; they break up each cycle, distributing the energy to the next group. They are flexible; they can move in many directions easily, darting around obstacles.

Each sign has a polarity, an electrical charge that generates energy on to the next sign that continues around the zodiac, which becomes like a giant circular battery. Polarity refers to opposites, which you could define as masculine/feminine, yin/yang, positive/negative, active/reactive. Alternating around the zodiac, the six fire and air signs are active, positive, masculine, and yang in polarity. These signs are open, expanding, and outward. Structure and form come from the six earth and water signs, which are reactive, negative, and yin—in other words, nurturing and receptive in polarity, allowing the energy to develop and take shape. Having all positive energy would be like having a car without brakes! All negative energy will go nowhere. Both are needed in balanced proportion.

Once you understand the basic raw material of astrology—what makes up a sign—you're ready to move onto the big stage, the actual horoscope. The analogy of a theater has often been used to make the many different astrological components, which can be confusing to the lay person, easier to understand. In the theatrical context, there is a stage, which is the horoscope chart, divided in areas of specific activity. The actors are the planets, each with a distinct character to play. The plot is determined by the angles or aspects between the planets, which show how they interact.

Depending on the position of the actors on the stage, some will perform major roles, with domineering personalities, and others will be minor supporting players, but each will have distinct and separate characteristics that add up to your total astrological personality.

The Horoscope Chart—Your Stage Set

The round horoscope wheel is divided into twelve sections, where different kinds of action take place. These slices of the horoscope are called houses. Each house is characterized by a sign of the zodiac, but ruled by the sign that is passing over the house at the time when the chart was set up. Therefore, the activities of each house will be colored by two signs (unless the ruling sign is the same as the sign passing over the house); you must consider both the sign governing the nature of each house and the sign passing over it when you interpret a chart. Each planet also has a house it calls home—the house of the sign it rules—where it operates especially well.

Quadrants—The Four Main Divisions

Two critical dividing lines bisect the wheel horizontally and vertically, splitting up the chart into four quarters of three houses each. These quarters are called quadrants and each house within a quadrant has a special way of operating, which corresponds to the qualities of a sign (cardinal, fixed and mutable). Rather than study the houses in consecutive order, you may find it easiest to understand them in terms of how they operate, as we have grouped them here:

The Action Houses

The houses that fall on the lines of each quadrant set the wheel of the chart in motion and are called the angular houses. It should be no surprise that the activities of these houses are those of the active cardinal signs.

The First House—Natural Place of Aries and Mars. Imagine the house where active pioneering Aries would naturally feel at home. This is the house of firsts—the first gasp of independence, the first impression you make, how you initiate matters, the image you choose to project. Planets that fall here have a strong impact on how you come across. The sign passing over this house is known as your ascendant or rising sign, which will show you how you come across to others.

The Fourth House—Natural Place of Cancer and the Moon. Located at the bottom of the chart, the fourth house, like the home, shows the foundation of life, the psychological underpinnings. Here is where you have the deepest confrontations with who you are and how you make yourself feel secure. It shows your early home environment and the circumstances of the end of your life, your final home.

The Seventh House—Natural Place of Libra and Venus. The seventh house brings you into one-on-one relationships with others. Here are your attitudes towards others (the direct opposite of those involved with the first house of the self). Here you handle contracts or partnership agreements (such as marriage). Therefore, it is not the place for love affairs or casual romances (those belong to the fifth house).

16

The Tenth House—Natural Place of Capricorn and Saturn. Jumping to the top of the chart, the tenth house is located directly overhead at the high moon position. This is the most visible house in the chart, the one dealing with your public image, your career, and your reputation in the eyes of the world. Here is where you go public, take on responsibilties, as opposed to the fourth house, where you stay home. The tenth house will strongly affect your choice of career and your relations with the outer world.

The Consolidating Houses

The houses in the middle of each quadrant are called the succedent houses. As the chart unfolds around the zodiac, energy pulsates from the active cadent houses into these more restful consolidating places, naturally ruled by the fixed signs Taurus (second house), Leo (fifth), Scorpio (eighth), and Aquarius (eleventh).

The Second House—Home of Taurus and Venus. Here is where your values—your sense of material security—begin: This house shows what you appreciate and how you feel about the material world, money, and finances. It also shows your sense of self-worth. Happenings here involve possessions, material resources, and your earning capacity.

The Fifth House—Home of Leo and the Sun. The Leo House is where creativity develops. It is the house where you express yourself, where you create and procreate. It is the inner child who delights in play. Security within yourself has been established by the time you reach this house, so you are free to have fun, enjoying romance and love affairs. It is where you give love.

The Eighth House—Home of Scorpio and Pluto (also Mars). The eighth house is where you share experience with another; it shows how you unite with others and what happens when two people or energies merge and you relinquish control. It follows that this is the house of sex, of shared resources, of taxes (you share with the government). Here are issues of control—the transformation from *I* to *we* often involves power struggles. Deep psychological transformative work takes place here as we deal with the issue of bonding. Uses of shared resources, including the environment, also happen here. This is often called the psychic house because it is where we transcend ourselves in dreams, experience the psychic or collective unconscious, and identify with group symbols. Drug experiences are also part of losing control here.

The Eleventh House—Home of Aquarius and Uranus. Here you are going beyond yourself to identify with something larger—a group, a goal, a belief system. This house is where you define what you really want, what kinds of friends you have, what kind of groups you identify with as an equal. Here is where you could become a socially conscious humanitarian, a team player, or a partygoing social butterfly. It's where you look to others to stimulate you and where you discover your kinship to the rest of humanity.

The Houses of Change and Growth

The cadent houses fall at the end of each quadrant. Their activities prepare us for growth and change and are ruled by the mutable signs: Gemini (third house), Virgo (sixth), Sagittarius (ninth), and Pisces (twelfth).

The Third House—Home of Gemini and Mercury. The third house shows how you interact with your immediate environment and how you reach out to others nearby. It shows your first relationships with brothers and sisters, and how you deal with people close to you, such as your neighbors or pals. It's where you take short trips, write letters, or use the telephone. It shows how your mind works in terms of left-brain logical and analytical functions. This is the Gemini part of your life.

The Sixth House—Home of Virgo and Mercury. The sixth house describes how you get things done and how you look after others and fulfill responsibilities such as taking care of pets. Here is your daily survival, your job (as opposed to your career, which is the domain of the tenth house), your diet, and your health and fitness regimens. This house shows how you take care of your body and maintenance systems so you can perform better in the world.

The Ninth House—Home of Sagittarius and Jupiter. As the third house is affiliated with the lower mind, its opposite place, the ninth house, relates to the higher mind—the abstract, intuitive, spiritual mind that asks big questions like "Why we are here?" The third house explored what was close at hand; its opposite house, the ninth, stretches out to explore more exotic territory, either by actually traveling, by stretching mentally with higher education, or by stretching spiritually with religious activity. Here is where you write a book or extensive thesis, where you pontificate, philosophize, or preach.

The Twelfth House—Home of Pisces and Neptune. The final house symbolizes the withdrawal and dissolution that happens before a rebirth, a place where the accumulated experiences are processed in the unconscious. Mysticism; the occult; mental health; confinement in religious, mental or penal institutions; and spiritual work belong to the twelfth house. In your daily life, the twelfth house reveals hidden enemies, deepest intimacies, and your best-kept secrets. It is where the boundaries between yourself and others become blurred. It symbolizes self-undoing, surrendering the sense of a separate self to a deep feeling of wholeness, such as selfless service in religion or any activity that involves merging with the greater whole. Many sports stars have important planets in the twelfth house that enable them to merge with the energy flow of the game, to go beyond a sense of competition to find an almost mystical strength that transcends their limitations. This house is also associated with past lives and karma.

Now that you've got the territory mapped out, it's time to learn the language and meet the players. Read the following chapters for an introduction to the glyphs and the planets.

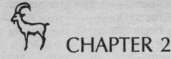 **CHAPTER 2**

Glyphs: Some Odd Characters that Can Make Your Life Easier

The first time you look at a horoscope, you'll realize that astrology has a language all its own, written in strange-looking characters that represent the planets and signs. These symbols or glyphs are used by astrologers all over the world and they are also used in all the new astrology programs available for your computer. So if you want to progress in astrology enough to read a print-out of a horoscope, you've got to know the meaning of the glyphs.

Learning to decipher the glyphs can not only help you read a computer chart, but can help you understand the meaning of the signs and planets, because each symbol contains clues to what it represents. And since there are only twelve signs and ten planets (not counting a few asteroids and other space creatures some astrologers use), it's a lot easier than learning to read than, say, Chinese!

Here's a code-cracker for the glyphs, beginning with the glyphs for the planets. But even if you already know your glyphs, don't just skim over the chapter. There are hidden meanings to discover, so test your glyph-ese.

The Glyphs for the Planets

The glyphs for the planets are easy to learn. They're simply combinations of the circle, the semicircle or arc, and the cross. Each component of a glyph has a special meaning in relation to the others, and they combine to create the total meaning of the symbol.

The circle, which has no beginning or end, is one of the oldest symbols of spirit or spiritual forces. All of the early diagrams of the heavens—spiritual territory—are shown in circular form. The semicircle or arc symbolizes the receptive, finite soul, which contains spiritual potential in the curving line. The vertical line of the cross symbolizes movement from heaven to earth. The horizontal line describes temporal movement, here and now, in time and space. Superimposed together, the vertical and horizontal planes symbolize manifestation in the material world.

The Sun Glyph ☉

The sun is always shown by this powerful solar symbol, a circle with a point in the center. The point is you, your spiritual center, and the symbol represents your infinite personality incarnating (the point) into the finite cycles of birth and death.

This symbol was brought into common use in the sixteenth century, after a German occultist and scholar, Cornelius Agrippa (1486–1535) wrote a book called *Die Occulta Philosophia,* which became accepted as the standard work in its field. In his book, Agrippa collected many medieval astrological and magical symbols, which have been copied by astrologers ever since.

The Moon Glyph ☽

This is surely the easiest symbol to spot on a chart. The Moon glyph is a left-facing arc stylized into the crescent moon, which perfectly captures the reactive, receptive, emotional nature of the moon.

As part of a circle, the arc symbolizes the potential fulfillment of the entire circle. It is the life force that is still incomplete.

The Mercury Glyph ☿

Mercury contains all three elemental symbols—the crescent, the circle, and the cross in vertical order. This is the "Venus with a hat" glyph (compare with the symbol of Venus). With another stretch of the imagination, can't you see the winged cap of Mercury the messenger? Think of the upturned crescent as antennae that tune in and transmit messages from the sun, reminding you that Mercury is the way you communicate and the way your mind works. The upturned arc is receiving energy into the spirit or solar circle, which will later be translated into action on the material plane, symbolized by the cross. All the elements are equally sized because neutral Mercury doesn't play favorites. This planet symbolizes objective, detached, unemotional thinking.

The Venus Glyph ♀

Here the relationship is between two elements, the circle or spirit above the cross of matter. Spirit is elevated over matter, pulling it upward. Venus asks, "What is beautiful? What do you like best? What do you love to have done to you?" Venus determines both your ideal of beauty and what feels good sensually. It governs your own allure and power to attract, as well as what attracts and pleases you.

The Mars Glyph ♂

In this glyph, the cross of matter is stylized into an arrowhead pointed up and outward, propelled by the circle of spirit. You can deduce that Mars embodies your spiritual energy projected into the outer world. It's your assertiveness, your initiative, your aggressive drive, what you like to do to others, your temper. If you know someone's Mars, you know whether they'll blow up when angry or do a slow burn. Your task is to use your outgoing Mars energy wisely and well.

The Jupiter Glyph ♃

Jupiter is the basic cross of matter, with a large stylized crescent perched on the left side of the horizontal, temporal plane. You might think of the crescent as an open hand, for one meaning of Jupiter is "luck," what's handed to you. You don't work for what you get from Jupiter—it comes to you if you're open to it.

The Jupiter glyph might also remind you of a jumbo jet plane with a huge tail fin, about to take off. This is the planet of travel, both mental and spiritual, and the planet of expanding your horizons via new ideas, spiritual dimensions, and places. Jupiter embodies the optimism and enthusiasm of the traveler about to embark on an exciting adventure.

The Saturn Glyph ♄

Flip Jupiter over and you've got Saturn. (This might not be immediately apparent, because Saturn is usually stylized into an *h* form like the one shown here.) But the principle it expresses is the opposite of Jupiter's expansive tendencies. Saturn pulls you back to earth—the receptive arc is pushed down underneath the cross of matter. Before there are any rewards or expansion, the duties and obligations of the material world must be considered. Saturn says, "Stop, wait, finish your chores before you take off!"

Saturn's glyph also resembles the sickle of old Father Time. Saturn was first known as Chronos, the Greek god of time, for time brings all matter to an end. When it was thought to be the most distant planet (before the discovery of Uranus), Saturn was believed to be the place that time stopped. After the soul, having departed from earth, journeyed back to the outer reaches of the universe, it finally stopped at Saturn, "the end of time."

The Uranus Glyph ♅

The glyph for Uranus is often stylized to form a capital *H* after Sir William Hershel, the planet's discoverer. But the more esoteric version curves the two pillars of the H into crescent antennae, or "ears," resembling satellite discs receiving signals from space. These are perched on the horizonal material line of the cross (matter) and pushed from below by the circle of the spirit. To many sci-fi fans, Uranus looks like an orbiting satellite.

Uranus channels the highest energy of all, the white electrical light of the universal spiritual sun, the force that holds the cosmos together. This pure electrical energy is gathered from all over the universe. Because Uranian energy doesn't follow an ordinary celestial drumbeat, it can't be controlled or predicted (which is also true of those who are strongly influenced by this eccentric planet). In the symbol, this energy is manifested through the balance of polarities (the two opposite arms of the glyph) like the two polarized wires of a light bulb.

The Neptune Glyph Ψ

Neptune's glyph is usually stylized to look like a trident, the weapon of the Roman god Neptune. However, on a more esoteric level, it shows the large upturned crescent of the soul pierced through by the cross of matter. Neptune nails down, or materializes, soul energy, bringing impulses from the soul level into manifestation. That is why Neptune is associated with imagination or "imagining in," making an image of the soul. Neptune works through feeling, sensitivity, and mystical capacity to bring the divine into the earthly realm.

The Pluto Glyph ♇

Pluto is written two ways. One is a composite of the letters *PL,* the first two letters of the word Pluto and coincidentally the initials of Percival Lowell, one of the planet's discoverers. The other, more esoteric symbol is a small circle, above a large open crescent that surmounts the cross of matter. This depicts Pluto's power to regenerate—imagine a new little spirit emerging from the sheltering cup of the soul. Pluto rules the forces of life and death—after this Planet has passed a sensitive point in your chart, you are transformed, reborn in some way.

Sci-fi fans might visualize this glyph as a small satellite (the circle) being launched. It was shortly after Pluto's discovery that we learned how to harness the nuclear forces that made space exploration possible. Pluto rules the transformative power of atomic energy, which totally changed our lives and from which there was no turning back.

The Glyphs for the Signs

On an astrological chart, the glyph for the sign will appear after that of the planet. For example, when you see the moon glyph followed first by a number and then by another glyph representing the sign, this means that the moon was passing over a certain degree of that astrological sign at the time of the chart. On the dividing lines between the segments or houses on your chart, you'll find the symbol for the sign that rules the house.

Because sun-sign symbols do not contain the same basic geometric components of the planetary glyphs, we must look elsewhere for clues to their meanings. Many have been passed down from ancient Egyptian and Chaldean civilizations, with few modifications. Others have been adapted over the centuries. In deciphering many of the glyphs, you'll often find that the symbols reveal a dual nature of the sign, not always apparent in the usual sun-sign descriptions. For instance, the Gemini glyph is similar to the Roman numeral for two, and reveals this sign's longing to discover a twin soul. The Cancer glyph may be interpreted as resembling either the nurturing breasts or the self-protective claws of the crab—both symbols associated with the contrasting qualities of this sign. Libra's glyph embodies the duality of the spirit balanced with material reality. The Sagittarius glyph shows that the aspirant must also carry along the earthly animal nature in his quest. The Capricorn sea goat is another symbol with dual emphasis. The goat climbs high yet is always pulled back by the deep waters of the unconscious. Aquarius embodies the double waves of mental detachment, balanced by the desire for connection with others in a friendly way. And finally, the two fishes of Pisces, which are forever tied together, show the duality of the soul and the spirit that must be reconciled.

The Aries Glyph ♈

Since the symbol for Aries is the ram, this glyph's most obvious association is with a ram's horns, which characterizes one aspect of the Aries personality—an aggressive, me-first, leaping-head-first-attitude. But the symbol may have other meanings for you, too. Some astrologers liken it to a fountain of energy, which Aries people also embody. The first sign of the zodiac bursts on the scene eagerly, ready to go. Another analogy is to the eyebrows and nose of the human head, which Aries rules, and the thinking power that is initiated in the brain.

One theory of the origin of this symbol links it to the Egyptian god Amun, represented by a ram. As Amon-Ra, this god was believed to embody the creator of the universe, the leader of all the other gods. This relates easily to the position of Aries as the leader (or first sign) of the zodiac, which begins at the spring equinox, a time of the year when nature is renewed.

The Taurus Glyph ♉

This is another easy glyph to draw and identify. It takes little imagination to decipher the bull's head with long curving horns. Like the bull, the archetypal Taurus is slow to anger but ferocious when provoked, as well as stubborn, steady, and sensual. Another association is the larynx (and thyroid) of the throat area (ruled by Taurus) and the eustachian tubes running up to the ears, which coincides with the relationship of Taurus to the voice, song, and music. Many famous singers, musicians, and composers have prominent Taurus influences.

Many ancient religions involved a bull as the central figure in fertility rites or initiations, usually symbolizing the victory of man over his animal nature. Another possible origin is in the sacred bull of Egypt, who embodied the incarnate form of Osiris, god of death and resurrection. In early Christian imagery, the Taurean bull represented St. Luke.

The Gemini Glyph ♊

The standard glyph immediately calls to mind the Roman numeral for two and the symbol for Gemini, the "twins." In almost all images for this sign, the relationship between two persons is emphasized. This is the sign of communication and human contact; it manifests the desire to share.

Many of the figurative images for Gemini show twins with their arms around each other, emphasizing that they are sharing the same ideas and the same ground. In the glyph, the top line indicates mental communication, while the bottom line indicates shared physical space.

The most famous Gemini legend is that of the twin sons, Castor and Pollux. One of them had a mortal father, while the other was the son of Zeus, king of the gods. When it came time for the mortal twin to die, his grief-stricken brother pleaded with Zeus, who agreed to let them spend half the year on earth, in mortal form, and half in immortal life, with the gods on Mt. Olympus. This reflects the basic nature of humankind, which possesses an immortal soul yet is also subject to the limits of mortality.

The Cancer Glyph ♋

Two convenient images relate to the Cancer glyph. The easiest to picture is the curving claws of the Cancer symbol, the crab. Like the crab, Cancer's element is water. This sensitive sign also has a hard protective shell to protect its tender interior. It must be wily to escape predators, scampering sideways and hiding shyly under rocks. The crab also responds to the cycles of the moon, as do all shellfish. The other image is that of two female breasts, which Cancer rules, showing that this is a sign that nurtures and protects others as well as itself.

In ancient Egypt, Cancer was also represented by the scarab beetle, a symbol of regeneration and eternal life.

The Leo Glyph ♌

Notice that the Leo glyph seems to be an extension of Cancer's glyph, with a significant difference. In the Cancer glyph, the lines curve inward protectively, while the Leo glyph expresses energy outwardly. There is no duality in the symbol—or in Leo.

Lions have belonged to the sign of Leo since earliest times and it is not difficult to imagine the king of beasts with his sweeping mane and curling tail from this glyph. The upward sweep of the glyph easily describes the positive energy of Leos—the flourishing tail and the flamboyant qualities. Another analogy, which is a stretch of the imagination, is that of a heart leaping up with joy and enthusiasm—also very typical of Leo, which rules the heart. In early Christian imagery, the Leo lion represented St. Mark.

The Virgo Glyph ♍

You can read much into this mysterious glyph. For instance, it could represent the initials of "Mary Virgin," or a young woman holding a staff of wheat, or stylized female genitalia—all common interpretations. The *M* shape might also remind you that Virgo is ruled by Mercury. The cross beneath the symbol could indicate the grounded, practical nature of this earth sign.

The earliest zodiacs link Virgo with the Egyptian goddess Isis, who gave birth to the god Horus after her husband Osiris had been killed, in the archetype of a miraculous conception. There are many statues of Isis nursing her baby son, which are reminiscent of medieval Virgin and Child motifs. This sign has also been associated with the image of the Holy Grail, substituting the Virgo symbol with a chalice.

The Libra Glyph ♎

It is not difficult to read the standard image for Libra, the scales, into this glyph. There is another meaning, however, that is equally relevant—the setting sun as it descends over the horizon. Libra's natural position on the zodiac wheel is the descendent or sunset position (as Aries' natural position is the ascendant, or rising sign). Both images relate to Libra's personality. Libra is always weighing pros and cons for a balanced decision. In the sunset image, the sun (male) hovers over the horizontal Earth (female) before setting. Libra is the space between these lines, harmonizing yin and yang, spiritual and material, male and female, ideal and real. The glyph has also been linked to the kidneys, which are ruled by Libra.

The Scorpio Glyph ♏

With its barbed tail, this glyph is easy to identify with the sign of the Scorpion. It also represents the male sexual parts, over which the sign rules. However, some earlier symbols for Scorpio, such as the Egyptian, represent it as an erect serpent. The arrowhead can also help you draw the conclusion that Mars is the ruler of this sign.

Another image for Scorpio, which is not identifiable in this glyph, is the eagle. Scorpios can go to extremes, soaring like the eagle or self-destructing like the Scorpion. In early Christian imagery, which often used zodiacal symbols, the Scorpio eagle was chosen to symbolize the intense apostle, St. John the Evangelist.

The Sagittarius Glyph ♐

This glyph is one of the easiest to spot and draw—an upward-pointing arrow lifting up a cross. The arrow is pointing skyward, while the cross represents the four elements of the material world, which the arrow must convey. Elevating materiality into spirituality is an important Sagittarius quality, which explains why this sign is associated with higher learning, religion, philosophy, and travel—the aspiring professions. Sagittarius can also send barbed arrows of frankness in their pursuit of truth. (This is also the sign of the super-salesman.)

Sagittarius is symbolically represented by the centaur, a mythological creature who is half-man, half-horse, aiming his arrow toward the skies. Though Sagittarius is motivated by spiritual aspiration, it also must balance the powerful appetites of the animal nature. The centaur Chiron, a figure in Greek mythology, became a wise teacher after many adventures and world travels.

The Capricorn Glyph ♑

One of the most difficult symbols to draw, this glyph may take some practice. It is a representation of the sea goat, a mytical animal that is a goat with a curving fish's tail. The goat part of Capricorn wants to leave the waters of the emotions and climb to the elevated areas of life. But the fish part is the unconscious, the deep chaotic psychic level that draws the goat back. Capricorn is often trying to escape the deep, feeling part of life by submerging himself in work, steadily climbing to the top. To some people, the glyph represents a seated figure with a bent knee, a reminder that Capricorn governs the knee area of the body.

An interesting aspect of this figure is how the sharp-pointed horns of the symbol, which represent the penetrating, shrewd, conscious side of Capricorn, contrast with the swishing tail, which represents its serpentine, unconscious, emotional force. One Capricorn legend, which dates from Roman times, tells of the earthy fertility god, Pan, who tried to save himself from uncontrollable sexual desires by jumping into the Nile. His upper body turned into a goat while the lower part became a fish. Later, Jupiter gave him a safe haven in the skies, as a constellation.

The Aquarius Glyph ≈

This ancient water symbol can be traced back to an Egyptian hieroglyph representing streams of life force. Symbolized by the water bearer, Aquarius is distributor of the waters of life—the magic liquid of regeneration. The two waves can also be linked to the positive and negative charges of the electrical energy that Aquarius rules, a sort of universal wavelength. Aquarius is tuned in intuitivety to higher forces via this electrical force. The duality of the glyph could also refer to the dual nature of Aquarius, a sign that runs hot and cold, is friendly but also detached in the mental world of air signs.

In Greek legends, Aquarius is represented by Ganymede, who was carried to heaven by an eagle in order to become the cup bearer of Zeus, and to supervise the annual flooding of the Nile. The sign became associated with aviation and notions of flight.

The Pisces Glyph)(

Here is an abstraction of the familiar image of Pisces, two fishes swimming in opposite directions, bound together by a cord. The fishes represent spirit, which yearns for the freedom of heaven, while the soul remains attached to the desires of the temporal world. During life on earth, the spirit and the soul are bound together. When they complement each other, instead of pulling in opposite directions, this facilitates the creative expression for which Pisceans are known. The ancient version of this glyph, taken from the Egyptians, had no connecting line; the line was added in the fourteenth century.

Another interpretation is that the left fish indicates the direction of involution or the beginning of the cycle; the right-hand fish denotes the direction of evolution, or the way to completion of a cycle. It's an appropriate meaning for Pisces, the last sign of the zodiac.

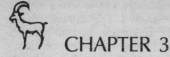

CHAPTER 3

Astrology's Top Ten: The Planetary Keys to Your Individual Horoscope

If you've been focusing on your sun sign, you may not realize that you've got nine other planets in your horoscope. All together, these are astrology's Top Ten, and each has a special type of energy to contribute to the total picture that is unique to you. (By the way, in astrology's special language, the sun and moon are often referred to as planets, though of course they're not.)

Use the tables following this chapter to find where your planets lie.

The Sun is Always Number One

Your Sun Sign will always be at the top of the list. It's the most obvious part of you, the part that shines brightest. But the other planets add special colorations that make you different from all other members of your sun sign. When you know a person's sun sign, you already know some very useful generic qualities. But when you know all the planets in a person's Top Ten, then you've got a much clearer picture of how that individual will act in a given situation. Learn the Top Ten to find out how you communicate, act and react, what moves you, what's likely to hold you back. The sun's just one card in your hand—when you know your other planets, you can really play to win!

Besides having its own unique kind of energy, a planet's personality is colored by the sign it is passing through at the time a horoscope is cast. For example, Mercury, the planet that rules the way you communicate, will express itself in a dynamic, headstrong Aries way, if it was passing through the sign of Aries when you were born. You would communicate in a much different way if it were passing through the slower, more patient, more sensual sign of Taurus.

In some signs, a planet's kind of energy operates very smoothly. It is at home in this kind of space. However, in other signs, the planet can be much more awkward, ill at ease, and slightly out of sorts. The signs that most correspond to the energies of the planet are said to be "ruled" by that planet.

Here are the planets and the signs they rule:

ARIES—Mars
TAURUS—Venus, in its most sensual form
GEMINI—Mercury, in its communicative role
CANCER—The Moon
LEO—The Sun
VIRGO—Also Mercury, this time in its critical capacity
LIBRA—Also Venus, in its aesthetic form
SCORPIO—Pluto, replacing the sign's original ruler, Mars
SAGITTARIUS—Jupiter
CAPRICORN—Saturn
AQUARIUS—Uranus, replacing Saturn
PISCES—Neptune, replacing Jupiter

Another great place for a planet to reside is in the sign of its exaltation. Here is where the planet's energy is lifted up to perfection. This is the sign where the planet can accomplish the most, be its most influential and creative. A person who has many planets in exalted signs is lucky indeed.

The SUN—exalted in Aries, where its energy creates action
The MOON—exalted in Taurus, where instincts and reactions operate on a highly creative level

MERCURY—exalted in Virgo, where it can reach analytical heights

VENUS—exalted in Pisces, a sign whose sensitivity encourages love and creativity

MARS—exalted in Capricorn, a sign that puts energy to work

JUPITER—exalted in Cancer, where it encourages nurturing and growth

SATURN—at home in Libra, where it steadies the scales of justice and promotes balanced, responsible judgement

URANUS—powerful in Scorpio, where it promotes transformation

NEPTUNE—especially favored in Cancer, where it gains the security to transcend to a higher state

PLUTO—exalted in Pisces, where it dissolves the old cycle, to make way for transition to the new

The Moon—The Inner You

The moon can teach you about the inner side of yourself, your needs and secrets, as well as those of others. It is your most personal planet, the receptive, reflective, female, nurturing side of you. And it reflects who you were nurtured *by*—the "Mother" or mother figure in your chart. In a man's chart, the moon position also describes his female, receptive, emotional side, and the woman in his life who will have the deepest effect. (Venus reveals the kind of woman who attracts him physically).

The sign the moon was passing through at your birth reflects your instinctive emotional nature, what appeals to you subconsciously. Since accurate moon tables are too extensive for this book, check through these descriptions to find the moon sign that feels most familiar, or better yet, have your chart calculated by a computer service to get your accurate moon placement.

Moon in Aries

You are an idealistic, impetuous person who falls in and out of love easily. This placement makes you both independent and ardent. You love a challenge, but could cool once your quarry is captured. You should cultivate patience and tolerance—or you might tend to gravitate toward those who treat you rough, just for the challenge and excitement.

Moon in Taurus

You are a sentimental soul who is very fond of the good life and gravitates toward solid, secure relationships. You like displays of affection and creature comforts— all the tangible trappings of a cozy, safe, calm atmosphere. You are sensual and steady emotionally, but very stubborn and determined. You can't be pushed. You should make an effort to broaden your horizons and to take a risk sometimes.

Moon in Gemini

You are a born flirt who loves social life and needs constant stimulation. You enjoy a lively professional and social life. You may marry more than once and have a rather chaotic emotional life due to your difficulty with commitment and settling down. Be sure to find a partner who is also outgoing. You will have to learn at some point to focus your energies and to keep on an even keel. You tend to be somewhat fragmented—to do two things at once, to have two homes or even two lovers. If you can find a creative way to express your many-faceted nature, you'll be ahead of the game.

Moon in Cancer

Your needs are very much associated with your reactions to the needs of others. You are very sensitive and self-protective, though some of you may mask this with a hard shell. This placement also gives an excellent memory and an uncanny ability to psyche out the needs of others. The moon is very strong in Cancer, so all of the lunar phases will affect you, especially full moons and eclipses. You are happiest at home and may work at home or turn your office into a second home, where you can nuture and comfort people—you may ·tend to mother the world. This is an extremely psychic, intuitive position, which could draw you to occult work in some way. Or you may get professionally involved with providing food and shelter.

Moon in Leo

This is a warm, passionate moon that takes everything to heart. You are attracted to the noble, generous, and aristocratic in life and may be a bit of a snob. You have an innate ability to take command emotionally, but you do need strong support, loyalty, and loud applause from those you love. You are possessive of your loved ones and your turf and will roar if anyone threatens to take over your territory.

Moon in Virgo

You are rather cool until you decide if others measure up. But once someone or something meets your ideal standards, you hold up your end of the arrangement perfectly. You may, in fact, drive yourself too hard to attain some notion of perfection. Try to be a bit easier on yourself and others. Don't always act the censor! You love to be the teacher and are drawn to situations where you can change others for the better. But sometimes you must learn to accept others for what they are and enjoy what you have.

Moon in Libra

This is a partnership-oriented placement—you may find it difficult to be alone or to do things alone. But you must learn to lean on yourself first. When you have learned emotional balance, you can have excellent relationships. It is best for you to avoid extremes or your love life can be precarious. You thrive in a rather conservative, traditional, romantic relationship, where you receive attention and flattery—but not possessiveness—from your partner. You'll be your most charming in an elegant, harmonious atmosphere.

Moon in Scorpio

This is a moon that enjoys and responds to intense, passionate feelings. You may go to extremes and have a very dramatic emotional life, full of ardor, suspicion, jealousy, and obsession. It would be much healthier to channel your need for power and control into meaningful work. This is a good position for anyone in the fields of medicine, police work, research, the occult, psychoanalysis, or intuitive work, because life-and-death situations don't faze you. However, you do take disappointments very hard.

Moon in Sagittarius

You take life's ups and downs with good humor and the proverbial grain of salt. You'll love 'em and leave 'em, and take off on a great adventure at a moment's notice. "Born free" could be your slogan. You can't stand to be possessed emotionally by anyone. Attracted by the exotic, you have wanderlust mentally and physically. You may be too much in search of new mental and spiritual stimulation to ever settle down.

Moon in Capricorn

Are you ever accused of being too cool and calculating? You have an earthy side, but you take prestige and position very seriously. Your strong drive to succeed extends to your romantic life, where you will be devoted to improving your lifestyle, rising to the top. You may be attracted to someone older or very much younger or from a different social world. It may be difficult to look at the lighter side of emotional relationships. You are very dutiful and responsible to those you care for.

Moon in Aquarius

You are a people collector with many friends of all backgrounds. You are happiest surrounded by people and are uneasy when left alone. You usually stay friends with those with whom you get involved. Though tolerant and understanding, you are unpredictable. You don't like anything to be too rigid. You may resist working on schedule or you may have a very unconventional love life. With pleny of space, you will be able to sustain relationships. But you'll blow away from possessive types.

Moon in Pisces

You are very responsive and empathetic to others, especially if they have problems. (You may have to be on guard against attracting too many people with sob stories.) You'll be happiest if you can find a way to express your creative imagination in the arts or in the spiritual or healing professions. You may tend to escape in a fantasy world or be attracted to exotic places or people. You need an emotional anchor, as you are very sensitive to the moods of others. You are happiest near water, working in a field that gives you emotional variety. But steer clear of too much escapism (especially in alcohol) and keep a firm foothold in reality.

Three Close Neighbors—Mercury, Venus, and Mars

These are the planets that work in your immediate personal life. Mercury affects how you communicate and how your mental processes work. Are you a quick study who grasps information rapidly, or do you learn more slowly and thoroughly? How is your concentration? Can you express yourself easily? Are you a good writer? All these questions can be answered by your Mercury placement.

Venus shows what you react to. What turns you on? What appeals to you aesthetically? Are you charming to others? Are you attractive to look at? Your taste, your refinement, your sense of balance and proportion are all Venus ruled.

Mars is your outgoing energy, your drive and ambition. Do you reach out for new adventures? Are you assertive? Are you motivated? Self-confident? Hot-tempered? How you channel your energy and drive is revealed by your Mars placement.

Mercury—The Communicator, the Genius, the Gossip

Since Mercury never travels far from the sun, read Mercury in your sun sign, the sign preceding and following it. Then decide which most reflects the way your mind works.

Mercury in Aries: Your mind is very active and assertive. You never hesitate to say exactly what you think or shy away from a battle. In fact, you may relish a verbal confrontation.

Mercury in Taurus: You may be a slow learner, but you have good concentration and mental stamina. You want to make your ideas really happen. You'll attack a problem methodically and consider every angle thoroughly, never jumping to conclusions. You'll stick with a subject until you master it.

Mercury in Gemini: You are a wonderful communicator, with a great facility for expressing yourself verbally and in writing. Though you learn fast, you may lack focus and discipline. Watch a tendency to jump from subject to subject.

Mercury in Cancer: You are very intuitive rather than logical. Your mental processes are usually colored by your emotions. This gives you the advantage of great imagination and empathy for others.

Mercury in Leo: You are enthusiastic and very dramatic in the way you express yourself. You like to hold the attention of groups, and could be a great public speaker. Your mind thinks big and likes to deal with the overall picture rather than details.

Mercury in Virgo: This is one of the best places for Mercury. This gives you critical ability, attention to details, and thorough analysis. Your mind focuses on the pratical side of things. You are an excellent teacher and editor.

Mercury in Libra: You are a born diplomat who smoothes over ruffled feathers; you may be a talented debater or lawyer. However, you vacillate when it comes to taking a stand or making decisions; you're forever weighing the pros and cons.

Mercury in Scorpio: This is the investigative mind, which stops at nothing to get the answer. You may have a sarcastic, stinging wit—a gift for the cutting remark. There is always a grain of truth to your verbal sallies, thanks to your penetrating insight.

Mercury in Sagittarius: You are a super-salesman with a tendency to expound. You are very broad minded, but you could be dogmatic when it comes to telling others what's good for them. You won't hesitate to tell the truth as you see it, so watch a tendency toward tactlessness. On the plus side, you have a great sense of humor.

Mercury in Capricorn: This placement endows good mental discipline. You have a love of learning and a very orderly approach to your subjects. You will patiently plod through facts and figures until you master your tasks. You grasp structured situations easily but may be short on creativity.

Mercury in Aquarius: You are an independent thinker who won't hesitate to break the rules to find the most original, innovative approach to problems. But once your mind is made up, it is difficult to change.

Mercury in Pisces: You have the psychic, intuitive mind of a natural poet. You should learn to make use of your creative imagination. You also think in terms of helping others, but check a tendency to be vague and forgetful of details.

Venus—The Designer, the Lover, the Socialite

Venus tells how you relate to others and to your environment. It shows where you receive pleasure, what you love to do. It is never more than two or three signs away from the sun.

Find your Venus placement on the chart in this book by looking for the year of your birth in the left hand column. Then follow the line of that year across the page until you reach the time period of your birthday. The sign heading that column will be your Venus. If you were born on a day when Venus was changing signs, check the signs preceding or following that day to determine if that feels more like your Venus nature.

Venus in Aries: Oh, do you love excitement! You can't stand to be bored, confined, or ordered around. But a good challenge, maybe even a rousing row turns you on. Confess—don't you pick a fight now and then just to get everyone moving? You're attracted by the chase, not the catch, which could create problems in your love life if the object of your affection becomes too attainable. You like to wear red and to be first with the very latest fashion. You'll spot a trend before anyone else.

Venus in Taurus: All your senses work in high gear. You love to be surrounded by glorious tastes, smells, textures, sounds, and visuals. Austerity is not for you, neither is being rushed. You like time to enjoy your pleasures. Soothing surroundings with plenty of creature comforts are your cup of tea. You like to feel secure in your nest, with no sudden jolts or surprises.

Venus in Gemini: You are a lively, sparkling personality that thrives in a situation that affords constant variety and a frequent change of scenes. A varied social life is important to you, with plenty of stimulation and a chance to engage in some light flirtation. Commitment may be difficult for you; playing the field is so much more fun.

Venus in Cancer: An atmosphere where you feel protected, coddled, and mothered is best for you. You love to be surrounded by children in a cozy, homelike situation. You are attracted to those who are tender and nurturing, who make you feel secure and well provided

41

for. You may also be quite secretive about your emotional life, or be attracted to clandestine relationships.

Venus in Leo: First-class attention in large doses turns you on. And so does the glitter of real gold and the flash of mirrors. You like to feel like a star at all times, surrounded by your admiring audience. The side effect is that you may be attracted to flatterers and tinsel, while the real gold requires some digging.

Venus in Virgo: Everything neatly in its place? On the surface, you are attracted to an atmosphere where everything is in perfect order, but underneath are some basic earthy urges. You are attracted to those who appeal to your need to teach or to play out a Pygmalion fantasy. You're at your best when you are busy doing something useful.

Venus in Libra: Elegance and harmony are your key words. You can't abide an atmosphere of contention. Your taste tends toward the classic, with light harmonies of color—nothing clashing, too trendy, or outrageous. You love doing things with a partner and should be careful to pick one who is decisive but patient enough to let you weigh the pros and cons. And steer clear of argumentative types.

Venus in Scorpio: Hidden mysteries intrigue you—in fact, anything that is too open and above board is a bit of a bore. You surely have a stack of whodunits by the bed (along with an erotic magazine or two). You may also be fascinated with the occult, crime or scientific research. Intense, all-or-nothing situations add spice to life, but you could get burned by your flair for living dangerously. The color black, spicy food, dark wood furniture, and heady perfume all get you in the right mood.

Venus in Sagittarius: If you are not actually a world traveler, your surroundings are sure to reflect your love of faraway places. You like a casual outdoor atmosphere and a dog or two to pet. There should be plenty of room for athletic equipment and suitcases. You're attracted to kindred souls who love to travel and who share your freedom-loving philosophy of life. Athletics, spiritual, or New Age pursuits are other interests.

Venus in Capricorn: No fly-by-night relationships for you! You want substance in life. You are attracted to whatever will help you get where you are going. Status objects turn you on. So do those who have a serious responsible, businesslike approach or who remind you of a beloved parent. It is characteristic of this placement to be attracted to someone of a different generation. Antiques, traditional clothing, and dignified behavior favor you.

Venus in Aquarius: This Venus wants to make friends more than to make love. You like to be in a group, particularly one pushing a worthy cause. You feel quite at home surrounded by people, remaining detached from any intense commitment. Original ideas and unpredictable people fascinate you. You don't like everything to be planned out in advance, preferring spontaneity and delightful surprises.

Venus in Pisces: This Venus is attracted to being of service. You love to give of yourself and you find plenty of takers. Stray animals and people appeal to your heart and your pocketbook. Be careful to look at their motives realistically once in a while. Fantasy, theater, and psychic or spiritual activities also speak to you.

Mars—The Go-Getter, the Athlete, the Competitor

Mars is the mover and shaker in your life. It shows how you pursue your goals, and whether you have energy to burn or proceed in a slow, steady pace. Or are you nervous, restless, and unable to sit still. It will also show how you get angry: Do you explode, or do a slow burn, or hold everything inside, then get revenge later?

To find your Mars, turn to the chart on page 70. Find your birth year in the left-hand column and trace the line across horizontally until you come to the column headed by the month of your birth. There you will find an abbreviation of your Mars sign. If the description of your Mars sign doesn't ring true, read the descriptions of the sign preceding and following it. You may have been born on a day when Mars was changing signs, so your Mars would be in the adjacent sign.

Mars in Aries: In the sign it rules, Mars shows its brilliant, fiery nature. You have an explosive temper and can be quite impatient, but on the other hand, you have tremendous courage, energy, and drive. You'll let nothing stand in your way as you race to be first! Obstacles are met head on and broken through by force. However, those that require patience and persistence can have you exploding in rage. You're a great starter, but not necessarily around for the finish.

Mars in Taurus: Slow, steady, concentrated energy gives you the power. You have great stamina and you won't give up. Your tactic is to wear away obstacles with your persistance. Often you come out a winner because you've had the patience to hang in there. When angered, you do a slow burn.

Mars in Gemini: You can't sit still for long. This Mars craves variety. You often have two or more things going on at once—it's all an amusing game to you. Your life can get very complicated, but that only adds spice and stimulation. What drives you into a nervous hyper state? Boredom, sameness, routine, and confinement. You can do wonderful things with your hands and you have a way with words.

Mars in Cancer: You rarely attack head on—instead, you'll keep things to yourself, make plans in secret, and always cover your actions. This might be interpreted by some as manipulative, but you are only being self-protective. You get furious when anyone knows too much about you. But you do like to know all about them. Your mothering and feeding instincts can be put to good use in your work in food, hotel, or child-care related businesses. You may have to overcome your fragile sense of security, which prompts you not to take risks and to get physically upset when criticized. Don't take things so personally!

Mars in Leo: You have a very dominant personality that takes center stage—modesty is not one of your traits, nor is taking a backseat. You prefer giving the orders and have been known to make a dramatic scene if they are not obeyed. Properly used, this Mars confers leadership ability, endurance, and courage.

Mars in Virgo: You are the fault-finder of the zodiac, who notices every detail. Mistakes of any kind make you very nervous. You may worry even if everything is going smoothly. You may not express your anger directly, but you sure can nag. You have definite likes and dislikes and you are sure you can do the job better than anyone else. You are certainly more industrious than most other signs. Why do't you express your Mars energy by teaching instead of criticizing?

Mars in Libra: This Mars will have a passion for beauty, justice, and art. But you will generally avoid confrontations at all costs. You prefer to spend your energy finding a diplomatic solution or weighing pros and cons. Your other techniques are passive aggression, or you'll exercise your well-known charm to get people to do what you want.

Mars in Scorpio: This is a powerful placement, so intense that it demands careful channeling into worthwhile activities. Otherwise, you could be obsessed with your sexuality or may use your need for power and control to manipulate others emotionally. You are strong willed, shrewd, and very private about your affairs, and you'll usually have a secret agenda behind your actions. Your great stamina, focus, and discipline are excellent assets for careers in the military or medical fields, especially research or surgery. When angry, you don't get mad, you get even!

Mars in Sagittarius: This expansive Mars often propels people into sales, travel, athletics, or philosophy. Your energies function well when you are on the move. You have a hot temper and are inclined to say what you think before you consider the consequences. You shoot for high goals—and talk endlessly about them—but you may be weak on groundwork. This Mars needs a solid foundation. Watch a tendency to take unnecessary risks.

Mars in Capricorn: This is an ambitious Mars with an excellent sense of timing. You have an eye for those who can be of use to you, and you may dismiss people ruthlessly when angry. But you drive yourself hard and deliver full value. This is a good placement for an executive. You'll aim for status and a high material position in life, and keep climbing despite the odds.

Mars in Aquarius: This is the most rebellious Mars. You seem to have a drive to assert yourself against the status quo. You may enjoy provoking people, shocking them out of traditional views. Or this placement could express itself in an offbeat sex life. Others could find you a bit eccentric; somehow, you often find yourself in unconventional situations. You enjoy being a leader of an active group, which pursues forward-looking studies or goals.

Mars in Pisces: This Mars is a good actor who knows just how to appeal to the sympathies of others. You can create and project wonderful fantasies or use your sensitive antennae to crusade for those less fortunate. You get what you want through creating a veil of illusion and glamor. This is a good Mars for a dancer, performer, photographer, or someone in motion pictures. Many famous film stars, such as Jane Fonda, have this placement. Watch a tendency to manipulate by making others feel sorry for you.

Jupiter—Expansion, Luck, Optimism

Jupiter is the planet in your horoscope that makes you want more. This big, bright, swirling mass of gases is associated with abundance, prosperity, and the kind of windfall you get without too much hard work. You're optimistic under Jupiter's influence—anything seems possible. You'll travel, expand your mind with higher education, and publish to share your knowledge widely.

But a strong Jupiter has its down side, too. Jupiter's influence is neither discriminating nor disciplined. It represents the principle of growth without judgement, and could result in extravagance, weight gain, laziness, and carelessness, if not kept in check.

Be sure to look up your Jupiter in the tables in this book. When the current position of Jupiter is favorable, you may get that lucky break. At any rate, it's a great time to try new things, take risks, travel, or get more education. Opportunities seem to open up at this time, so take advantage of them.

Once a year, Jupiter changes signs. That means you are due for an expansive time every twelve years, when Jupiter travels through your sun sign. You'll also have up periods every four years, when Jupiter is in the same element as your sun sign.

Jupiter in Aries: You are the soul of enthusiasm and optimism. Your luckiest times are when you are getting started on an exciting project or selling an idea that you really believe in. You may have to watch a tendency to be arrogant with those who do not share your enthusiasm. You follow your impulse, often ignoring budget or other common-sense limitations. To produce real, solid benefits, you'll need patience and follow-through wherever this Jupiter falls in your horoscope.

Jupiter in Taurus: You may be especially lucky in matters of real estate. You'll spend on beautiful material things, especially those that come from nature—minerals or precious gems, for instance. You can't have too much comfort or too many sensual pleasures. Watch a tendency to overindulge in good food, or to over-pamper yourself with nothing but the best. Spartan living is not for you!

Jupiter in Gemini: You are the great talker of the zodiac; you may be a great writer, too. But restlessness could be your weak point. You jump around, talk too much, and could be a jack-of-all-trades. Keeping a secret is especially difficult so you'll also have to watch a tendency to spill the beans. Since you love to be in the center of a beehive of activity, you'll have a vibrant social life. Your best opportunities will come through your talent for language—speaking, writing, communicating, and selling.

Jupiter in Cancer: You are luckiest in situations where you can find emotional closeness or deal with basic security needs such as food, nuturing, or shelter. You may be a great collector and you may simply love to accumulate things. You are the one who stashes things away for a rainy day. You probably have a very good memory and love children. In fact, you may have many children to care for. The food, hotel, child care, or shipping businesses hold good opportunities for you.

Jupiter in Leo: You are a natural showman who loves to live in a larger than life way. Yours is a personality full of color that always finds its way into the limelight. You can't have too much attention or applause. Show biz is a natural place for you, and any area where you can exercise your flair for drama, your natural playfulness, and your romantic nature brings you good fortune. But watch a tendency to be overly extravagant or to monopolize center stage.

Jupiter in Virgo: You actually love those minute details others find boring. To you, they make all the difference between the perfect and the ordinary. You are the fine craftsman who spots every flaw. You expand your awareness by finding the most practical methods, and by being of service to others. A great teacher, you'll have luck in education, nutrition, publishing, crafts, and health promotion. Watch a tendency to overwork.

Jupiter in Libra: This is an other-directed Jupiter that develops best with a partner. The stimulation of others helps you grow. You are also most comfortable in harmonious, beautiful situations, and you work well with artistic people. You have a great sense of fair play and an ability to evaluate the pros and cons of a situation. You usually prefer to play the role of diplomat rather than adversary.

Jupiter in Scorpio: You love the feeling of power and control, of taking things to their limit. You can't resist a mystery. Your shrewd, penetrating mind sees right through to the heart of most situations and people. You have luck in work that probes for solutions to matters of life and death. You may be drawn to undercover work, behind-the-scenes intrigue, psychotherapy, the occult, and sex-related ventures. Your challenge will be to develop a sense of moderation and tolerance for others' beliefs. This Jupiter can be fanatical. You may have luck in handling others' money—insurance, taxes, and inheritance can bring you a windfall.

Jupiter in Sagittarius: Independent, outgoing, and idealistic, you'll shoot for the stars. This Jupiter compels you to travel far and wide, both physically and mentally, via higher education. You may have luck while traveling in an exotic place. You also have luck with outdoor ventures, exercise, and animals (particularly horses). Since you tend to be very open about your opinions, watch a tendency to be tactless and to exaggerate. Instead, use your wonderful sense of humor to make your point.

Jupiter in Capricorn: Jupiter is much more restrained in Capricorn. Here, Jupiter can make you overwork, and heighten any ambition or sense of duty you may have. You'll expand in areas that advance your position, putting you farther up the social or corporate ladder. You are lucky working within the establishment in a very structured situation, where you can show off your ability to organize and which will provide rewards for your hard work.

Jupiter in Aquarius: This is another freedom-loving Jupiter with great tolerance and originality. You are at your best when you are working for a humanitarian cause and in the company of many supporters. This is a good Jupiter for a political career. You'll relate to all kinds of people on all social levels. You have an abundance of original ideas. However, you are best off away from routine and any situation that imposes rigid rules. You need mental stimulation!

Jupiter in Pisces: You are a giver whose feelings and pocketbook are easily touched by others, so choose your companions with care. You could be the original sucker for a hard-luck story. Better find a worthy hospital or charity to appreciate your selfless support. You have a great creative imagination and may attract good fortune in fields related to oil, perfume, pharmaceuticals, petroleum, dance, footwear, and alcohol. But beware of over-indulgence in drugs or alcohol—focus on a creative outlet instead.

Saturn—Discipline, Order, Structure

Jupiter speeds you up with lucky breaks, then along comes Saturn to slow you down with the disciplinary brakes. Saturn has unfairly been called a malific planet, one of the bad guys of the zodiac. On the contrary, Saturn is one of our best friends, the kind that tells you what's wrong with you for your own good. Under a Saturn transit, we grow up, take responsibility for our lives, and emerge from whatever test this planet has in store far wiser, more capable, and mature.

When Saturn hits a critical point in your horoscope, you can count on an experience that will make you slow up, pull back, and reexamine your life. If is a call to eliminate what is not working and to shape up. By the end of its twenty-eight-year trip around the zodiac, Saturn will have tested you in all areas of your life. The major tests usually happen in seven-year cycles, when Saturn passes over the angles of your chart—your rising sign, midheaven, descendant, and nadir. This is when the real life-changing experiences happen. But you are also in for a testing period whenever Saturn passes a planet in your chart or stresses that planet from a distance. Therefore, it is useful to check your planetary positions with the travel schedule of Saturn to prepare in advance, or at least to brace yourself.

When Saturn returns to its location at the time of your birth, at approximately age twenty-eight, you will have your first Saturn return. At this time, a person usually takes stock or settles down to find his mission in life and assume full adult duties and responsibilities.

Another way Saturn helps us is to reveal the karmic

lessons from previous lives, and give us the chance to overcome them. So look at Saturn's challenges as much-needed opportunities for self-improvement. Under a Jupiter influence you'll have more fun, but Saturn gives you solid, long-lasting results.

Look up your natal Saturn in the tables in this book for clues on where you need work.

Saturn in Aries: Saturn here gives you great ambition and independence. You don't let anyone push you around. And you know what's best for you. Following orders is not your strong point. Neither is diplomacy. Because no one quite lives up to your standards, you often wind up doing everything yourself. You are best off running your own business, though you may be quite lonely at times.

Saturn in Taurus: A big issue with you is getting control of the cash flow. There will be lean periods which can be frightening, but you have the patience and endurance to stick them out and the methodical drive to prosper in the end. Learn to take a philosophical attitude like Ben Franklin, who also had this placement and who said, "A penny saved is a penny earned."

Saturn in Gemini: You are a rather cold, detached, serious student. You may not be inclined to communicate or share your knowledge. You dwell in the realms of science, theory, or abstract analysis, even when you are dealing with the emotions, like Sigmund Freud, who had this placement.

Saturn in Cancer: Your tests come with establishing a secure emotional base. In doing so, you may have to deal with some very basic fears centering around your early home environment. Most of your Saturn tests will have emotional roots in those early childhood experiences. You may have difficulty remaining objective in terms of what you try to achieve. So it will be especially important for you to deal with negative feelings such as guilt, paranoia, jealousy, resentment, and suspicion. Galileo and Michaelangelo also navigated these murky waters.

Saturn in Leo: This is an authoritarian Saturn—a strict, demanding parent who may deny the pleasure principle in your zeal to see that rules are followed. Though you may feel guilty about taking the spotlight, you are very ambitious and loyal. You have to watch a tendency toward rigidity, also toward overwork and holding back affection. Joseph Kennedy and Billy Graham share this placement.

Saturn in Virgo: This is a cautious exacting Saturn, intensely hard on yourself, most of all. You give yourself the roughest time with your constant worries about every little detail, often making yourself sick. Your tests will come in learning tolerance and understanding of others. Charles DeGaulle and Nathaniel Hawthorne had this meticulous Saturn.

Saturn in Libra: Saturn is exalted here, which makes this planet an ally. You may choose very serious, older partners in life. Perhaps that stems from a fear of dependency. You need to learn to stand solidly on your own before you commit to another. You are extremely cautious as you deliberate every involvement, with good reason. It is best that you find an occupation that makes good use of your sense of duty and honor. Steer clear of fly-by-night situations. Khrushchev and Mao Tse Tung had this placement, too.

Saturn in Scorpio: You have great staying power. This Saturn tests you in matters of control and transformation. You may feel drawn to some kind of intrigue or undercover work, like J. Edgar Hoover. Or there may be an air or mystery surrounding your life and death like Marilyn Monroe and Robert Kennedy, who had this placement. There are lessons to be learned from your sexual involvements—often sex is used for manipulation here, or is somehow out of the ordinary. The mad Roman emperor Caligula and the transvestite Christine Jorgenson are extreme cases.

Saturn in Sagittarius: Your challenges and lessons will come from tests of your spiritual and philosophical values, as happened to Martin Luther King and Gandhi.

You are high minded and sincere, with this reflective, moral placement. Uncompromising in your ethical standards, you could be a benevolent despot.

Saturn in Capricorn: With the help of Saturn at maximum strength, your judgment will improve with age. And, like Spencer Tracy's screen image, you'll be the gray-haired hero with a strong sense of responsibility. You advance in life slowly but steadily, always with a strong hand at the helm and an eye for the advantagious situation. Negatively, you may be a loner, prone to periods of melancholy.

Saturn in Aquarius: Your tests come from your relationships with groups. Do you care too much about what others think? You may fear being different from others, and therefore slight your own unique, forward-looking gifts or, like Lord Byron and Howard Hughes, take the opposite tack and rebel in the extreme. You can apply discipline to accomplish great humanitarian goals, like Albert Schweitzer.

Saturn in Pisces: Your fear of the unknown and the irrational may lead you to a secluded solitary lifestyle. You may go on the run like Jesse James, who had this placement—to avoid looking too deeply inside. Or you may take refuge in institutions, especially hospitals, charity, or religious work. Queen Victoria, who also had this placement, symbolized an era in which institutions of all kinds were sustained. Discipline applied to artistic work, especially poetry and dance, or spiritual work, such as yoga and meditation, can help you.

Uranus, Neptune, and Pluto Affect Your Whole Generation

These three planets remain in signs such a long time that a whole generation bears the imprint of the sign. Mass movements, great sweeping changes, fads that characterize a generation, even the issues of the conflicts and wars of the time are influenced by the "outer three." When one of these distant planets changes signs, there is a definite shift in the atmosphere, the feeling of the end of an era.

Since these planets are so far away from the sun—too far to be seen by the naked eye—they pick up signals from the universe at large. These planetary receivers literally link the sun with distant energies, and they perform a similar function in your horoscope by linking your central character with intuitive, spiritual, transformative forces from the cosmos. Each planet has a special domain and will reflect this in the area of your life where it falls.

Uranus—The 'Aha!' Planet

There is nothing ordinary about this quirky green planet that seems to be traveling on its side, surrounded by a swarm of at least fifteen moons. Is it any wonder that astrologers assigned it to Aquarius, the most eccentric and gregarious sign? Uranus seems to wend its way around the sun, marching to its own tune.

Uranus energy is electrical, happening in sudden flashes. It is not influenced by karma or past events, nor does it regard tradition, sex, or sentiment. The Uranian key words are surprise and awakening. Uranus wakes you up, jolts you out of your comfortable rut. Suddenly, there's that flash of inspiration, that bright idea, that totally new approach to revolutionize whatever scheme you were undertaking. The Uranus place in your life is where you awaken and become your own person. And it is probably the most unconventional place in your chart.

Look up the sign of Uranus at the time of your birth and see where you follow your own tune.

Uranus in Aries—a Fiery Shocker: Birth date: March 31–November 4, 1927; January 13, 1928–June 6, 1934; October 10, 1934–March 28, 1935. Your generation is original, creative, pioneering, developing the computer, the airplane, and the cyclotron. You let nothing hold you back from exploring the unknown and have powerful mixture of fire and electricity behind you. Women of your generation were among the first to be liberated. You were the unforgettable style-setters. You have a surprise in store for everyone. Like Yoko Ono, Grace Kelly, and Jacqueline Onassis, your life may be jolted by sudden and violent changes.

Uranus in Taurus—Sudden Shakeups: Birth date: June 6, 1934–October 10, 1934; March 28, 1935–August 7, 1941; October 5, 1941–May 15, 1942. You are probably self-employed or would like to be. You have original ideas about making money, and you brace yourself for sudden changes of fortune. This Uranus can cause shakeups, particularly in finances, but it can also make you a born entrepreneur, like Jane Fonda.

Uranus in Gemini—The Walking Talk Show: Birth date: August 7–October 5, 1941; May 15, 1942–August 30, 1948; November 12, 1948–June 10, 1949. You were the first children to be influenced by television. And in your adult years, your generation stocks up on answering machines, cordless phones, automobile phones, computers, and fax machines—any new way you can communicate. You have an inquiring mind, but your interests are rather short-lived. This Uranus can be easily fragmented if there is no structure and focus.

Uranus in Cancer—Domestic Disturbances: Birth date: August 30–November 12, 1948; June 10, 1949–August 24, 1955; January 28–June 10, 1956. This generation came at a time when divorce was becoming commonplace, so your home image is unconventional. You may have an unusual relationship with your parents, have come from a broken home or an unconventional one. You'll have unorthodox ideas about parenting, intimacy, food, and shelter. You may also be interested in dreams, psychic phenomena, and memory work.

Uranus in Leo—A Flashy Performer: Birth date: August 24, 1955–January 28, 1956; June 10, 1956–November 1, 1961; January 10–August 10, 1962. This generation understood how to use electronic media. Many of your group are now leaders in the high-tech industries. You also understand how to use the new media to promote yourself. Like Isadora Duncan, you may have a very eccentric kind of charisma and a life that is sparked by unusual love affairs. Your children, too, may have traits that are out of the ordinary. Where this planet falls in your chart, you'll have a love of freedom, be a bit of an egomaniac, show the full force of your personality in a unique way, like tennis great Martina Navratilova.

Uranus in Virgo—Eccentric Genius: Birth date: November 1, 1961–January 10, 1962; August 10, 1962–September 28, 1968; May 20, 1969–June 24, 1969. You'll have highly individual work methods. Many will be finding newer, more practical ways to use computers. Like Einstein, who had this placement, you'll break the rules brilliantly. Your generation came at a time of student rebellions, the civil rights movement, and the general acceptance of health foods. Chances are, you are concerned about pollution and cleaning up the environment. You may also be involved with nontraditional healing methods. Heavyweight champ Mike Tyson has this placement.

Uranus in Libra—On Again, Off-Again Partners: Birth date: September 28, 1968–May 20, 1969; June 24, 1969–November 21, 1974; May 1–September 8, 1975. Your generation will be always changing partners. Born during the time of women's liberation, you may have come from a broken home and have no clear image of what a marriage entails. There will be many sudden splits and experiments before you settle down. Your generation will be much involved in legal and political reforms and in changing artistic and fashion looks.

Uranus in Scorpio—The New Age: Birth date: November 21, 1974–May 1, 1975; September 8, 1975–February 17, 1981; March 20–November 16, 1981. Interest in transformation, meditation, and life after death signaled the beginning of New Age consciousness. Your generation recognizes no boundaries, no limits or external controls. You'll have new attitudes toward death and dying, psychic phenomena, and the occult. Like Mae West and Casanova, you'll shock 'em sexually, too.

Uranus in Sagittarius—Space Trippers: Birth date: February 17–March 20, 1981; November 16, 1981–February

15, 1988; May 27, 1988–December 2, 1988. Could this generation be the first to travel in outer space? The last generation with this placement included Charles Lindbergh. At that time, the first Zeppelins and the Wright Brothers were conquering the skies. Uranus here forecasts great discoveries, mind expansion, and long distance travel. Like Galileo and Martin Luther, those born in these years will generate new theories about the cosmos and man's relation to it.

Uranus in Capricorn—Movers and Shakers: Birth date: December 20, 1904–January 30, 1912; September 4–November 12, 1912; February 15–May 27, 1988; December 2, 1988–April 1, 1995; June 9, 1995–January 12, 1996. This generation will challenge traditions with the help of electronic gadgets. In these years, we got organized with the help of technology put to practical use. Great leaders, who were movers and shakers of history, like Julius Caesar and Henry VIII were born under this placement.

Uranus in Aquarius—The Innovators: Birth date: January 20–September 4, 1912; November 12, 1912–April 1, 1919; August 16, 1919–January 22, 1920; January 12, 1996 through the end of this century. The last generation with this placement produced great innovative minds such as Leonard Bernstein and Orson Welles. The next, after the year 2000, will be another radical breakthrough generation, much concerned with global issues that involve all humanity. Intuition, innovation, and sudden changes will surprise everyone when Uranus is in its home sign. This will be a time of experimentation on every level.

Uranus in Pisces—That's Entertainment: Birth date: April 1–August 16, 1919; January 22, 1920–March 31, 1927; November 4, 1927–January 13, 1928. In this century, Uranus in Pisces focused attention on the rise of electrical entertainment—radio and the cinema, and the secretiveness of Prohibition. This produced a generation of idealists exemplified by Judy Garland's theme, "Over the Rainbow."

Neptune—Dreams, Imagination, Illusions

Under Neptune's influence, you see what you want to see. But Neptune also encourages you to create, let your fantasies and daydreams run free. Neptune is often maligned as the planet of illusions, drugs and alcohol, where you can't bear to face reality. But it also embodies the energy of glamour, subtlety, mystery, and mysticism and governs anything that takes you out of the mundane world, including out-of-body experiences.

Neptune acts to break through your ordinary perceptions and take you to another level of reality, where you can experience either confusion or ecstasy. Neptune's force can pull you off course, like this planet affects its neighbor Uranus, but only if you allow this to happen. Those who use Neptune wisely can translate their daydreams into poetry, theater, design, or inspired moves in the business world, avoiding the tricky con artist side of this planet.

Find your Neptune listed here:

Neptune in Cancer: Birth date: July 19–December 25, 1901; May 21, 1902–September 23, 1914; December 14, 1914–July 19, 1915; March 19–May 2, 1916. Dreams of the homeland, idealistic patriotism, and glamorization of the nurturing assets of women characterized this age.

Neptune in Leo: Birth date: September 23–December 14, 1914; July 19, 1915–March 19, 1916; May 2, 1916–September 21, 1928; February 19, 1929–July 24, 1929. This sign brought us the glamor of the 1920s and the big spenders. Gambling, seduction, theater, and lavish entertaining distracted from the realities of the age.

Neptune in Virgo: Birth date: September 21, 1928—February 19, 1929; July 24, 1929–October 3, 1942; April 17–August 2, 1943. Neptune in Virgo encompassed the great depression and World War II. Those born at this time later spread the gospel of health and fitness. This generation's devotion to spending hours at the office inspired the term "workaholic."

Neptune in Libra: Birth date: October 2, 1942–April 17, 1943; August 2, 1943–December 24, 1955; March 12–October 19, 1956; June 15–August 6, 1957. Neptune in Libra was the romantic generation who would later be concerned with "relating." As this generation matured there was a new trend toward marriage and commitment. Racial and sexual equality became an important issue, as they redesigned traditional roles to suit modern times.

Neptune in Scorpio: Birth date: December 24, 1955–March 12, 1956; October 19, 1956–June 15, 1957; August 6, 1957–January 4, 1970; May 3–November 6, 1970. Neptune in Scorpio brought in a generation that would become interested in transformative power. Born in an era that glamorized sex, drugs, rock and roll, and Eastern religion, they matured in a more sobering time of AIDS, cocaine abuse, and New Age spirituality. As they mature, they will become active in transforming the environment and healing the planet from the results of the abuse of power.

Neptune in Sagittarius: Birth date: January 4–May 3, 1970; November 6, 1970–January 19, 1984; June 23–November 21, 1984. Neptune in Sagittarius was the time when space and astronaut travel became a reality. The Neptune influence glamorized new approaches to mysticism, religion and mind expansion. This generation will take a new approach to spiritual life, with emphasis on visions, mysticism, and clairvoyance.

Neptune in Capricorn: Birth date: January 19, 1984–June 23, 1984; November 21, 1984–January 29, 1998. Neptune in Capricorn, which began in 1984 and will stay until 1998, brought a time when delusions about material power were first glamorized, then dashed on the rocks of reality. It was also a time when the psychic world and the material world merged in the commercial marketplace. The occult gained an aura of respectibility, while material values went topsy-turvy.

Pluto—Power, Control, Transformation

Pluto is a mysterious, far-out little planet with a strange elliptical orbit that occasionally runs inside the orbit of its neighbor Neptune. Because of its eccentric path, Pluto can vary the length of time in a sign from thirteen to thirty-two years. Though it is a tiny planet, its influence is great. When Pluto zaps a strategic point in your horoscope, your life changes dramatically.

This little planet is the power behind the scenes; it affects you at deep levels of consciousness, causing events to come to the surface that will transform you and your generation. The Pluto place in your horoscope is where you have invisible power (Mars governs the visible power), where you can transform, heal, and affect the unconscious needs of the masses. Pluto governs your need to control, your attitudes toward death and immortality. Much of the strength of Pluto will depend on its position in your chart and the aspects it makes to other planets.

Pluto in Gemini (Late 1800's–May 28, 1914): This was a time of mass suggestion and breakthroughs in communications, when many brilliant writers, such as Ernest Hemingway and F. Scott Fitzgerald, were born. Henry Miller, D. H. Lawrence, and James Joyce scandalized by using explicit sex in their literature.

Pluto in Cancer (May 28, 1914–June 14, 1939): Dictators and mass media arose to wield emotional power over the masses. Women's rights was a popular issue. Deep sentimental feelings, acquisitiveness, and possessiveness characterized these times and people.

Pluto in Leo (June 14, 1939–August 19, 1957): The performing arts played on the emotions of the masses. Mick Jagger, John Lennon, and rock and roll were born at this time. Those born here were self-centered, powerful, and boisterous. This generation does its own thing, for better or for worse.

Pluto in Virgo (August 19, 1957–October 5, 1971; April 17, 1972–July 30, 1972): This is the "yuppie" generation that sparked a mass movememt toward fitness, health, and career. During this time, machines were invented to process the detail work perfectly. Inventions took on a practical turn, as answering machines, fax machines, car telephones, home office equipment all contributed to transform the workplace.

Pluto in Libra (October 5, 1971–April 17, 1972; July 30, 1972–August 28, 1984): People born at this time will be concerned with partnerships, working together and finding diplomatic solutions to problems. Marriage is becoming redefined along more traditional, but equal partnership lines. This was a time of women's liberation, gay rights, ERA, and abortion legislation, all of which transformed our ideas about relationships.

Pluto in Scorpio (August 28, 1984–January 17, 1995): Pluto was in its ruling sign for a comparatively short period of time. In 1989, it was at its perihelion or closest point to the sun and Earth. We have all felt the transforming power somewhere in our lives. This is a time of record achievements, destructive sexually transmitted diseases, nuclear power controversies, explosive political issues. Pluto destroys in order to create new understanding—the phoenix rising from the ashes, which should be some consolation for those of you who have felt Pluto's force before 1995.

Pluto's entry into Sagittarius (January 17, 1995): This had us rolling down the information superhighway into the future. This should signal a time of great optimism and spiritual development, bringing the century to an optimistic close. In Sagittarius, the sign that rules travel, there's a good possibility that Pluto, the planet of extremes, will make space travel a reality for many of us. New dimensions in electronic publishing, concern with animal rights and the environment, and an increasing emphasis on extreme forms of religion could signal this period. We'll be developing far-reaching philosophies designed to elevate our lives with a new sense of purpose.

VENUS SIGNS 1901–2000

	Aries	Taurus	Gemini	Cancer	Leo	Virgo
1901	3/29–4/22	4/22–5/17	5/17–6/10	6/10–7/5	7/5–7/29	7/29–8/23
1902	5/7–6/3	6/3–6/30	6/30–7/25	7/25–8/19	8/19–9/13	9/13–10/7
1903	2/28–3/24	3/24–4/18	4/18–5/13	5/13–6/9	6/9–7/7	7/7–8/17
						9/6–11/8
1904	3/13–5/7	5/7–6/1	6/1–6/25	6/25–7/19	7/19–8/13	8/13–9/6
1905	2/3–3/6	3/6–4/9	7/8–8/6	8/6–9/1	9/1–9/27	9/27–10/21
	4/9–5/28	5/28–7/8				
1906	3/1–4/7	4/7–5/2	5/2–5/26	5/26–6/20	6/20–7/16	7/16–8/11
1907	4/27–5/22	5/22–6/16	6/16–7/11	7/11–8/4	8/4–8/29	8/29–9/22
1908	2/14–3/10	3/10–4/5	4/5–5/5	5/5–9/8	9/8–10/8	10/8–11/3
1909	3/29–4/22	4/22–5/16	5/16–6/10	6/10–7/4	7/4–7/29	7/29–8/23
1910	5/7–6/3	6/4–6/29	6/30–7/24	7/25–8/18	8/19–9/12	9/13–10/6
1911	2/28–3/23	3/24–4/17	4/18–5/12	5/13–6/8	6/9–7/7	7/8–11/8
1912	4/13–5/6	5/7–5/31	6/1–6/24	6/24–7/18	7/19–8/12	8/13–9/5
1913	2/3–3/6	3/7–5/1	7/8–8/5	8/6–8/31	9/1–9/26	9/27–10/20
	5/2–5/30	5/31–7/7				
1914	3/14–4/6	4/7–5/1	5/2–5/25	5/26–6/19	6/20–7/15	7/16–8/10
1915	4/27–5/21	5/22–6/15	6/16–7/10	7/11–8/3	8/4–8/28	8/29–9/21
1916	2/14–3/9	3/10–4/5	4/6–5/5	5/6–9/8	9/9–10/7	10/8–11/2
1917	3/29–4/21	4/22–5/15	5/16–6/9	6/10–7/3	7/4–7/28	7/29–8/21
1918	5/7–6/2	6/3–6/28	6/29–7/24	7/25–8/18	8/19–9/11	9/12–10/5
1919	2/27–3/22	3/23–4/16	4/17–5/12	5/13–6/7	6/8–7/7	7/8–11/8
1920	4/12–5/6	5/7–5/30	5/31–6/23	6/24–7/18	7/19–8/11	8/12–9/4
1921	2/3–3/6	3/7–4/25	7/8–8/5	8/6–8/31	9/1–9/25	9/26–10/20
	4/26–6/1	6/2–7/7				
1922	3/13–4/6	4/7–4/30	5/1–5/25	5/26–6/19	6/20–7/14	7/15–8/9
1923	4/27–5/21	5/22–6/14	6/15–7/9	7/10–8/3	8/4–8/27	8/28–9/20
1924	2/13–3/8	3/9–4/4	4/5–5/5	5/6–9/8	9/9–10/7	10/8–11/12
1925	3/28–4/20	4/21–5/15	5/16–6/8	6/9–7/3	7/4–7/27	7/28–8/21

Libra	Scorpio	Sagittarius	Capricorn	Aquarius	Pisces
8/23–9/17	9/17–10/12	10/12–1/16	1/16–2/9 11/7–12/5	2/9 12/5–1/11	3/5–3/29
10/7–10/31	10/31–11/24	11/24–12/18	12/18–1/11	2/6–4/4	1/11–2/6 4/4–5/7
8/17–9/6 11/8–12/9	12/9–1/5			1/11–2/4	2/4–2/28
9/6–9/30	9/30–10/25	1/5–1/30 10/25–11/18	1/30–2/24 11/18–12/13	2/24–3/19 12/13–1/7	3/19–4/13
10/21–11/14	11/14–12/8	12/8–1/1/06			1/7–2/3
8/11–9/7	9/7–10/9 12/15–12/25	10/9–12/15 12/25–2/6	1/1–1/25	1/25–2/18	2/18–3/14
9/22–10/16	10/16–11/9	11/9–12/3	2/6–3/6 12/3–12/27	3/6–4/2 12/27–1/20	4/2–4/27
11/3–11/28	11/28–12/22	12/22–1/15			1/20–2/4
8/23–9/17	9/17–10/12	10/12–11/17	1/15–2/9 11/17–12/5	2/9–3/5 12/5–1/15	3/5–3/29
10/7–10/30	10/31–11/23	11/24–12/17	12/18–12/31	1/1–1/15 1/29–4/4	1/16–1/28 4/5–5/6
11/19–12/8	12/9–12/31		1/1–1/10	1/11–2/2	2/3–2/27
9/6–9/30	1/1–1/4 10/1–10/24	1/5–1/29 10/25–11/17	1/30–2/23 11/18–12/12	2/24–3/18 12/13–12/31	3/19–4/12
10/21–11/13	11/14–12/7	12/8–12/31		1/1–1/6	1/7–2/2
8/11–9/6	9/7–10/9 12/6–12/30	10/10–12/5 12/31	1/1–1/24	1/25–2/17	2/18–3/13
9/22–10/15	10/16–11/8	1/1–2/6 11/9–12/2	2/7–3/6 12/3–12/26	3/7–4/1 12/27–12/31	4/2–4/26
11/3–11/27	11/28–12/21	12/22–12/31		1/1–1/19	1/20–2/13
8/22–9/16	9/17–10/11	1/1–1/14 10/12–11/6	1/15–2/7 11/7–12/5	2/8–3/4 12/6–12/31	3/5–3/28
10/6–10/29	10/30–11/22	11/23–12/16	12/17–12/31	1/1–4/5	4/6–5/6
11/9–12/8	12/9–12/31		1/1–1/9	1/10–2/2	2/3–2/26
9/5–9/30	1/1–1/3 9/31–10/23	1/4–1/28 10/24–11/17	1/29–2/22 11/18–12/11	2/23–3/18 12/12–12/31	3/19–4/11
10/21–11/13	11/14–12/7	12/8–12/31		1/1–1/6	1/7–2/2
8/10–9/6	9/7–10/10 11/29–12/31	10/11–11/28	1/1–1/24	1/25–2/16	2/17–3/12
9/21–10/14	1/1 10/15–11/7	1/2–2/6 11/8–12/1	2/7–3/5 12/2–12/25	3/6–3/31 12/26–12/31	4/1–4/26
11/13–11/26	11/27–12/21	12/22–12/31		1/1–1/19	1/20–2/12
8/22–9/15	9/16–10/11	1/1–1/14 10/12–11/6	1/15–2/7 11/7–12/5	2/8–3/3 12/6–12/31	3/4–3/27

VENUS SIGNS 1901–2000

	Aries	Taurus	Gemini	Cancer	Leo	Virgo
1926	5/7–6/2	6/3–6/28	6/29–7/23	7/24–8/17	8/18–9/11	9/12–10/5
1927	2/27–3/22	3/23–4/16	4/17–5/11	5/12–6/7	6/8–7/7	7/8–11/9
1928	4/12–5/5	5/6–5/29	5/30–6/23	6/24–7/17	7/18–8/11	8/12–9/4
1929	2/3–3/7	3/8–4/19	7/8–8/4	8/5–8/30	8/31–9/25	9/26–10/19
	4/20–6/2	6/3–7/7				
1930	3/13–4/5	4/6–4/30	5/1–5/24	5/25–6/18	6/19–7/14	7/15–8/9
1931	4/26–5/20	5/21–6/13	6/14–7/8	7/9–8/2	8/3–8/26	8/27–9/19
1932	2/12–3/8	3/9–4/3	4/4–5/5	5/6–7/12	9/9–10/6	10/7–11/1
			7/13–7/27	7/28–9/8		
1933	3/27–4/19	4/20–5/28	5/29–6/8	6/9–7/2	7/3–7/26	7/27–8/20
1934	5/6–6/1	6/2–6/27	6/28–7/22	7/23–8/16	8/17–9/10	9/11–10/4
1935	2/26–3/21	3/22–4/15	4/16–5/10	5/11–6/6	6/7–7/6	7/7–11/8
1936	4/11–5/4	5/5–5/28	5/29–6/22	6/23–7/16	7/17–8/10	8/11–9/4
1937	2/2–3/8	3/9–4/17	7/7–8/3	8/4–8/29	8/30–9/24	9/25–10/18
	4/14–6/3	6/4–7/6				
1938	3/12–4/4	4/5–4/28	4/29–5/23	5/24–6/18	6/19–7/13	7/14–8/8
1939	4/25–5/19	5/20–6/13	6/14–7/8	7/9–8/1	8/2–8/25	8/26–9/19
1940	2/12–3/7	3/8–4/3	4/4–5/5	5/6–7/4	9/9–10/5	10/6–10/31
			7/5–7/31	8/1–9/8		
1941	3/27–4/19	4/20–5/13	5/14–6/6	6/7–7/1	7/2–7/26	7/27–8/20
1942	5/6–6/1	6/2–6/26	6/27–7/22	7/23–8/16	8/17–9/9	9/10–10/3
1943	2/25–3/20	3/21–4/14	4/15–5/10	5/11–6/6	6/7–7/6	7/7–11/8
1944	4/10–5/3	5/4–5/28	5/29–6/21	6/22–7/16	7/17–8/9	8/10–9/2
1945	2/2–3/10	3/11–4/6	7/7–8/3	8/4–8/29	8/30–9/23	9/24–10/18
	4/7–6/3	6/4–7/6				
1946	3/11–4/4	4/5–4/28	4/29–5/23	5/24–6/17	6/18–7/12	7/13–8/8
1947	4/25–5/19	5/20–6/12	6/13–7/7	7/8–8/1	8/2–8/25	8/26–9/18
1948	2/11–3/7	3/8–4/3	4/4–5/6	5/7–6/28	9/8–10/5	10/6–10/31
			6/29–8/2	8/3–9/7		
1949	3/26–4/19	4/20–5/13	5/14–6/6	6/7–6/30	7/1–7/25	7/26–8/19
1950	5/5–5/31	6/1–6/26	6/27–7/21	7/22–8/15	8/16–9/9	9/10–10/3
1951	2/25–3/21	3/22–4/15	4/16–5/10	5/11–6/6	6/7–7/7	7/8–11/9

Libra	Scorpio	Sagittarius	Capricorn	Aquarius	Pisces
10/6–10/29	10/30–11/22	11/23–12/16	12/17–12/31	1/1–4/5	4/6–5/6
11/10–12/8	12/9–12/31	1/1–1/7	1/8	1/9–2/1	2/2–2/26
9/5–9/28	1/1–1/3	1/4–1/28	1/29–2/22	2/23–3/17	3/18–4/11
	9/29–10/23	10/24–11/16	11/17–12/11	12/12–12/31	
10/20–11/12	11/13–12/6	12/7–12/30	12/31	1/1–1/5	1/6–2/2
8/10–9/6	9/7–10/11	10/12–11/21	1/1–1/23	1/24–2/16	2/17–3/12
	11/22–12/31				
9/20–10/13	1/1–1/3	1/4–2/6	2/7–3/4	3/5–3/31	4/1–4/25
	10/14–11/6	11/7–11/30	12/1–12/24	12/25–12/31	
11/2–11/25	11/26–12/20	12/21–12/31		1/1–1/18	1/19–2/11
8/21–9/14	9/15–10/10	1/1–1/13	1/14–2/6	2/7–3/2	3/3–3/26
		10/11–11/5	11/6–12/4	12/5–12/31	
10/5–10/28	10/29–11/21	11/22–12/15	12/16–12/31	1/1–4/5	4/6–5/5
11/9–12/7	12/8–12/31		1/1–1/7	1/8–1/31	2/1–2/25
9/5–9/27	1/1–1/2	1/3–1/27	1/28–2/21	2/22–3/16	3/17–4/10
	9/28–10/22	10/23–11/15	11/16–12/10	12/11–12/31	
10/19–11/11	11/12–12/5	12/6–12/29	12/30–12/31	1/1–1/5	1/6–2/1
8/9–9/6	9/7–10/13	10/14–11/14	1/1–1/22	1/23–2/15	2/16–3/11
	11/15–12/31				
9/20–10/13	1/1–1/3	1/4–2/5	2/6–3/4	3/5–3/30	3/31–4/24
	10/14–11/6	11/7–11/30	12/1–12/24	12/25–12/31	
11/1–11/25	11/26–12/19	12/20–12/31		1/1–1/18	1/19–2/11
8/21–9/14	9/15–10/9	1/1–1/12	1/13–2/5	2/6–3/1	3/2–3/26
		10/10–11/5	11/6–12/4	12/5–12/31	
10/4–10/27	10/28–11/20	11/21–12/14	12/15–12/31	1/1–4/4	4/6–5/5
11/9–12/7	12/8–12/31		1/1–1/7	1/8–1/31	2/1–2/24
9/3–9/27	1/1–1/2	1/3–1/27	1/28–2/20	2/21–3/16	3/17–4/9
	9/28–10/21	10/22–11/15	11/16–12/10	12/11–12/31	
10/19–11/11	11/12–12/5	12/6–12/29	12/30–12/31	1/1–1/4	1/5–2/1
8/9–9/6	9/7–10/15	10/16–11/7	1/1–1/21	1/22–2/14	2/15–3/10
	11/8–12/31				
9/19–10/12	1/1–1/4	1/5–2/5	2/6–3/4	3/5–3/29	3/30–4/24
	10/13–11/5	11/6–11/29	11/30–12/23	12/24–12/31	
11/1–1/25	11/26–12/19	12/20–12/31		1/1–1/17	1/18–2/10
8/20–9/14	9/15–10/9	1/1–1/12	1/13–2/5	2/6–3/1	3/2–3/25
		10/10–11/5	11/6–12/5	12/6–12/31	
10/4–10/27	10/28–11/20	11/21–12/13	12/14–12/31	1/1–4/5	4/6–5/4
11/10–12/7	12/8–12/31		1/1–1/7	1/8–1/31	2/1–2/24

VENUS SIGNS 1901–2000

	Aries	Taurus	Gemini	Cancer	Leo	Virgo
1952	4/10–5/4	5/5–5/28	5/29–6/21	6/22–7/16	7/17–8/9	8/10–9/3
1953	2/2–3/13	3/4–3/31	7/8–8/3	8/4–8/29	8/30–9/24	9/25–10/18
	4/1–6/5	6/6–7/7				
1954	3/12–4/4	4/5–4/28	4/29–5/23	5/24–6/17	6/18–7/13	7/14–8/8
1955	4/25–5/19	5/20–6/13	6/14–7/7	7/8–8/1	8/2–8/25	8/26–9/18
1956	2/12–3/7	3/8–4/4	4/5–5/7	5/8–6/23	9/9–10/5	10/6–10/31
			6/24–8/4	8/5–9/8		
1957	3/26–4/19	4/20–5/13	5/14–6/6	6/7–7/1	7/2–7/26	7/7–8/19
1958	5/6–5/31	6/1–6/26	6/27–7/22	7/23–8/15	8/16–9/9	9/10–10/3
1959	2/25–3/20	3/21–4/14	4/15–5/10	5/11–6/6	6/7–7/8	7/9–9/20
					9/21–9/24	9/25–11/9
1960	4/10–5/3	5/4–5/28	5/29–6/21	6/22–7/15	7/16–8/9	8/10–9/2
1961	2/3–6/5	6/6–7/7	7/8–8/3	8/4–8/29	8/30–9/23	9/24–10/17
1962	3/11–4/3	4/4–4/28	4/29–5/22	5/23–6/17	6/18–7/12	7/13–8/8
1963	4/24–5/18	5/19–6/12	6/13–7/7	7/8–7/31	8/1–8/25	8/26–9/18
1964	2/11–3/7	3/8–4/4	4/5–5/9	5/10–6/17	9/9–10/5	10/6–10/31
			6/18–8/5	8/6–9/8		
1965	3/26–4/18	4/19–5/12	5/13–6/6	6/7–6/30	7/1–7/25	7/26–8/19
1966	5/6–6/31	6/1–6/26	6/27–7/21	7/22–8/15	8/16–9/8	9/9–10/2
1967	2/24–3/20	3/21–4/14	4/15–5/10	5/11–6/6	6/7–7/8	7/9–9/9
					9/10–10/1	10/2–11/9
1968	4/9–5/3	5/4–5/27	5/28–6/20	6/21–7/15	7/16–8/8	8/9–9/2
1969	2/3–6/6	6/7–7/6	7/7–8/3	8/4–8/28	8/29–9/22	9/23–10/17
1970	3/11–4/3	4/4–4/27	4/28–5/22	5/23–6/16	6/17–7/12	7/13–8/8
1971	4/24–5/18	5/19–6/12	6/13–7/6	7/7–7/31	8/1–8/24	8/25–9/17
1972	2/11–3/7	3/8–4/3	4/4–5/10	5/11–6/11	9/9–10/5	10/6–10/30
			6/12–8/6	8/7–9/8		
1973	3/25–4/18	4/18–5/12	5/13–6/5	6/6–6/29	7/1–7/25	7/26–8/19
1974						
	5/5–5/31	6/1–6/25	6/26–7/21	7/22–8/14	8/15–9/8	9/9–10/2
1975	2/24–3/20	3/21–4/13	4/14–5/9	5/10–6/6	6/7–7/9	7/10–9/2
					9/3–10/4	10/5–11/9

Libra	Scorpio	Sagittarius	Capricorn	Aquarius	Pisces
9/4–9/27	1/1–1/2	1/3–1/27	1/28–2/20	2/21–3/16	3/17–4/9
	9/28–10/21	10/22–11/15	11/16–12/10	12/11–12/31	
10/19–11/11	11/12–12/5	12/6–12/29	12/30–12/31	1/1–1/5	1/6–2/1
8/9–9/6	9/7–10/22	10/23–10/27	1/1–1/22	1/23–2/15	2/16–3/11
	10/28–12/31				
9/19–10/13	1/1–1/6	1/7–2/5	2/6–3/4	3/5–3/30	3/31–4/24
	10/14–11/5	11/6–11/30	12/1–12/24	12/25–12/31	
11/1–11/25	11/26–12/19	12/20–12/31		1/1–1/17	1/18–2/11
8/20–9/14	9/15–10/9	1/1–1/12	1/13–2/5	2/6–3/1	3/2–3/25
		10/10–11/5	11/6–12/16	12/7–12/31	
10/4–10/27	10/28–11/20	11/21–12/14	12/15–12/31	1/1–4/6	4/7–5/5
11/10–12/7	12/8–12/31		1/1–1/7	1/8–1/31	2/1–2/24
9/3–9/26	1/1–1/2	1/3–1/27	1/28–2/20	2/21–3/15	3/16–4/9
	9/27–10/21	10/22–11/15	11/16–12/10	12/11–12/31	
10/18–11/11	11/12–12/4	12/5–12/28	12/29–12/31	1/1–1/5	1/6–2/2
8/9–9/6	9/7–12/31		1/1–1/21	1/22–2/14	2/15–3/10
9/19–10/12	1/1–1/6	1/7–2/5	2/6–3/4	3/5–3/29	3/30–4/23
	10/13–11/5	11/6–11/29	11/30–12/23	12/24–12/31	
11/1–11/24	11/25–12/19	12/20–12/31		1/1–1/16	1/17–2/10
8/20–9/13	9/14–10/9	1/1–1/12	1/13–2/5	2/6–3/1	3/2–3/25
		10/10–11/5	11/6–12/7	12/8–12/31	
10/3–10/26	10/27–11/19	11/20–12/13	2/7–2/25	1/1–2/6	4/7–5/5
			12/14–12/31	2/26–4/6	
11/10–12/7	12/8–12/23		1/1–1/6	1/7–1/30	1/31–2/23
9/3–9/26	1/1	1/2–1/26	1/27–2/20	2/21–3/15	3/16–4/8
	9/27–10/21	10/22–11/14	11/15–12/9	12/10–12/31	
10/18–11/10	11/11–12/4	12/5–12/28	12/29–12/31	1/1–1/4	1/5–2/2
8/9–9/7	9/8–12/31		1/1–1/21	1/22–2/14	2/15–3/10
9/18–10/11	1/1–1/7	1/8–2/5	2/6–3/4	3/5–3/29	3/30–4/23
	10/12–11/5	11/6–11/29	11/30–12/23	12/24–12/31	
	11/25–12/18	12/19–12/31		1/1–1/16	1/17–2/10
10/31–11/24					
8/20–9/13		1/1–1/12	1/13–2/4	2/5–2/28	3/1–3/24
		10/9–11/5	11/6–12/7	12/8–12/31	
			1/30–2/28	1/1–1/29	
10/3–10/26	10/27–11/19	11/20–12/13	12/14–12/31	3/1–4/6	4/7–5/4
			1/1–1/6	1/7–1/30	1/31–2/23
11/10–12/7	12/8–12/31				

VENUS SIGNS 1901–2000

	Aries	Taurus	Gemini	Cancer	Leo	Virgo
1976	4/8–5/2	5/2–5/27	5/27—6/20	6/20–7/14	7/14–8/8	8/8–9/1
1977	2/2–6/6	6/6–7/6	7/6–8/2	8/2–8/28	8/28–9/22	9/22–10/17
1978	3/9–4/2	4/2–4/27	4/27–5/22	5/22–6/16	6/16–7/12	7/12–8/6
1979	4/23–5/18	5/18–6/11	6/11–7/6	7/6–7/30	7/30–8/24	8/24–9/17
1980	2/9–3/6	3/6–4/3	4/3–5/12 6/5–8/6	5/12–6/5 8/6–9/7	9/7–10/4	10/4–10/30
1981	3/24–4/17	4/17–5/11	5/11–6/5	6/5–6/29	6/29–7/24	7/24–8/18
1982	5/4–5/30	5/30–6/25	6/25–7/20	7/20–8/14	8/14–9/7	9/7–10/2
1983	2/22–3/19	3/19–4/13	4/13–5/9	5/9–6/6	6/6–7/10 8/27–10/5	7/10–8/27 10/5–11/9
1984	4/7–5/2	5/2–5/26	5/26–6/20	6/20–7/14	7/14–8/7	8/7–9/1
1985	2/2–6/6	6/8–7/6	7/6–8/2	8/2–8/28	8/28–9/22	9/22–10/16
1986	3/9–4/2	4/2–4/26	4/26–5/21	5/21–6/15	6/15–7/11	7/11–8/7
1987	4/22–5/17	5/17–6/11	6/11–7/5	7/5–7/30	7/30–8/23	8/23–9/16
1988	2/9–3/6	3/6–4/3	4/3–5/17 5/27–8/6	5/17–5/27 8/6–9/7	9/7–10/4	10/4–10/29
1989	3/23–4/16	4/16–5/11	5/11–6/4	6/4–6/29	6/29–7/24	7/24–8/18
1990	5/4–5/30	5/30–6/25	6/25–7/20	7/20–8/13	8/13–9/7	9/7–10/1
1991	2/22–3/18	3/18–4/13	4/13–5/9	5/9–6/6	6/6–7/11 8/21–10/6	7/11–8/21 10/6–11/9
1992	4/7–5/1	5/1–5/26	5/26–6/19	6/19–7/13	7/13–8/7	8/7–8/31
1993	2/2–6/6	6/6–7/6	7/6–8/1	8/1–8/27	8/27–9/21	9/21–10/16
1994	3/8–4/1	4/1–4/26	4/26–5/21	5/21–6/15	6/15–7/11	7/11–8/7
1995	4/22–5/16	5/16–6/10	6/10–7/5	7/5–7/29	7/29–8/23	8/23–9/16
1996	2/9–3/6	3/6–4/3	4/3–8/7	8/7–9/7	9/7–10/4	10/4–10/29
1997	3/23–4/16	4/16–5/10	5/10–6/4	6/4–6/28	6/28–7/23	7/23–8/17
1998	5/3–5/29	5/29–6/24	6/24–7/19	7/19–8/13	8/13–9/6	9/6–9/30
1999	2/21–3/18	3/18–4/12	4/12–5/8	5/8–6/5	6/5–7/12 8/15–10/7	7/12–8/15 10/7–11/9
2000	4/6–5/1	5/1–5/25	5/25–6/13	6/13–7/13	7/13–8/6	8/6–8/31

Libra	Scorpio	Sagittarius	Capricorn	Aquarius	Pisces
9/1–9/26	9/26–10/20	1/1–1/26	1/26–2/19	2/19–3/15	3/15–4/8
		10/20–11/14	11/14–12/6	12/9–1/4	
10/17–11/10	11/10–12/4	12/4–12/27	12/27–1/20		1/4–2/2
8/6–9/7	9/7–1/7			1/20–2/13	2/13–3/9
9/17–10/11	10/11–11/4	1/7–2/5	2/5–3/3	3/3–3/29	3/29–4/23
		11/4–11/28	11/28–12/22	12/22–1/16	
10/30–11/24	11/24–12/18	12/18–1/11			1/16–2/9
8/18–9/12	9/12–10/9	10/9–11/5	1/11–2/4	2/4–2/28	2/28–3/24
			11/5–12/8	12/8–1/23	
10/2–10/26	10/26–11/18	11/18–12/12	1/23–3/2	3/2–4/6	4/6–5/4
			12/12–1/5		
11/9–12/6	12/6–1/1			1/5–1/29	1/29–2/22
9/1–9/25	9/25–10/20	1/1–1/25	1/25–2/19	2/19–3/14	3/14–4/7
		10/20–11/13	11/13–12/9		
10/16–11/9	11/9–12/3	12/3–12/27			1/4–2/2
8/7–9/7	9/7–1/7			1/20–3/13	2/13–3/9
9/16–10/10	10/10–11/3	1/7–2/5	2/5–3/3	3/3–3/28	3/28–4/22
		11/3–11/28	11/28–12/22	12/22–1/15	
10/29–11/23	11/23–12/17	12/17–1/10			1/15–2/9
8/18–9/12	9/12–10/8	10/8–11/5	1/10–2/3	2/3–2/27	2/27–3/23
			11/5–12/10	12/10–1/16	
10/1–10/25	10/25–11/18	11/18–12/12	1/16–3/3	3/3–4/6	4/6–5/4
			12/12–1/5		
8/21–12/6	12/6–12/31	12/21–1/25/92		1/5–1/29	1/29–2/22
8/31–9/25	9/25–10/19	10/19–11/13	1/25–2/18	2/18–3/13	3/13–4/7
			11/13–12/8	12/8–1/3	
10/16–11/9	11/9–12/2	12/2–12/26	12/26–1/19		1/3–2/2
8/7–9/7	9/7–1/7			1/19–2/12	2/12–3/8
9/16–10/10	10/10–11/13	1/7–2/4	2/4–3/2	3/2–3/28	3/28–4/22
		11/3–11/27	11/27–12/21	12/21–1/15	
10/29–11/23	11/23–12/17	12/17–1/10/97			1/15–2/9
8/17–9/12	9/12–10/8	10/8–11/5	1/10–2/3	2/3–2/27	2/27–3/23
			11/5–12/12	12/12–1/9	
9/30–10/24	10/24–11/17	11/17–12/11	1/9–3/4	3/4–4/6	4/6–5/3
11/9–12/5	12/5–12/31	12/31–1/24		1/4–1/28	1/28–2/21
8/31–9/24	9/24–10/19	10/19–11/13	1/24–2/18	2/18–3/12	3/13–4/6
			11/13–12/8	12/8	

1901	MAR	1	Leo
	MAY	11	Vir
	JUL	13	Lib
	AUG	31	Scp
	OCT	14	Sag
	NOV	24	Cap
1902	JAN	1	Aqu
	FEB	8	Pic
	MAR	19	Ari
	APR	27	Tau
	JUN	7	Gem
	JUL	20	Can
	SEP	4	Leo
	OCT	23	Vir
	DEC	20	Lib
1903	APR	19	Vir
	MAY	30	Lib
	AUG	6	Scp
	SEP	22	Sag
	NOV	3	Cap
	DEC	12	Aqu
1904	JAN	19	Pic
	FEB	27	Ari
	APR	6	Tau
	MAY	18	Gem
	JUN	30	Can
	AUG	15	Leo
	OCT	1	Vir
	NOV	20	Lib
1905	JAN	13	Scp
	AUG	21	Sag
	OCT	8	Cap
	NOV	18	Aqu
	DEC	27	Pic
1906	FEB	4	Ari
	MAR	17	Tau
	APR	28	Gem
	JUN	11	Can
	JUL	27	Leo
	SEP	12	Vir
	OCT	30	Lib
	DEC	17	Scp
1907	FEB	5	Sag
	APR	1	Cap
	OCT	13	Aqu
	NOV	29	Pic
1908	JAN	11	Ari
	FEB	23	Tau
	APR	7	Gem
	MAY	22	Can
	JUL	8	Leo
	AUG	24	Vir
	OCT	10	Lib
	NOV	25	Scp
1909	JAN	10	Sag
	FEB	24	Cap
	APR	9	Aqu
	MAY	25	Pic
	JUL	21	Ari
	SEP	26	Pic
	NOV	20	Ari
1910	JAN	23	Tau
	MAR	14	Gem
	MAY	1	Can
	JUN	19	Leo
	AUG	6	Vir
	SEP	22	Lib
	NOV	6	Scp
	DEC	20	Sag
1911	JAN	31	Cap
	MAR	14	Aqu
	APR	23	Pic
	JUN	2	Ari
	JUL	15	Tau
	SEP	5	Gem
	NOV	30	Tau
1912	JAN	30	Gem
	APR	5	Can
	MAY	28	Leo
	JUL	17	Vir
	SEP	2	Lib
	OCT	18	Scp

	NOV	30	Sag		MAY	26	Gem
1913	JAN	10	Cap		JUL	8	Can
	FEB	19	Aqu		AUG	23	Leo
	MAR	30	Pic		OCT	10	Vir
	MAY	8	Ari		NOV	30	Lib
	JUN	17	Tau	1920	JAN	31	Scp
	JUL	29	Gem		APR	23	Lib
	SEP	15	Can		JUL	10	Scp
1914	MAY	1	Leo		SEP	4	Sag
	JUN	26	Vir		OCT	18	Cap
	AUG	14	Lib		NOV	27	Aqu
	SEP	29	Scp	1921	JAN	5	Pic
	NOV	11	Sag		FEB	13	Ari
	DEC	22	Cap		MAR	25	Tau
1915	JAN	30	Aqu		MAY	6	Gem
	MAR	9	Pic		JUN	18	Can
	APR	16	Ari		AUG	3	Leo
	MAY	26	Tau		SEP	19	Vir
	JUL	6	Gem		NOV	6	Lib
	AUG	19	Can		DEC	26	Scp
	OCT	7	Leo	1922	FEB	18	Sag
1916	MAY	28	Vir		SEP	13	Cap
	JUL	23	Lib		OCT	30	Aqu
	SEP	8	Scp		DEC	11	Pic
	OCT	22	Sag	1923	JAN	21	Ari
	DEC	1	Cap		MAR	4	Tau
1917	JAN	9	Aqu		APR	16	Gem
	FEB	16	Pic		MAY	30	Can
	MAR	26	Ari		JUL	16	Leo
	MAY	4	Tau		SEP	1	Vir
	JUN	14	Gem		OCT	18	Lib
	JUL	28	Can		DEC	4	Scp
	SEP	12	Leo	1924	JAN	19	Sag
	NOV	2	Vir		MAR	6	Cap
1918	JAN	11	Lib		APR	24	Aqu
	FEB	25	Vir		JUN	24	Pic
	JUN	23	Lib		AUG	24	Aqu
	AUG	17	Scp		OCT	19	Pic
	OCT	1	Sag		DEC	19	Ari
	NOV	11	Cap	1925	FEB	5	Tau
	DEC	20	Aqu		MAR	24	Gem
1919	JAN	27	Pic		MAY	9	Can
	MAR	6	Ari		JUN	26	Leo
	APR	15	Tau		AUG	12	Vir

	SEP	28	Lib	1932	JAN	18	Aqu
	NOV	13	Scp		FEB	25	Pic
	DEC	28	Sag		APR	3	Ari
1926	FEB	9	Cap		MAY	12	Tau
	MAR	23	Aqu		JUN	22	Gem
	MAY	3	Pic		AUG	4	Can
	JUN	15	Ari		SEP	20	Leo
	AUG	1	Tau		NOV	13	Vir
1927	FEB	22	Gem	1933	JUL	6	Lib
	APR	17	Can		AUG	26	Scp
	JUN	6	Leo		OCT	9	Sag
	JUL	25	Vir		NOV	19	Cap
	SEP	10	Lib		DEC	28	Aqu
	OCT	26	Scp	1934	FEB	4	Pic
	DEC	8	Sag		MAR	14	Ari
1928	JAN	19	Cap		APR	22	Tau
	FEB	28	Aqu		JUN	2	Gem
	APR	7	Pic		JUL	15	Can
	MAY	16	Ari		AUG	30	Leo
	JUN	26	Tau		OCT	18	Vir
	AUG	9	Gem		DEC	11	Lib
	OCT	3	Can	1935	JUL	29	Scp
	DEC	20	Gem		SEP	16	Sag
1929	MAR	10	Can		OCT	28	Cap
	MAY	13	Leo		DEC	7	Aqu
	JUL	4	Vir	1936	JAN	14	Pic
	AUG	21	Lib		FEB	22	Ari
	OCT	6	Scp		APR	1	Tau
	NOV	18	Sag		MAY	13	Gem
	DEC	29	Cap		JUN	25	Can
1930	FEB	6	Aqu		AUG	10	Leo
	MAR	17	Pic		SEP	26	Vir
	APR	24	Ari		NOV	14	Lib
	JUN	3	Tau	1937	JAN	5	Scp
	JUL	14	Gem		MAR	13	Sag
	AUG	28	Can		MAY	14	Scp
	OCT	20	Leo		AUG	8	Sag
1931	FEB	16	Can		SEP	30	Cap
	MAR	30	Leo		NOV	11	Aqu
	JUN	10	Vir		DEC	2	1Pic
	AUG	1	Lib	1938	JAN	30	Ari
	SEP	17	Scp		MAR	12	Tau
	OCT	30	Sag		APR	23	Gem
	DEC	10	Cap		JUN	7	Can

	JUL	22	Leo		FEB	14	Aqu
	SEP	7	Vir		MAR	25	Pic
	OCT	25	Lib		MAY	2	Ari
	DEC	11	Scp		JUN	11	Tau
1939	JAN	29	Sag		JUL	23	Gem
	MAR	21	Cap		SEP	7	Can
	MAY	25	Aqu		NOV	11	Leo
	JUL	21	Cap		DEC	26	Can
	SEP	24	Aqu	1946	APR	22	Leo
	NOV	19	Pic		JUN	20	Vir
1940	JAN	4	Ari		AUG	9	Lib
	FEB	17	Tau		SEP	24	Scp
	APR	1	Gem		NOV	6	Sag
	MAY	17	Can		DEC	17	Cap
	JUL	3	Leo	1947	JAN	25	Aqu
	AUG	19	Vir		MAR	4	Pic
	OCT	5	Lib		APR	11	Ari
	NOV	20	Scp		MAY	21	Tau
1941	JAN	4	Sag		JUL	1	Gem
	FEB	17	Cap		AUG	13	Can
	APR	2	Aqu		OCT	1	Leo
	MAY	16	Pic		DEC	1	Vir
	JUL	2	Ari	1948	FEB	12	Leo
1942	JAN	11	Tau		MAY	18	Vir
	MAR	7	Gem		JUL	17	Lib
	APR	26	Can		SEP	3	Scp
	JUN	14	Leo		OCT	17	Sag
	AUG	1	Vir		NOV	26	Cap
	SEP	17	Lib	1949	JAN	4	Aqu
	NOV	1	Scp		FEB	11	Pic
	DEC	15	Sag		MAR	21	Ari
1943	JAN	26	Cap		APR	30	Tau
	MAR	8	Aqu		JUN	10	Gem
	APR	17	Pic		JUL	23	Can
	MAY	27	Ari		SEP	7	Leo
	JUL	7	Tau		OCT	27	Vir
	AUG	23	Gem		DEC	26	Lib
1944	MAR	28	Can	1950	MAR	28	Vir
	MAY	22	Leo		JUN	11	Lib
	JUL	12	Vir		AUG	10	Scp
	AUG	29	Lib		SEP	25	Sag
	OCT	13	Scp		NOV	6	Cap
	NOV	25	Sag		DEC	15	Aqu
1945	JAN	5	Cap	1951	JAN	22	Pic

	MAR	1	Ari		SEP	24	Lib
	APR	10	Tau		NOV	8	Scp
	MAY	21	Gem		DEC	23	Sag
	JUL	3	Can	1958	FEB	3	Cap
	AUG	18	Leo		MAR	17	Aqu
	OCT	5	Vir		APR	27	Pic
	NOV	24	Lib		JUN	7	Ari
1952	JAN	20	Scp		JUL	21	Tau
	AUG	27	Sag		SEP	21	Gem
	OCT	12	Cap		OCT	29	Tau
	NOV	21	Aqu	1959	FEB	10	Gem
	DEC	30	Pic		APR	10	Can
1953	FEB	8	Ari		JUN	1	Leo
	MAR	20	Tau		JUL	20	Vir
	MAY	1	Gem		SEP	5	Lib
	JUN	14	Can		OCT	21	Scp
	JUL	29	Leo		DEC	3	Sag
	SEP	14	Vir	1960	JAN	14	Cap
	NOV	1	Lib		FEB	23	Aqu
	DEC	20	Scp		APR	2	Pic
1954	FEB	9	Sag		MAY	11	Ari
	APR	12	Cap		JUN	20	Tau
	JUL	3	Sag		AUG	2	Gem
	AUG	24	Cap		SEP	21	Can
	OCT	21	Aqu	1961	FEB	5	Gem
	DEC	4	Pic		FEB	7	Can
1955	JAN	15	Ari		MAY	6	Leo
	FEB	26	Tau		JUN	28	Vir
	APR	10	Gem		AUG	17	Lib
	MAY	26	Can		OCT	1	Scp
	JUL	11	Leo		NOV	13	Sag
	AUG	27	Vir		DEC	24	Cap
	OCT	13	Lib	1962	FEB	1	Aqu
	NOV	29	Scp		MAR	12	Pic
1956	JAN	14	Sag		APR	19	Ari
	FEB	28	Cap		MAY	28	Tau
	APR	14	Aqu		JUL	9	Gem
	JUN	3	Pic		AUG	22	Can
	DEC	6	Ari		OCT	11	Leo
1957	JAN	28	Tau	1963	JUN	3	Vir
	MAR	17	Gem		JUL	27	Lib
	MAY	4	Can		SEP	12	Scp
	JUN	21	Leo		OCT	25	Sag
	AUG	8	Vir		DEC	5	Cap

1964	JAN	13	Aqu		JUL	18	Leo
	FEB	20	Pic		SEP	3	Vir
	MAR	29	Ari		OCT	20	Lib
	MAY	7	Tau		DEC	6	Scp
	JUN	17	Gem	1971	JAN	23	Sag
	JUL	30	Can		MAR	12	Cap
	SEP	15	Leo		MAY	3	Aqu
	NOV	6	Vir		NOV	6	Pic
1965	JUN	29	Lib		DEC	26	Ari
	AUG	20	Scp	1972	FEB	10	Tau
	OCT	4	Sag		MAR	27	Gem
	NOV	14	Cap		MAY	12	Can
	DEC	23	Aqu		JUN	28	Leo
1966	JAN	30	Pic		AUG	15	Vir
	MAR	9	Ari		SEP	30	Lib
	APR	17	Tau		NOV	15	Scp
	MAY	28	Gem		DEC	30	Sag
	JUL	11	Can	1973	FEB	12	Cap
	AUG	25	Leo		MAR	26	Aqu
	OCT	12	Vir		MAY	8	Pic
	DEC	4	Lib		JUN	20	Ari
1967	FEB	12	Scp		AUG	12	Tau
	MAR	31	Lib		OCT	29	Ari
	JUL	19	Scp		DEC	24	Tau
	SEP	10	Sag	1974	FEB	27	Gem
	OCT	23	Cap		APR	20	Can
	DEC	1	Aqu		JUN	9	Leo
1968	JAN	9	Pic		JUL	27	Vir
	FEB	17	Ari		SEP	12	Lib
	MAR	27	Tau		OCT	28	Scp
	MAY	8	Gem		DEC	10	Sag
	JUN	21	Can	1975	JAN	21	Cap
	AUG	5	Leo		MAR	3	Aqu
	SEP	21	Vir		APR	11	Pic
	NOV	9	Lib		MAY	21	Ari
	DEC	29	Scp		JUL	1	Tau
1969	FEB	25	Sag		AUG	14	Gem
	SEP	21	Cap		OCT	17	Can
	NOV	4	Aqu		NOV	25	Gem
	DEC	15	Pic	1976	MAR	18	Can
1970	JAN	24	Ari		MAY	16	Leo
	MAR	7	Tau		JUL	6	Vir
	APR	18	Gem		AUG	24	Lib
	JUN	2	Can		OCT	8	Scp

Year	Month	Day	Sign		Year	Month	Day	Sign
	NOV	20	Sag			FEB	25	Ari
1977	JAN	1	Cap			APR	5	Tau
	FEB	9	Aqu			MAY	16	Gem
	MAR	20	Pic			JUN	29	Can
	APR	27	Ari			AUG	13	Leo
	JUN	6	Tau			SEP	30	Vir
	JUL	17	Gem			NOV	18	Lib
	SEP	1	Can		1984	JAN	11	Scp
	OCT	26	Leo			AUG	17	Sag
1978	JAN	26	Can			OCT	5	Cap
	APR	10	Leo			NOV	15	Aqu
	JUN	14	Vir			DEC	25	Pic
	AUG	4	Lib		1985	FEB	2	Ari
	SEP	19	Scp			MAR	15	Tau
	NOV	2	Sag			APR	26	Gem
	DEC	12	Cap			JUN	9	Can
1979	JAN	20	Aqu			JUL	25	Leo
	FEB	27	Pic			SEP	10	Vir
	APR	7	Ari			OCT	27	Lib
	MAY	16	Tau			DEC	14	Scp
	JUN	26	Gem		1986	FEB	2	Sag
	AUG	8	Can			MAR	28	Cap
	SEP	24	Leo			OCT	9	Aqu
	NOV	19	Vir			NOV	26	Pic
1980	MAR	11	Leo		1987	JAN	8	Ari
	MAY	4	Vir			FEB	20	Tau
	JUL	10	Lib			APR	5	Gem
	AUG	29	Scp			MAY	21	Can
	OCT	12	Sag			JUL	6	Leo
	NOV	22	Cap			AUG	22	Vir
	DEC	30	Aqu			OCT	8	Lib
1981	FEB	6	Pic			NOV	24	Scp
	MAR	17	Ari		1988	JAN	8	Sag
	APR	25	Tau			FEB	22	Cap
	JUN	5	Gem			APR	6	Aqu
	JUL	18	Can			MAY	22	Pic
	SEP	2	Leo			JUL	13	Ari
	OCT	21	Vir			OCT	23	Pic
	DEC	16	Lib			NOV	1	Ari
1982	AUG	3	Scp		1989	JAN	19	Tau
	SEP	20	Sag			MAR	11	Gem
	OCT	31	Cap			APR	29	Can
	DEC	10	Aqu			JUN	16	Leo
1983	JAN	17	Pic			AUG	3	Vir

Year	Month	Day	Sign		Year	Month	Day	Sign
	SEP	19	Lib			SEP	7	Scp
	NOV	4	Scp			OCT	20	Sag
	DEC	18	Sag			NOV	30	Cap
1990	JAN	29	Cap		1996	JAN	8	Aqu
	MAR	11	Aqu			FEB	15	Pic
	APR	20	Pic			MAR	24	Ari
	MAY	31	Ari			MAY	2	Tau
	JUL	12	Tau			JUN	12	Gem
	AUG	31	Gem			JUL	25	Can
	DEC	14	Tau			SEP	9	Leo
1991	JAN	21	Gem			OCT	30	Vir
	APR	3	Can		1997	JAN	3	Lib
	MAY	26	Leo			MAR	8	Vir
	JUL	15	Vir			JUN	19	Lib
	SEP	1	Lib			AUG	14	Scp
	OCT	16	Scp			SEP	28	Sag
	NOV	29	Sag			NOV	9	Cap
1992	JAN	9	Cap			DEC	18	Aqu
	FEB	18	Aqu		1998	JAN	25	Pic
	MAR	28	Pic			MAR	4	Ari
	MAY	5	Ari			APR	13	Tau
	JUN	14	Tau			MAY	24	Gem
	JUL	26	Gem			JUL	6	Can
	SEP	12	Can			AUG	20	Leo
1993	APR	27	Leo			OCT	7	Vir
	JUN	23	Vir			NOV	27	Lib
	AUG	12	Lib		1999	JAN	26	Scp
	SEP	27	Scp			MAY	5	Lib
	NOV	9	Sag			JUL	5	Scp
	DEC	20	Cap			SEP	2	Sag
1994	JAN	28	Aqu			OCT	17	Cap
	MAR	7	Pic			NOV	26	Aqu
	APR	14	Ari		2000	JAN	4	Pic
	MAY	23	Tau			FEB	12	Ari
	JUL	3	Gem			MAR	23	Tau
	AUG	16	Can			MAY	3	Gem
	OCT	4	Leo			JUN	16	Can
	DEC	12	Vir			AUG	1	Leo
1995	JAN	22	Leo			SEP	17	Vir
	MAY	25	Vir			NOV	4	Lib
	JUL	21	Lib			DEC	23	Scp

JUPITER SIGN 1901–2000

Year	Month	Day	Sign		Year	Month	Day	Sign
1901	JAN	19	Cap		1932	AUG	11	Vir
1902	FEB	6	Aqu		1933	SEP	10	Lib
1903	FEB	20	Pic		1934	OCT	11	Scp
1904	MAR	1	Ari		1935	NOV	9	Sag
	AUG	8	Tau		1936	DEC	2	Cap
	AUG	31	Ari		1937	DEC	20	Aqu
1905	MAR	7	Tau		1938	MAY	14	Pic
	JUL	21	Gem			JUL	30	Aqu
	DEC	4	Tau			DEC	29	Pic
1906	MAR	9	Gem		1939	MAY	11	Ari
	JUL	30	Can			OCT	30	Pic
1907	AUG	18	Leo			DEC	20	Ari
1908	SEP	12	Vir		1940	MAY	16	Tau
1909	OCT	11	Lib		1941	MAY	26	Gem
1910	NOV	11	Scp		1942	JUN	10	Can
1911	DEC	10	Sag		1943	JUN	30	Leo
1913	JAN	2	Cap		1944	JUL	26	Vir
1914	JAN	21	Aqu		1945	AUG	25	Lib
1915	FEB	4	Pic		1946	SEP	25	Scp
1916	FEB	12	Ari		1947	OCT	24	Sag
	JUN	26	Tau		1948	NOV	15	Cap
	OCT	26	Ari		1949	APR	12	Aqu
1917	FEB	12	Tau			JUN	27	Cap
	JUN	29	Gem			NOV	30	Aqu
1918	JUL	13	Can		1950	APR	15	Pic
1919	AUG	2	Leo			SEP	15	Aqu
1920	AUG	27	Vir			DEC	1	Pic
1921	SEP	25	Lib		1951	APR	21	Ari
1922	OCT	26	Scp		1952	APR	28	Tau
1923	NOV	24	Sag		1953	MAY	9	Gem
1924	DEC	18	Cap		1954	MAY	24	Can
1926	JAN	6	Aqu		1955	JUN	13	Leo
1927	JAN	18	Pic			NOV	17	Vir
	JUN	6	Ari		1956	JAN	18	Leo
	SEP	11	Pic			JUL	7	Vir
1928	JAN	23	Ari			DEC	13	Lib
	JUN	4	Tau		1957	FEB	19	Vir
1929	JUN	12	Gem			AUG	7	Lib
1930	JUN	26	Can		1958	JAN	13	Scp
1931	JUL	17	Leo			MAR	20	Lib

Year	Month	Day	Sign		Year	Month	Day	Sign
	SEP	7	Scp		1975	MAR	18	Ari
1959	FEB	10	Sag		1976	MAR	26	Tau
	APR	24	Scp			AUG	23	Gem
	OCT	5	Sag			OCT	16	Tau
1960	MAR	1	Cap		1977	APR	3	Gem
	JUN	10	Sag			AUG	20	Can
	OCT	26	Cap			DEC	30	Gem
1961	MAR	15	Aqu		1978	APR	12	Can
	AUG	12	Cap			SEP	5	Leo
	NOV	4	Aqu		1979	FEB	28	Can
1962	MAR	25	Pic			APR	20	Leo
1963	APR	4	Ari			SEP	29	Vir
1964	APR	12	Tau		1980	OCT	27	Lib
1965	APR	22	Gem		1981	NOV	27	Scp
	SEP	21	Can		1982	DEC	26	Sag
	NOV	17	Gem		1984	JAN	19	Cap
1966	MAY	5	Can		1985	FEB	6	Aqu
	SEP	27	Leo		1986	FEB	20	Pic
1967	JAN	16	Can		1987	MAR	2	Ari
	MAY	23	Leo		1988	MAR	8	Tau
	OCT	19	Vir			JUL	22	Gem
1968	FEB	27	Leo			NOV	30	Tau
	JUN	15	Vir		1989	MAR	11	Gem
	NOV	15	Lib			JUL	30	Can
1969	MAR	30	Vir		1990	AUG	18	Leo
	JUL	15	Lib		1991	SEP	12	Vir
	DEC	16	Scp		1992	OCT	10	Lib
1970	APR	30	Lib		1993	NOV	10	Scp
	AUG	15	Scp		1994	DEC	9	Sag
1971	JAN	14	Sag		1996	JAN	3	Cap
	JUN	5	Sc		1997	JAN	21	Aqu
	SEP	11	Sag		1998	FEB	4	Pic
1972	FEB	6	Cap		1999	FEB	13	Ari
	JUL	24	Sag			JUN	28	Tau
	SEP	25	Cap			OCT	23	Ari
1973	FEB	23	Aqu		2000	FEB	14	Tau
1974	MAR	8	Pic			JUN	30	Gem

1903	JAN	19	Aqu	1948	SEP	19	Vir
1905	APR	13	Pic	1949	APR	3	Leo
	AUG	17	Aqu		MAY	29	Vir
1906	JAN	8	Pic	1950	NOV	20	Lib
1908	MAR	19	Ari	1951	MAR	7	Vir
1910	MAY	17	Tau		AUG	13	Lib
	DEC	14	Ari	1953	OCT	22	Scp
1911	JAN	20	Tau	1956	JAN	12	Sag
1912	JUL	7	Gem		MAY	14	Scp
	NOV	30	Tau		OCT	10	Sag
1913	MAR	26	Gem	1959	JAN	5	Cap
1914	AUG	24	Can	1962	JAN	3	Aqu
	DEC	7	Gem	1964	MAR	24	Pic
1915	MAY	11	Can		SEP	16	Aqu
1916	OCT	17	Leo		DEC	16	Pic
	DEC	7	Can	1967	MAR	3	Ari
1917	JUN	24	Leo	1969	APR	29	Tau
1919	AUG	12	Vir	1971	JUN	18	Gem
1921	OCT	7	Lib	1972	JAN	10	Tau
1923	DEC	20	Scp		FEB	21	Gem
1924	APR	6	Lib	1973	AUG	1	Can
	SEP	13	Scp	1974	JAN	7	Gem
1926	DEC	2	Sag		APR	18	Can
1929	MAR	15	Cap	1975	SEP	17	Leo
	MAY	5	Sag	1976	JAN	14	Can
	NOV	30	Cap		JUN	5	Leo
1932	FEB	24	Aqu	1977	NOV	17	Vir
	AUG	13	Cap	1978	JAN	5	Leo
	NOV	20	Aqu		JUL	26	Vir
1935	FEB	14	Pic	1980	SEP	21	Lib
1937	APR	25	Ari	1982	NOV	29	Scp
	OCT	18	Pic	1983	MAY	6	Lib
1938	JAN	14	Ari		AUG	24	Scp
1939	JUL	6	Tau	1985	NOV	17	Sag
	SEP	22	Ari	1988	FEB	13	Cap
1940	MAR	20	Tau		JUN	10	Sag
1942	MAY	8	Gem		NOV	12	Cap
1944	JUN	20	Can	1991	FEB	6	Aqu
1946	AUG	2	Leo	1993	MAY	21	Pic

	JUN	30	Aqu		OCT	25	Ari
1994	JAN	28	Pic	1999	MAR	1	Tau
1996	APR	7	Ari	2000	AUG	10	Gem
1998	JUN	9	Tau		OCT	16	Tau

How to Use the Uranus, Neptune, and Pluto Tables

Find your birthday in the list following each sign.

Look up your Uranus placement by finding your birthday on the following lists.

URANUS IN ARIES BIRTH DATES

March 31–November 4, 1927
January 13, 1928–June 6, 1934
October 10, 1934–March 28, 1935

URANUS IN TAURUS BIRTH DATES

June 6, 1934–October 10, 1934
March 28, 1935–August 7, 1941
October 5, 1941–May 15, 1942

URANUS IN GEMINI BIRTH DATES

August 7–October 5, 1941
May 15, 1942–August 30, 1948
November 12, 1948–June 10, 1949

URANUS IN CANCER BIRTH DATES

August 30–November 12, 1948
June 10, 1949–August 24, 1955
January 28–June 10, 1956

URANUS IN LEO BIRTH DATES

August 24, 1955–January 28, 1956
June 10, 1956–November 1, 1961
January 10–August 10, 1962

URANUS IN VIRGO BIRTH DATES

November 1, 1961–January 10, 1962
August 10, 1962–September 28, 1968
May 20, 1969–June 24, 1969

URANUS IN LIBRA BIRTH DATES

September 28, 1968–May 20, 1969
June 24, 1969–November 21, 1974
May 1–September 8, 1975

URANUS IN SCORPIO BIRTH DATES

November 21, 1974–May 1, 1975
September 8, 1975–February 17, 1981
March 20–November 16, 1981

URANUS IN SAGITTARIUS BIRTH DATES

February 17–March 20, 1981
November 16, 1981–February 15, 1988
May 27, 1988–December 2, 1988

URANUS IN CAPRICORN BIRTH DATES

December 20, 1904–January 30, 1912
September 4–November 12, 1912
February 15–May 27, 1988
December 2, 1988–April 1, 1995
June 9, 1995–January 12, 1996

URANUS IN AQUARIUS BIRTH DATES

January 30–September 4, 1912
November 12, 1912–April 1, 1919
August 16, 1919–January 22, 1920

URANUS IN PISCES BIRTH DATES

April 1–August 16, 1919
January 22, 1920–March 31, 1927
November 4, 1927–January 13, 1928

Look up your Neptune placement by finding your birthday on the following lists.

NEPTUNE IN CANCER BIRTH DATES

July 19–December 25, 1901
May 21, 1902–September 23, 1914
December 14, 1914–July 19, 1915
March 19–May 2, 1916

NEPTUNE IN LEO BIRTH DATES

September 23–December 14, 1914
July 19, 1915–March 19, 1916
May 2, 1916–September 21, 1928
February 19, 1929–July 24, 1929

NEPTUNE IN VIRGO BIRTH DATES

September 21, 1928–February 19, 1929
July 24, 1929–October 3, 1942
April 17–August 2, 1943

NEPTUNE IN LIBRA BIRTH DATES

October 3, 1942–April 17, 1943
August 2, 1943–December 24, 1955
March 12–October 19, 1956
June 15–August 6, 1957

NEPTUNE IN SCORPIO BIRTH DATES

December 24, 1955–March 12, 1956
October 19, 1956–June 15, 1957
August 6, 1957–January 4, 1970
May 3–November 6, 1970

NEPTUNE IN SAGITTARIUS BIRTH DATES

January 4–May 3, 1970
November 6, 1970–January 19, 1984
June 23–November 21, 1984

NEPTUNE IN CAPRICORN BIRTH DATES

January 19, 1984–June 23, 1984
November 21, 1984–January 29, 1998

Find your Pluto placement in the following list:
Pluto in Gemini—Late 1800s until May 28, 1914
Pluto in Cancer—May 26, 1914–June 14, 1939
Pluto in Leo—June 14, 1939–August 19, 1957
Pluto in Virgo—August 19, 1957–October 5, 1971
              April 17, 1972–July 30, 1972
Pluto in Libra—October 5, 1971—April 17, 1972
              July 30, 1972–August 28, 1984
Pluto in Scorpio—August 28, 1984–January 17, 1995
Pluto in Sagittarius—starting January 17, 1995

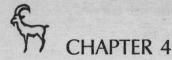 **CHAPTER 4**

Top Trends of '97—Including Full and New Moon Timing & Mercury Retrogrades

As you become more and more involved with astrology, you may be able to sense a certain coordination between the pace of your life and the rhythm of the moon and planets, and you may then wonder if arranging your schedule according to this dance of nature could make a positive difference. If you know the dates that the tricky planet Mercury will be creating havoc with communications, you'll back up that vital fax with a duplicate by Express Mail, read between the lines of contracts, and put off closing that deal until you have double-checked all the information.

This year begins on a hesitant beat, with Mars, the planet of action, swinging into reverse motion in Libra, a sign where it tends to be wavering and indecisive anyway. Is it a great time to start a new venture? Or better for doing research? Wouldn't it behoove you to keep an eye on relationships and legal matters—all areas ruled by Libra, which could suddenly become stalled or switch into reverse gear until late April?

Why not find out for yourself if there's truth to the saying "timing is everything," by marking your own calendar for love, career, moves, vacations, and important events, using the following information and lists in this chapter and the one titled "Look Up Your Planets," as well as the moon sign listings under your daily forecast. Here are some special times to note on your calendar:

- Dates of your sun sign (high energy period)
- The month previous to your sun sign (low energy period)

- Dates of planets in your sign this year
- Full and new moons (pay special attention when these fall in your sun sign)
- Eclipses (see the eclipse chapter in this book)
- Moon in your sun sign every month, as well as moon in the opposite sign (listed in your daily forecast)
- Mercury retrogrades
- Other retrograde periods, especially if the planet is in your sun sign.

Your Most Vital Sign

Every birthday starts a cycle of solar energy for you. You should feel a new surge of vitality as the powerful sun enters your sign. This is the time when predominant energies are most favorable to you. So go for it! Start new projects, make your big moves. You'll get the recognition you deserve now, when everyone is attuned to your sun sign. Look in the tables in this book to see if other planets will also be passing through your sun sign at this time. Venus (love, beauty), Mars (energy, drive), or Mercury (communication, mental sharpness) reinforce the sun and give an extra boost to your life in the areas they affect. Venus will rev up your social and love life, making you seem especially attractive. Mars gives you extra energy and drive. Mercury fuels your brain power and helps you communicate. Jupiter signals an especially lucky period of expansion.

There are two down times related to the sun. During the month before your birthday period, when you are winding up your annual cycle, you could be feeling especially vulnerable and depleted, so get extra rest, watch your diet, and don't overstress yourself. Use this time to gear up for a big push when the sun enters your sign.

Another down time is when the sun is the opposite sign (six months from your birthday) and the prevailing energies are very different from yours. You may feel at odds with the world, and things might not come easily. You'll have to work harder for recognition because people are not on your wavelength. However, this could be a good time to work in cooperation with others or behind the scenes.

Phasing In and Out with the Moon

Working with the phases of the moon is as easy as looking up at the night sky. At the new moon, when both sun and moon are in the same sign, it's the best time to begin new ventures, especially the activities that are favored by that sign. You'll have powerful energies pulling you in the same direction. You'll be focused outward, toward action. Postpone breaking off, terminating, deliberating, or reflecting, activities that require introspection and passive work.

Get your project under way during the first quarter, then go public at the full moon, a time of high intensity, when feelings come out into the open. This is your time to shine, to express yourself. Be aware, however, that because pressures are being released, other people are also letting off steam and confrontations are possible. So try to avoid arguments. Traditionally, astrologers often advise against surgery at this time, for it could produce heavier bleeding.

During the last quarter until the next new moon, you'll be most controlled. This is a winding-down phase, a time to cut off unproductive relationships and to do serious thinking and inward-directed activities.

You'll feel some new and full moons more strongly than others, especially those new moons that fall in your sun sign and full moons in your opposite sign. Because that full moon happens at your low-energy time of year, it is likely to be an especially stressful time in a relationship, when any hidden problems or unexpressed emotions could surface.

1997 Full and New Moons

New Moon in Capricorn—January 8
Full Moon in Leo—January 23rd
New Moon in Aquarius—February 7
Full Moon in Virgo—February 22
New Moon in Pisces—March 8 (Solar Eclipse)
Full Moon in Libra—April 23 (Lunar Eclipse)
New Moon in Aries—April 7
Full Moon in Scorpio—April 22

New Moon in Taurus—May 6
Full Moon in Sagittarius—May 22
New Moon in Gemini—June 5
Full Moon in Sagittarius (Second Time)—June 20
New Moon in Cancer—July 4
Full Moon in Capricorn—July 20
New Moon in Leo—August 3
Full Moon in Aquarius—August 18
New Moon in Virgo—September 1 (Solar Eclipse)
Full Moon in Pisces—September 16 (Lunar Eclipse)
New Moon in Libra—October 1
Full Moon in Aries—October 16
New Moon in Scorpio—October 31
Full Moon in Taurus—November 14
New Moon in Sagittarius—November 30
Full Moon in Gemini—December 14
New Moon in Capricorn—December 29

Forecasting with the Daily Moon Sign

To forecast the daily emotional "weather," to determine your monthly high and low days, or to synchronize your activities with the cycles and the sign of the moon, take note of the moon's daily sign under your daily forecast at the end of the book. Here are some of the activities favored and moods you are likely to encounter under each sign.

Moon in Aries

Get moving! The new moon in Aries is an ideal time to start new projects. Everyone is pushy, raring to go, rather impatient and short-tempered. Leave details and follow-up for later. Competitive sports or marital arts are great ways to let off steam. Quiet types could use some assertiveness, but it's a great day for dynamos. Be careful not to step on too many toes.

Moon in Taurus

It's time to do solid, methodical tasks. This is the time to tackle follow-through or backup work. Lay the foundations for success. Make investments, buy real estate, do appraisals, do some hard bargaining. Attend to your property—get out in the country. Spend some time in your garden. Enjoy creature comforts, your favorite music, a delicious dinner, sensual lovemaking. Forget starting a diet.

Moon in Gemini

Talk means action today. Telephone, write letters, fax! Make new contacts, stay in touch with steady customers. You can handle lots of tasks at once. It's a great day for mental activity of any kind. Don't try to pin people down—they too are feeling restless. Keep it light. Flirtations and socializing are good. Watch gossip, and don't give away secrets.

Moon in Cancer

This is a moody, sensitive, emotional time. People respond to personal attention and mothering. Stay at home, have a family dinner, call your mother. Nostalgia, memories, and psychic powers are heightened. You'll want to hang on to people and things (don't clean out your closets now). You could have some shrewd insights into what others really need and want now. Pay attention to dreams, intuition, and gut reactions.

Moon in Leo

Everybody is in a much more confident, warm, generous mood. It's a good day to ask for a raise, so show what you can do and dress like a star. People will respond to flattery, enjoy a bit of drama and theatre. You may be extravagent—treat yourself royally and show off a bit but don't break the bank! Be careful that you don't promise more than you can deliver.

Moon in Virgo

Do practical down-to-earth chores. Review your budget. Make repairs. Be an efficiency expert. This is not a day to ask for a raise. Have a health checkup, revamp your diet, and buy vitamins or health food. Make your home spotless as you take care of details and piled-up chores. Reorganize your work and life so they run more smoothly, efficiently, and economically. Be prepared for others to be in a critical, fault-finding mood.

Moon in Libra

Attend to legal matters, negotiating contracts and arbitrating. Do things with your favorite partner—socialize, be romantic, and buy a special gift or a beautiful object. Decorate yourself or your surroundings. Buy new clothes. Throw a party or plan an elegant, romantic evening. Smooth over any ruffled feathers and be sure to avoid confrontations and stick to civilized discussions.

Moon in Scorpio

This is a day to do things with passion. You'll have excellent concentration and focus. Try not to get too intense emotionally, however, and avoid sharp exchanges with loved ones. Others may tend to go to extremes, get jealous, overreact. It's a great day for troubleshooting, problem-solving, research, scientific work, and making love. Pay attention to psychic vibes.

Moon in Sagittarius

It's a great time for travel. Have philosophical discussions. Set long-range career goals. Work out, do sports, or buy athletic equipment. Others will be feeling upbeat, exuberant, and adventurous. Risk taking is favored—you may feel like taking a gamble, betting on the horses, visiting a local casino, or buying a lottery ticket. Teaching, writing, and spiritual activities also get the green light. Relax outdoors, and take care of animals.

Moon in Capricorn

You can accomplish a lot today, so get on the ball! Issues concerning your basic responsibilties, duties, family, and parents could crop up. You'll be expected to deliver on promises now, so weed out the dead wood from your life. Get a dental checkup.

Moon in Aquarius

It's a great day for doing things with groups—clubs, meetings, outings, politics, parties. Campaign for your candidate or work for a worthy cause. Deal with larger issues that affect humanity, such as the environment or metaphysical questions. Buy a computer or electronic gadget. Watch TV. Wear something outrageous. Try something you've never done before or present an original idea. Don't stick to a rigid schedule—go with the flow. Take a class in meditation, mind control, or yoga.

Moon in Pisces

This can be a very creative day, so let your imagination work overtime. Film, theater, music, or ballet could inspire you. Spend some time alone, resting and reflecting, reading or writing poetry. Daydreams can also be profitable. Help those less fortunate or lend a listening ear to someone who may be feeling blue. Don't overindulge in self-pity or escapism, however. People are especially vulnerable to substance abuse now. Turn your thoughts to romance and someone special.

When the Planets Go Backward

All the planets, except for the sun and moon, have times when they appear to move backward—or retrograde— in the sky, or so it seems from our point of view on earth. At these times, planets do not work as they usually do, so it's best to take a break from that planet's energies and do some work on an inner level.

Mercury Retrograde

Mercury goes retrograde most often, and its effects can be especially irritating. When it reaches a short distance ahead of the sun three times a year, it seems to move backward from our point of view. Astrologers often compare retrograde motion to the optical illusion that occurs when we ride on a train that passes another train traveling at a different speed—the second train appears to be moving in reverse.

What this means to you is that the Mercury-ruled areas of your life—analytical thought processes, communications, scheduling, and such—are subject to all kinds of confusion. Be prepared. People will change their minds or renege on commitments. Communications equipment can break down and schedules must be changed on short notice. People are late for appointments or don't show up at all. Traffic is terrible. Major purchases malfunction, don't work out, or get delivered in the wrong color. Letters don't arrive or are delivered to the wrong address. Employees will make errors that have to be corrected later. Contracts don't work out or must be renegotiated.

Since most of us can't put our lives on hold for nine weeks every year (3 Mercury retrograde periods), we should learn to tame the trickster and make it work for us. The key is in the prefix "re." this is the time to go back over things in your life. Reflect on what you've done during the previous months. Look for deeper insights, spot errors you've missed, take time to review and reevaluate what has happened. This time is very good for inner spiritual work and meditations. Rest and reward yourself—it's a good time to take a vacation, especially if you revisit a favorite place. Reorganize your work and finish up projects that are backed up. Clean out your desk and closets. Throw away what you can't recycle. If you must sign contracts or agreements, do so with a contingency clause that lets you reevaluate the terms later.

Postpone major purchases or commitments. Don't get married (unless you're remarrying the same person). Try not to rely on other people keeping appointments, contracts, or agreements to the letter—have several alternatives. Double-check and read between the lines. Don't buy anything connected with communications or transportation (if you must, be sure to cover yourself). Mercury retrograding through your sun sign will intensify its effect on your life.

If Mercury was retrograde when you were born, you may be one of the lucky people who don't suffer the frustration of this period. If so, your mind probably works in a very intuitive, insightful way.

The sign Mercury is retrograding through can give you an idea of what's in store, as well as the sun signs that will be especially challenged.

Mercury Retrograde Periods in 1997

As the year begins, Mercury will be retrograding in Capricorn.

Mercury Turns Direct in Capricorn—January 12
Mercury Retrograde in Taurus—April 15
Mercury Turns Direct—May 8
Mercury Retrograde in Virgo—August 17
Mercury Turns Direct—September 10
Mercury Retrograde in Capricorn—December 7
Mercury Turns Direct in Sagitarrius—December 27

Mars Retrograde in 1997

Mars shows how and when to get where you want to go. Timing your moves with Mars on your side can give you a big push. On the other hand, pushing Mars the wrong way can guarantee that you'll run into frustrations in every corner. Your best times to forge ahead are during the weeks when Mars is traveling through your sun sign or your Mars sign (look these up in the chapter on how to find your planets). Also consider times when Mars is in a compatible sign (fire with air signs, or earth with water signs). You'll be sure to have planetary power on your side.

Hold your fire, however, when Mars retrogrades this year, especially if your sun or Mars is in either Libra or Virgo. This is the time to exercise patience and to let someone else run with the ball, especially if it's the opposing team. You may feel that you're not accomplishing much, but that's the right idea. Slow down and work off any frustrations at the gym. It's also best to postpone buying mechanical devices, which are Mars-ruled, and to take extra care when handling sharp objects. Sports, especially those requiring excellent balance, should be played with care. Be sure to use the appropriate protective gear and don't take unnecessary chances. This is not the time for daredevil moves! Pace yourself and pay extra attention to your health, since you may be especially vulnerable at this time.

Mars Retrograde Dates:

Mars Turns Retrograde in Libra—February 6
Mars Retrograde Moves Back Into Virgo—March 8
Mars Turns Direct—April 27 in Virgo

When Other Planets Retrograde

The slower-moving planets stay retrograde for months at a time (Saturn, Jupiter, Neptune, Uranus, and Pluto). When Saturn is retrograde, you may feel more like hanging out at the beach than getting things done. It's an uphill battle with self-discipline at this time. Neptune retrograde promotes a dreamy escapism from reality, whereas Uranus retrograde may mean setbacks in areas where there have been sudden changes. Think of this as an adjustment period, a time to think things over and allow new ideas to develop. Pluto retrograde is a time to work on establishing proportion and balance in areas where there have been recent dramatic transformations.

When the planets start moving forward again, there's a shift in the atmosphere. Activities connected with each planet start moving ahead, plans that were stalled get rolling. Make a special note of those days on your calendar and proceed accordingly.

Other Retrogrades in 1997

Pluto Turns Retrograde in Sagittarius—March 8
Neptune Turns Retrograde in Capricorn—May 1
Uranus Retrograde in Aquarius—May 13
Jupiter Turns Retrograde in Aquarius—June 10
Saturn Turns Retrograde in Aries—August 1
Pluto Turns Direct in Sagittarius—August 13
Jupiter Direct in Aquarius—October 8
Neptune Direct in Capricorn—October 9
Uranus Direct in Aquarius—October 14
Saturn Turns Direct in Aries—December 16

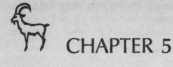 **CHAPTER 5**

The Power of Eclipses

Have you ever considered the amazing fact that one of the smallest bodies in our solar system, our moon, appears almost the same size as the sun, the largest body in our solar system? This is most evident during a total solar eclipse, when the moon so neatly covers the sun that scientists can study the solar flares that light up the rim of the eclipse. Imagine what would happen if the moon were somehow caused to change its orbit, perhaps by a bombarding asteroid. What would happen to the tides and to ocean and plant life, which respond to the moon? What would happen to our own bodies, which are mostly water? Life on earth would be impossible!

In case we've been taking the moon for granted, the eclipse seasons, which occur about every six months, remind us how important the moon is for our survival. Perhaps that is why eclipses have always had an ominous reputation. Folklore all over the world blames eclipses for catastrophes such as birth defects, crop failures, and hurricanes. Villagers on the peninsula of Baja, California paint their fruit trees red and wear red ribbons and underwear to deflect "evil rays." During the total eclipse of July 1991, everyone retreated safely indoors to follow the eclipse on television. In other native societies, people play drums and make loud noises to frighten off heavenly monsters believed to destroy the light of the sun and moon. Only the romantic Tahitians seem to have positive feelings about an eclipse. In this sensual tropical paradise, legend declares that the lights go out when the sun and moon make love and procreate the stars.

Ancient Chaldean astrologer-priests were the first to time eclipses accurately. They discovered that 6,585 days after an eclipse, another eclipse would happen. By counting ahead after all the eclipses in a given year, they could predict eclipses eighteen years into the future. This technique was practiced by navigators through the centuries, including Christopher Columbus, who used his knowledge of an upcoming lunar eclipse to extort food from the frightened inhabitants of Jamaica in 1504. In ancient Mexico, Mayan astronomer-priests also discovered that eclipses occur at regular intervals and recorded them with a hieroglyph of a serpent swallowing the sun.

What Causes an Eclipse?

A solar eclipse is the passage of the new moon directly across the face of the sun. It is a very exciting and awesome event, which causes the sky to darken suddenly. Though the effect lasts only a few minutes, it is enough to strike panic in the uniformed viewer.

A lunar eclipse happens when the full moon passes through the shadow of the Earth on the opposite side from the sun; as a result, the Earth keeps the sun's light from reaching the moon. The moon must be in level alignment with the sun and Earth for a lunar eclipse to occur.

Conditions are ripe for an eclipse twice a year, when a full or new moon is most likely to cross the path of the sun at two points known as the nodes.

What to Know About Nodes

To understand the nodes, visualize two rings, one inside the other. As you move the rings, you'll notice that the two circles intersect at opposite points. Now imagine one ring as the moon's orbit and the other as the sun's orbit as seen from Earth. The crossing points are called the moon's nodes.

For an eclipse to happen, two conditions must be met. First, the path of the orbiting moon must be close enough to a node. Second, this must happen at a time when there is either a new or full moon. (Not every new or full moon happens close enough to the nodes to create an eclipse.) The axis of the nodes is continually moving backward through the zodiac at the rate of about one and a half degrees per month; therefore, eclipses will eventually occur in every sign of the zodiac.

How Often Do Eclipses Occur?

Whenver the sun draws close to one of the nodes, any new or full moon happening near that time will create an eclipse. This eclipse season happens twice a year, approximately every six months. There are at least four eclipses each year, and there can be as many as seven.

Eclipses Have Family Ties

One of the most interesting things about eclipses is that they have "families." Each eclipse is a member of a string of related eclipses that pop up regularly. As mentioned before, the ancient Chaldeans, who were the first great sky watchers, discovered that eclipses reoccur in patterns, repeating themselves after approximately eighteen years plus nine to eleven days, in a cycle lasting a total of approximately 1300 years. Much later, in the eleventh century AD, these patterns became known as the "Saros Series." (In ancient Greek, saros means repetition.)

Because each Saros Series begins at a moment in time, the initial eclipse has a horoscope, and therefore a personality that goes through stages of development as the series of eclipses progresses over its 1300-year lifetime. So as a Saros Series moves through your chart, it will produce an eclipse with a similar personality every eighteen years. In the interim, you'll experience eclipses belonging to other Saros Series, which will exhibit their own special family characteristics. Therefore, there can be no one generic interpretation for eclipses, since each affects your horoscope in a different way, according to the personality of its particular Saros Series. This year, four eclipses will happen, so here is a brief description of their personalities. It might be useful to check the times of previous eclipses in the series to see what influences in your life might reoccur.

Saros Series #17 South will create a solar eclipse on the evening of March 8 in Pisces and a lunar eclipse on March 24 in Libra. The interpretation for this series seems to be quite beneficial, since the initial eclipse horoscope is blessed by a well-placed Jupiter and Venus, which favors relationships, romance, and creativity. Since the previous eclipses in this series happened in February and March of 1979, check what was happening in your life at that time for clues.

Saros Series #18 North will create a solar eclipse on September 1 in Virgo and a lunar eclipse on September 16 in Pisces. This eclipse series has quite a different and more stressful horoscope than the one earlier this year, highlighted by Pluto and Uranus, bringing potential for much tension, illnesses, accidents, and obsessive—compulsive tendencies. Review your experiences during the previous eclipses on August 22 (solar) and September 6 (lunar) 1979.

How Does a Solar Eclipse Interpretation Differ From a Lunar One?

The lineup of energy is quite different between a solar and a lunar eclipse. Lunar eclipses happen at the full moon, a time in the normal monthly lunar cycle when it's natural for emotions (ruled by the moon) to come to a head and be released. At a lunar eclipse, however, when the Earth passes between the sun and moon, the tense pull of energy created by the powerful opposition is temporarily short-circuited. During this time, we might become more objective and find relief from destructive emotional patterns, such as addictions, which would normally be intensified. The momentary turn-off of the full moon's emotional energies could give us a different perspective that might help us turn our lives around. On the other hand, this break in the normal cycle could cause a bewildering disorientation that intensifies insecurities and sends us off balance.

The solar eclipse occurs when the moon and sun are directly aligned, with the moon temporarily blocking the sun's energy. It is now the moon's forces that dominate, interfering with the normal communication between the Earth and the sun. When subconscious lunar forces take over, we are more likely to be ruled by our emotions and to make decisions based on subconscious feelings rather than on reason. Our self-esteem may also be weakened, as the sun (our ego force) darkens. However, this can be an opportunity to work on a deep inner spiritual level. Psychic experiences are also possibilities as the doorway to the unconscious opens wide.

Because eclipses bring about such a concentration of energy, these can be intense, unbalanced times, when the rhythms of everything in nature—birds, animal, fish, even oysters—are thrown off. But if we look behind a crisis that occurs at this time, we often find that there is some deep positive force bubbling beneath the surface that needed some kind of upheaval to manifest.

What is the Purpose of an Eclipse in my Life?

Eclipses can bring on milestone events in your life if they aspect a key point in your horoscope. In general, they shake up the status quo, bringing hidden areas out into the open. During this time, problems you've been avoiding or have brushed aside can surface to demand your attention. A good coping strategy is to accept whatever comes up as a challenge—it could make a big difference in your life. And don't forget the power of your sense of humor. If you can laugh at something, you'll never be afraid of it.

Second-guessing the eclipses is easy if you have a copy of your horoscope calculated by a computer. This enables you to pinpoint the area of your life that will be affected. However, you can make an educated guess, by setting up a rough diagram on your own. If you'd like to find out which area of your life this year's eclipses are most likely to affect, follow these easy steps. First, you must know the time of day you were born and look up your rising sign listed on the tables in this book. Then set up an estimated horoscope by drawing a circle, then dividing it into four parts by making a cross directly through the center. Continue to divide each of the parts into thirds, as if you were dividing a cake, until you have twelve slices. Write your rising sign on the middle left-hand slice, which would be the 9 o'clock point, if you were looking at your watch. Then continue counter-clockwise until you have listed all twelve signs of the zodiac.

You should now have a basic diagram of your horoscope chart (minus the planets, of course). Starting with your rising sign "slice," number each portion consecutively, working counter-clockwise. Since this year's eclipses will fall in Pisces, Virgo, and Libra, find the number of these slices, or "houses," on the chart and read the following descriptions for the kinds of issues that are likely to be emphasized.

If an Eclipse Falls in Your First House

Events cause you to examine the ways you are acting independently and push you to become more visible and to assert yourself. This is a time when you feel compelled to make your own decisions and do your own thing. There is an emphasis on how you are coming across to others. You may want to change your physical appearance, body image, or style of dress in some way. Under affliction, there might be illness or physical harm.

If an Eclipse Falls in Your Second House

This is the place where you consider all matters of security. You consolidate your resources, earn money, acquire property, and decide what you value and what you want to own. On a deeper level, this house reveals your sense of self-worth, the inner values that draw wealth in various forms.

If an Eclipse Falls in Your Third House

Here you communicate, reach out to others, express your ideas, and explore different courses of action. You may feel especially restless and have confrontations with neighbors or siblings. In your search for more knowledge, you may decide to improve your skills, get more education, or sign up for a course that interests you. Local transportation, especially your car, might be affected by an eclipse here.

If an Eclipse Falls in Your Fourth House

Here is where you put down roots, establishing your home base. You'll consider what home really means to you. Issues involving parents, the physical setup or location of your home, and your immediate family demand your attention. You may be especially concerned with parenting or relationships with your own mother. You may consider moving your home to a new location or leaving home.

If an Eclipse Falls in Your Fifth House

Here is where you express yourself, either through your personal talents or through procreating children. You are interested in making your special talents visible. This is also the house of love affairs and the romantic aspect of life, where you flirt, have fun, and enjoy the excitement of love. Hobbies and crafts, along with the ways you explore the playful child within, fall in this area.

If an Eclipse Falls in Your Sixth House

This is your care and maintenance department, where you take care of your health, organize your life, and set up a daily routine. It is also the place where you perfect your skills and add polish to your life. The chores you do every day, the skills you learn, and the techniques you use fall here. If something doesn't work in your life, an eclipse is sure to bring this to light. If you've been neglecting your health, diet, and fitness, you'll probably pay the consequences during an eclipse. Or you may be faced with work that requires much routine organization and steady effort, rather than creative ability. Or you may be required to perform services for others. (In ancient astrology, this was the place of slavery!)

If an Eclipse Falls in Your Seventh House

This is the area of committed relationships, of those which involve legal agreements, of working in a close relationship with another. Here you'll be dealing with how you relate, what you'll be willing to give up for the sake of a marriage or partnership. Eclipses here can put extra pressure on a relationship, and, if it's not working, precipitate a breakup. Lawsuits and open enemies also reside here.

If an Eclipse Falls in Your Eighth House

This area is concerned with power and control. Consider what are you willing to give up in order that something might happen. Power struggles, intense relationships, and the desire to penetrate a deeper mystery belong here. Debts, loans, or financial matters that involve another party, as well as wheeling and dealing, also come into focus. So does sex, where you surrender your individual power to create a new life together. Matters involving birth and death are also involved here.

If an Eclipse Falls in Your Ninth House

Here is where you look at the big picture, at the way everything relates to form a pattern. You'll seek information that helps you find meaning in life—higher education, religion, travel, global issues. Eclipses here can push you to get out of your rut, explore something you've never done before, and expand your horizons.

In an Eclipse Falls in Your Tenth House

This is the high-profile point in your chart. Here is where you consider how society looks at you and what your position is in the outside world. You'll be concerned about whether you receive proper credit for your work and if you're recognized by supervisors. Promotions, raises, and other forms of recognition can be given or denied. Your standing in your career or community can be challenged, or you'll be publicly acknowledged for achieving a goal. An eclipse here can make you famous—or burst your balloon if you've been too ambitious or neglecting other areas of your life.

If an Eclipse Falls in Your Eleventh House

Your relationship with groups of people comes under scrutiny during an eclipse. You'll focus on who you are identified with, who you socialize with, and how well are you accepted by other members of your team. Activities of clubs and political parties, as well as networking and other social interactions, become important. You'll be concerned about what other people think, asking "Do they like me?" and "Will I make the team or win the election?"

If an Eclipse Falls in Your Twelfth House

This is the time when the focus turns to your inner life. An especially favorable eclipse here might bring you great insight and inspiration, or events may happen that cause you to retreat from public life. Here is where we go to be alone, to do spiritual or reparatory work in retreats, hospitals, religious institutions, or psychotherapy. Here is where you deliver selfless service, through charitable acts. Good aspects from an eclipse could promote an ability to go with the flow, to rise above the competition and find an inner, almost mystical strength that enables you to connect with the deepest needs of others.

What is the Best Thing to do During an Eclipse?

When the natural rhythms of the sun and moon are disturbed, it's best to postpone important activities. Be sure to mark eclipse days on your calendar, especially if the eclipse falls in your birth sign. This year, those born under Pisces, Virgo, and Libra should take special note of the conscious and unconscious feelings that arise or are suppressed. With lunar eclipses, some possibilities could be a break from attachments, or the healing of an illness or substance abuse that had been triggered by the subconscious. The temporary event could be a healing time, helping you to gain perspective. During solar eclipses, when you could be in a highly subjective state, pay attention to the hidden subconscious patterns that surface, the emotional truth that is revealed in your feelings at this time.

The effect of the eclipse can reverberate for some time, often months after the event. But it is especially important to stay cool and make no major moves during the period known as the shadow of the eclipse, which begins about a week before and lasts until at least three days after the eclipse. After three days, the daily rhythms should be back to normal and you can proceed with business as usual.

Back in 1648, an astrologer named William Lilly wrote a treatise on eclipses that listed the effect of an eclipse in each of the astrological signs. Though his predictions stressed the negative side of the eclipse, some have been quite accurate. Solar eclipses in Pisces, for instance, were said to portend destruction and waste in sea towns, an earthquake, and churchmen "questioned and called to account for knavery." In 1989, there was a solar eclipse in Pisces (reinforced by a conjuction of Saturn and Neptune ruler of Pisces). In the following few months, there was a devastating earthquake in San Francisco, much concern about water pollution and oil spills, and the sensational trial of TV evangelist Jim Bakker, whose financial and sexual scandals surfaced and sent him to prison.

However, it is more positive to view eclipses as very special times when we can receive great insight through a changed perspective. By blacking out the emotional pressure of the full moon, a lunar eclipse could be a time of reason rather than confusion, a time when we can take a break from our problems. A solar eclipse, when the new moon blocks out the sun (or ego), could be a time when the moon's most positive qualities are expressed, bringing up a feeling of oneness, and compassion.

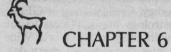

CHAPTER 6

Getting Connected: Your Resources for Joining the World of Astrology

Once you've caught the astrology bug, the worldwide astrology community welcomes you! You'll soon discover that there's no end to the fascinating techniques and aspects of our age-old art. What's more, you can connect with thousands of fellow astrology fans at club meetings, conferences, online classes and bulletin boards, or Inernet Web sites. There's always something new to learn, a lively debate or "flame war" to join, or information to share.

There are conferences all over the country, set up by very well organized groups of astrologers dedicated to promoting the image of astrology in the most positive way. The National Council for Geocosmic Research (NCGR) is one nationwide group that is dedicated to bringing astrologers together, promoting fellowship and a high quality education. They have an accredited course system, with study programs covering all levels from beginner to advanced. At this writing, they are sponsoring courses on the Internet, so check their Web site in the following resource list, if you're interested. Whether you'd like to know more about such specialities as financial astrology or techniques for timing by the stars, or if you'd prefer a psychological or mythological approach, you'll find all the experts at NCGR conferences or on their extensive backlog of conference tapes.

Those of you with computers have a terrific tool for connecting with other astrology buffs of all levels of expertise. If you have a modem, you can sign on to one of the major bulletin boards, such as the Microsoft Network, America Online, Prodigy, Compuserve, or GEnie, all of which have lively astrology areas. Access to the Internet will provide you with entry to the World Wide Web, which has astrology sites springing up every day. Or you can check into the astrology newsgroup (alt.astrology) for the latest happenings. If you'd like to buy some astrology software, you can get the opinions and advice of other astrologers. Some bulletin board groups even have demo versions of programs that you can download and preview.

If you do not yet own a computer and are thinking about buying a new or used one, have no fear. In spite of the breakneck pace of technology, there will still be plenty of software available for your computer. Even if you are using a dinosaur from the early 1980s, there are still excellent calculation and interpretation programs available.

If you are a newcomer to astrology, it is a good idea to learn the glyphs (astrology's special shorthand language) before you purchase a program. That way, you'll be able to read the charts without consulting a book. One program, however—Astrolabe's Solar Fire for Windows—has pop-up definitions. Just click your mouse on the glyph and a definition appears.

The most sophisticated astrology programs are more expensive (approximately $200–$250 at this writing), but you may not need all the features they provide. In that case, investigate some of the lower-priced programs—there are many available for under $100. You can also try out bargain-priced software at your local computer store. Expert Software has a widely available astrology program in computer stores for under $20 that is easy to use and will get you up and running. Call some of the companies on our list, state your needs and the type of computer you have, and they'll be happy to help you find the right program.

If you cannot go to conferences, you can still listen to many of the lectures and workshops on tape in your home or car. See the resource list to order catalogues for local or nationwide conferences. Taped instruction is also advertised in the most specialized astrology magazines, such as *Planet Earth* or *Mountain Astrologer*.

Another option, which might interest those who live in out-of-the-way places or are unable to fit classes into their schedule, are study-by-mail courses offered by several astrological computing services. Some courses will send you a series of tapes; others use workbooks or computer printouts.

Your Astrology Resource List

Nationwide Astrology Organizations

Contact these organizations for information on conferences, workshops, local meetings, conference tapes, and referrals.

NATIONAL COUNCIL FOR GEOCOSMIC RESEARCH
Educational workshops, tapes, conferences, and directory of professional astrologers available.
NCGR Membership Secretary
P.O. Box 501078
Malabar, FL 32950-1078
Phone: 407-722-9500
Fax: 407-728-2244
Internet—World Wide Web Site:
http://www.allware.com/ncgr

AMERICAN FEDERATION OF ASTROLOGERS (AFA)
P.O. Box 2240
Tempe, AZ 85382

A.F.A.N.
Networking, legal issues concerning astrology, news source concerning the astrology community.
8306 Wilshire Blvd., Suite 537
Beverly Hills, CA 90211
Fax: 213-799-2748

ARC DIRECTORY
Listing of astrologers worldwide.
2920 East Monte Vista
Tucson, AZ 85716
Phone: 602-321-1114

Conference and Lecture Tapes

Tapes are an excellent way to learn more about astrology. Here are some of the best resources for taped lectures by top astrologers.

NATIONAL COUNCIL FOR GEOCOSMIC RESEARCH

A favorite resource for great conferences all around the country, this is an extensive catalogue of tapes available. To order a catalogue contact:
Margie Herskovitz
5826 Greenspring Avenue
Baltimore, MD 21209
Phone: 410-466-1510

PEGASUS TAPES

Lectures from some of the most famous astrologers, conference tapes.
P.O. Box 419
Santa Ysabel, CA 92070

BULLDOG AUDIO

This company records lectures at main astrology conferences. To receive a brochure:
Phone: 208-667-8811
Fax: 208-664-9885

INTERNATIONAL SOCIETY OF ASTROLOGICAL REASEARCH

Lectures, workshops, seminars.
P.O. Box 38613
Los Angeles, CA 90038

ISIS INSTITUTE

P.O. Box 2122
El Sobrante, CA 94820-1222

ASTRO-ANALYTICS PRODUCTIONS

P.O. 16927
Encino, CA 91416-6927

Computer Programs

ASTROLABE
Check out their versatile, easy-to-use Windows program, Solar Fire for Windows. There's a variety of programs for all levels of expertise, wide selection of computer-generated readings, MAC program. A good source for innovative software, as well as programs for older computers.
Box 1750-R
Brewster, MA 02631
Phone: 800-843-6682

MATRIX SOFTWARE
Wide variety of software in all price ranges, demo disks at student and advanced levels, interesting readings. Check out WinStar for Windows.
315 Marion Avenue
Big Rapids, MI 49307
Phone: 800-PLANETS

ASTRO COMMUNICATIONS SERVICES
Very established, respected company with top-notch astrologers. Books, software for MAC and IBM compatibles, low-cost individual charts, telephone consultations. Extensive free catalogue.
Dept. AF693
P.O. Box 34487
San Diego, CA 92163-4487
Phone: 800-888-9983

AIR SOFTWARE
Some terrific programs from one of astrology's leading lights, Alphee Lavoie.
115 Caya Avenue
West Hartford, CT 06110
Phone: 800-659-1AIR

TIMECYCLES RESEARCH
Programs for IBM and MAC. Beautiful printouts. Ask about their Io Services software.
27 Dimmock Rd.
Waterford, CT 06385

Phone: 800-827-2240
E-mail: TimeCycles@aol.com

ASTRO-CARTOGRAPHY
Charts for location changes.
Astro-Numeric Service, Box 336-B
Ashland, OR 97520
Phone: 800-MAPPING

MICROCYCLES
Variety of programs; large catalogue.
P.O. Box 3175
Culver City, CA 90231
Phone: 800-829-2537

Astrology Online Resources

If you have a computer with a modem, then the world of online astrology is just a phone call away. By the time this book is in print, there may be many other active astrology areas, so check your favorite online service. If there is no astrology section, you may find astrologers hanging out under the New Age, Metaphysical, and Hobbies categories.

NATIONAL COUNCIL FOR GEOCOSMIC RESEARCH
Home Page
http://www.allware.com/ncgr

DELPHI
There is an astrology forum on this online service.
Starstuff@Delphi.com

MICROSOFT NETWORK
For those with Windows 95, there is a New Age Forum managed by Matrix Software, with twenty topic areas devoted to astrology at this writing.

AMERICA ONLINE
Check under New Age Resources or Clubs. This huge service has an especially easy-to-use World Wide Web

browser. At this writing, they are launching Astronet, a more expanded astrology area.

GEnie
You can meet and chat with professional astrologers, as well as beginning astrology buffs, on the astrology roundtable. There are hundreds of astrology-related files from beginner to professional-interest levels. There is also access to internet files, plus live online classes, conferences, and chats, as well as an astrology magazine. It's managed by professional astrologers who are available to answer your questions. In the extensive library, there are free calculation programs as well as demo programs for the PC and MAC formats. It's a great place to ask questions, find out the latest conference news, and meet other astrology buffs.

To join GEnie or get more information, call 800-638-9636 (GEnie client services) noon to midnight, eastern time.

COMPUSERVE
Check the NEW AGE category.

PRODIGY
Check out Astrology under Hobbies.

ASTROLOGY E-MAIL DISCUSSION GROUP
Correspond online with fellow astrology buffs in a focused discussion group. For information and guidelines, contact via your Internet server.
http://idirect.com/oracle/oracle-a-policy.html

METALOG YELLOW PAGES
An international online directory for consultant astrologers.
http:/www.astrologer.com

Astrology Magazines

Most have listings of conferences, events, and local happenings.

AMERICAN ASTROLOGY
475 Park Avenue South
NY, NY 10016

DELL HOROSCOPE
P.O. Box 53352
Boulder, CO 89321-3342

PLANET EARTH
The Great Bear
P.O. Box 5164
Eugene, OR 97405

MOUNTAIN ASTROLOGER
P.O. Box 970
Cedar Ridge, CA 95924-0970

ASPECTS
Aquarius Workshops
P.O. Box 260556
Encino, CA 91426

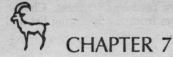

CHAPTER 7

Putting Venus and Mars—the Love Planets—to Work in Your Life

If you've been singing the blues and wondering, "What is this thing called love?" take heart! Though the sizzle in your relationship may have turned to fizzle, you might be able to rekindle the flame by applying some astrological first aid to your relationship.

For advice for the lovelorn, you have only to look as far as Venus and Mars for tips on how to improve your love life. The best sellers, *Men Are from Mars, Women Are from Venus* and *Mars and Venus in the Bedroom* by John Gray, Ph.D. illuminate the key differences in communication and love styles between men and women. According to the author, it's romance (that's the Venus in your life) that lures women and passion (the domain of Mars) that fuel's a man's drive.

Use the planet Venus as your key to romance and seduction. If you time your Venus moves well, you can win your lover's heart. You'll be at your most appealing when Venus is in your sign or in one that is harmonious with yours, when others will be likely to react to your charms. That's when you should create the atmosphere where love can bloom. Then pour on your passion when Mars is in your sign, fueling your sex drive and pushing you to take action.

Use the Venus and Mars tables in this book to create your agenda for love. Choose Venus times for seduction—the times when Venus is in the same Sign or Element as your Sun or Venus. Do the same for Mars, timing your moves for super sex and go-for-it maneuvers when Mars is in the most favorable element. Choose signs compatible with yours from the following list and get out your calendar!

- Fire signs are Aries, Leo, Sagittarius.
- Earth signs are Taurus, Virgo, Capricorn.
- Air signs are Gemini, Libra, Aquarius.
- Water signs are Cancer, Scorpio, Pisces.

Could You Be Making One of these Fatal Errors?

If you consider yourself unlucky in love, you may be looking for love in all the wrong places, as the song goes. There are certain places (or atmospheres) where you'll be most likely to encounter a specific sun sign. Try going to one on your Venus days to scout for someone compatible. Though they may not be your sign of choice, there might be other planets in the sign that are radiating attractiveness. Another possibility is that you may be unaware that you're doing the very thing that is sure to turn your lover off.

Here's a tip sheet to help your trouble shoot.

Aries

Where to find an Aries: Aries will go to the newest, trendiest places. They love action sports, tests of strength (join a gym) and competitive activities of all kinds. The sign is a participant rather than a spectator.

How to lose an Aries: Don't take your vitamins. Let yourself go, so you'll be run down, low on energy, and slow to get moving. Then whine and complain a lot. If that doesn't send Aries out the door, try being ultra-conservative, afraid to take a chance. Have no spontaneity. Take hours to get ready. Be always late, keeping Aries fuming impatiently.

Taurus

Where to find a Taurus: Anywhere there is good food, comfortable surroundings, and nature. Taurus likes country places, beautiful scenery, or luxurious resorts. You can find Taurus in decorating showrooms, home improvement stores, cooking or gardening classes, gourmet or speciality food stores, or your local bank or investment company. Attend auctions and antique shows. The opera, concerts, and record stores are other good bets. Join a choir or singing group or the local garden club. Invest in real estate.

How to lose a Taurus: It's a piece of cake. Just make Taurus uncomfortable. Be indifferent to food and surroundings. Wear stiff, untouchable clothes. Act cool physically. Dislike music, the arts, animals. Be pushy and impatient. Prefer the bustle of city to country living. Dislike animals and plants.

Gemini

Where to find a Gemini: Parties and social gatherings of all kinds. Through newspapers, telephone stores, gadget stores, book stores. At the latest hit show, a comedy club, where the action is. Invite a Gemini to an exciting social event—they'll never refuse.

How to lose a Gemini: Be a stay-at-home. Be old fashioned—don't keep up with the latest trends. Don't read and have nothing interesting to say. Look the same all the time. Have no curiosity about your surroundings. Be overly emotional or irrational. Act very dependent, possessive, and clingy. Make jealous scenes when Gemini flirts.

Cancer

Where to find a Cancer: Whenever there are events or things related to the house, architecture, cooking, interior design, or children. In the hotel or restaurant business. On a ship or at a yacht show or club. In a meditation or spiritual enlightenment class. At your local beach or pool. At a camera club or store.

How to lose a Cancer: Criticize them. Make them feel insecure or jealous. Flirt with others. Ridicule their moods. Be domineering. Act detached and unavailable emotionally. Throw out their favorite old hat or school prom photos. Criticize their family, especially their mother, or get along badly with her. Surround yourself with noisy pals and prefer going out to a cozy evening at home.

Leo

Where to find a Leo: At the theater, in any kind of show business event, in expensive stores and restaurants, at the beauty parlor or a suntan center. At an exclusive golf club, or at any jet-set watering hole or high-priced hotel. On the rooftop, by the pool or on the beach. Teaching, lecturing, performing, selling, demonstrating— any job that puts them before the public. At the town's best jewelry store. At an employment agency, hiring staff, or at a limousine or custom car rental.

How to lose a Leo: Be a tightwad. Compete with them for the spotlight—or the same territory. Look dowdy and unkempt, with messy hair. Make fun of them or ignore them. Forget birthdays or anniversaries. Be disloyal.

Virgo

Where to find a Virgo: Hospitals or any kind of medical care or healing setting, health food stores, a nutritionist's office. Accounting offices, bookstores, museums, adult education centers, classical music concerts, service organizations, or any of the helping professions. Office supply stores—wherever people go to get organized.

How to lose a Virgo: Tell them you don't need them. Give them nothing to do, and be more efficient than they are. Revel in disorder as you mess up their living quarters. Be loud and vulgar. Act overly emotional and irrational. Refuse to take their criticism seriously. Have no mental interests. Be the silent, uncommunicative type.

Libra

Where to find a Libra: Anywhere that sells the good life, especially beautiful objects and fine food. Entertaining graciously. Shopping for clothes, in bookstores, in law offices, record stores, antique dealers, or interior design resources. At parties—the more elegant, the better. Crusading against unfair practices, or in diplomatic circles.

How to lose a Libra: Act irrationally. Make emotional scenes—they hate confrontations. Have ugly, untidy surroundings. Look unattractive. Wear clashing colors. Have bad manners and an inconsiderate attitude. Forget birthdays and Valentine's Day.

Scorpio

Where to find a Scorpio: First try beaches, marinas, scuba shops, places where there is action on the water. If you're in the city, look in powerful political or business circles, competitive sports, sex shops, police stations—wherever there is an atmosphere of power, control, sex, or mystery. Occult or New Age Shops. Clothing stores that specialize in leather goods. Restaurants where VIPs hang out. At displays of power tools. At car races, sports with a dangerous edge, in aerobics classes. Doing research or investigative reporting—any kind of sleuthing. You might also meet your Scorpio in a psychotherapy or 12-step group.

How to lose a Scorpio: This is a sign that likes to be in control at all times, so work against this. Be flirtatious. Be sexually disinterested. Don't take the relationship seriously. Make them jealous. Be extravagant. Be indecisive and unreliable. Keep them waiting. Keep surprising them and changing plans—be unpredictable. In other words, give them no control. Act like a typical Gemini or Aquarius.

Sagittarius

Where to find a Sagittarius: Anywhere having to do with horses. At a casino or at an off-track betting or lottery counter. At a sporting event, especially tennis. At a sales convention. At a church or spiritual center. In a philosophy class or at any mind-expanding event. In the publishing business. In an animal rescue center or veterinarian's office or pet store—or walking the dog.

How to lose a Sagittarius: Fence them in. Be overly possessive. Make jealouse scenes. Don't laugh at their jokes. Belong to a different belief system. Be allergic to—or dislike animals. Be a stay-at-home and dislike travel.

Capricorn

Where to find a Capricorn: Meet them at work, or at the corporate or political center of town. At auctions, in a country music or rock and roll club, or in your local country club or university club. In a status store or designer department. In a gypsy tearoom. In the bank or broker's office. In a success seminar. In an organization that cares for the elderly, or at charity events.

How to lose a Capricorn: Treat your family, especially your partners, badly. Act rudely. Wear flashy clothes and too much makeup. Do not behave like a lady or gentleman, and have bad manners and make scenes. Show no appreciation for traditional values, antique furniture, or older buildings.

Aquarius

Where to find an Aquarius: At a political rally, organizing a charity event, or crusading for a controversial cause. Involve yourself in a team sport. Attend union meetings, participate in picket lines. Look in a high-tech store or gym, in a New Age or meditation class, or in a computer class or club. In an avant garde nightclub or art gallery. In mind-control classes or psychotherapy. At male-only or feminist events. Out with the boys or a group of girlfriends.

How to lose an Aquarius: Dislike their friends. Stay at home. Don't approve of their cause or support their crusades. Don't share with them, don't be a pal. Try to make them over or control and manipulate them. Keep telling them to shut up. Make emotional scenes. Cling, whine, and complain.

Pisces

Where to find a Pisces: Try your local watering hole: either the pub or the pool. Alcoholics Anonymous or any of the 12-step programs. Any event or class that involves the arts, particularly theater or dance. Esoteric or occult gathering places. New Age bookstores, astrology classes, health food stores, hospitals (either as a patient or a caregiver), the fashion business, shoe stores.

How to lose a Pisces: Show unkindness to an underdog, or to anyone, for that matter. Criticize their need to daydream. Pester them to get a steady job. Nag them about anything. Try to reform them. Run roughshod over their feelings. Don't leave them alone for a minute. Order them around, try to control them. The harder you grip, the faster they'll slip through your fingers.

CHAPTER 8

Check Out Your Passion Potential with *Every* Sign

You might be wondering if you can trust that first spark of chemistry—should you cut the relationship short if you're a Leo with a fatal attraction to a sexy Scorpio? You might be an Aquarius, already in a difficult relationship with an immaculate Virgo who complains that you rush off leaving a pile of towels on the bathroom floor. Or you're that Virgo, in love with Aquarius, who hadn't bargained for a lifetime of picking up after your mate. Old-fashioned astrologers would say, "This combination is doomed from the start!" It used to be that some sun sign combinations were treated like champagne and tomato juice—never the twain should meet. Others were blessed by the stars as perfectly compatible. Today's astrologers are more realistic, realizing that, although some combinations will be more challenging, too many long-lasting relationships happen between so-called incompatible sun signs to brand any combination as totally unworkable. We've gone far beyond stereotyping to respecting and enjoying the differences between people and using astrology to help us get along with them.

Find out your romance potential with each sign by checking the following turn-ons and turn-offs. With a little imagination you can apply other planets that could influence your relationship to these sun sign description. The moon (emotions), Mercury (communication), Mars (sex drive), and Venus (allure, tastes) can make a big difference on the longevity of a relationship.

There's a celebrity couple under every sign, so you can visualize a living example. Some have had enduring relationships; others have made show-business history;

still others have parted company. Note that many couples born under supposedly compatible sun signs have parted company, while other, more unlikely, combinations are still happily hitched. It stands to reason that hearts do not follow horoscopes. Or perhaps it is just that difficult edge to a relationship that keeps the sparks of love flying. Sometimes we are attracted to others who have what we are lacking in our charts. At any rate, the question of which sign makes your best partner is a difficult one to answer. But with astrological information, you can make an educated guess.

Aries

Aries/Aries

Turn-ons: At last someone who can keep up with you! This is the Scarlett O'Hara/Rhett Butler combination of two risk takers ready to take on the world. If you have the same mission in life but have staked out separate territory, you can function as passionate partners.

Turn-offs: The burning question between two fire signs is, who takes the lead? You can't fight fire with fire, so this romance could burn out. You may be so preoccupied with your own agenda that you may not have time for each other after the initial blaze of passion. And you both need backup support and may look for it elsewhere.

Celebrity Couple: Steven Seagal and Kelley Lebrock; Sarah Jessica Parker and Matthew Broderick.

Aries/Taurus

Turns-ons: Aries gets slow-moving Taurus up and at 'em, waving a red flag before the bull. Taurus is excited and ready to charge. Aries gets direction, follow-through, and solid backup support, as well as a warm, loving, sensual companion who is devoted and loyal.

Turn-offs: Adapting to each other's pace calls for compromise, as Aries learns that Taurus cannot be pushed, and Taurus learns that Aries is after instant gratification. You could lock horns over short-term versus long-term goals. Taurus might prefer comfortable surrounds, while Aries happily sacrifices comfort for adventure. Separate vacations could be the only solution.

Celebrity Couple: Imagine Aries Andy Garcia and Taurus Michelle Pfeiffer together.

Aries/Gemini

Turn-ons: There is plenty of excitements and fast-paced action here. Gemini gets a charge of excitement. Aries gets constant changes to keep up with. Both are spontaneous, optimistic, and energetic. Differences of opinion only keep the atmosphere stimulating.

Turn-offs: Juggling life with Gemini could have Aries seeing double. Aries is direct and to the point, but Gemini can't be pinned down. This hyperactive combination could get on both your nerves unless you give each other plenty of space. Gemini, tone down the flirting—Aries must be number one!

Celebrity Couple: Aries Warren Beatty and Gemini Annette Bening.

Aries/Cancer

Turn-ons: Cancer will give Aries hero worship and nurturing, plus shrewd business sense and a solid home base to operate from. Aries gives Cancer romance and enthusiasm, as well as positive energy and courage to coax out the cautious crab.

Turn-offs: Aries detests complaining or whining, so Cancer will have to suffer in silence. Sulking and possessive behavior are other Aries turn-offs. Cancer may balk when Aries pushes, and finds their behavior too insensitive and self-centered for delicate Cancerian feelings or stomach to bear.

Celebrity Couple: Aries Warren Beatty and Cancer Natalie Wood; Aries Marsha Mason and Cancer playwright Neil Simon.

Aries/Leo

Turn-ons: The heat's on with this pair of romantics who share high hopes, high energy, and high ideals. You can express your finest qualities if you learn to feed each other's egos and costar, rather than take over center stage. This could be a long-run relationship.

Turn-offs: The problems appear when romance turns to reality. Both of you are delegators—neither likes to do nitty-gritty follow-through. If either of you gets overly friendly, this romance could explode. Leo may long to be fussed over, while Aries will want to feel like number one sometimes. These two self-centered signs have to learn to give and occasionally give *in* to each other.

Celebrity Couple: Aries Warren Beatty and Leo Madonna; Aries Al and Leo Tipper Gore.

Aries/Virgo

Turn-ons: Aries' sexual magnetism and positive energy warms up Virgo. You both share high ideals in pursuit of love. Aries puts lovers on a pedestal, Virgo sees them as perfect. Aries' honesty and directness earn Virgo's trust.

Turn-offs: Aries can be recklessly impatient, which Virgo will find a serious weakness. Virgo's dedication to selfless service gets no credit from self-centered Aries, who wants recognition. Virgo may get tired and feel martyred. Unsympathetic Aries will see Virgo as a downer.

Celebrity Couple: Virgo singer Harry Connick Jr. and Aries "Victoria's Secret" model Jill Goodacre.

Aries/Libra

Turn-ons: This attraction of opposites is about sharing versus going it alone, the crusader versus the judge. Libra admires the decision maker in Aries and adores having a true romantic lead. In this combination, Aries supplies the push and energy, Libra the charm and diplomacy. Libra learns to take a stand; Aries learns to see the opposite point of view.

Turn-offs: Libra's indecisiveness can make Aries see red. Aries views vacillation as a serious weakness—he who hesitates is lost or last! Aries' lack of consideration and pushy manner is a Libra no-no. Aries enjoys a rousing confrontation, while Libra avoids disharmony. Possible solution: Discuss differences calmly in an elegant setting.

Celebrity Couple: Aries Simone Signoret and Libra Yves Montand.

Aries/Scorpio

Turn-ons: One of the zodiac's challenging pair-ups, your Mars-ruled chemistry could thrive on a battle of the sexes. You both love a dare! Neither of you gives in, but you'll never bore each other—though you might wear out. Aries' direct, uncomplicated forcefulness especially intrigues Scorpio, who's caught off guard for once.

Turn-offs: You could play so hard to get that you never really connect! Aries never quite trusts secretive Scorpio, while Scorpio's intrigues and power plays can fizzle under direct Aries fire. You are both jealous and controlling, but this dynamic duo can work if you focus on high ideals and mutual respect.

Celebrity Couple: Aries Rhea Pearlman and Scorpio Danny Devito; Aries Dennis Quaid and Scorpio Meg Ryan.

Aries/Sagittarius

Turn-ons: You're good buddies who love the great outdoors, risk-taking adventures, travel, and a high-action lifestyle. You'll support each other's goals. This works especially well if you share spiritual ideals. You're both independent and understand each other's need for space.

Turn-offs: You both tend to be self-involved and may not invest enough time in maintaining the relationship. Common goals may not be enough to keep you together, especially if you lack solid financial backup. Unless you become more available to each other, you may find yourself heading off in a different direction, in search of more ego support.

Celebrity Couple: Aries Alec Baldwin and Sagittarius Kim Basinger; Sagittarius Kenneth Branagh and Aries Emma Thompson.

Aries/Capricorn

Turn-ons: You're high achievers and hard workers who respect each other's stamina. Capricorn provides the solid organizational skills; Aries provides the enthusiasm and pioneering ideas. Capricorn's mature outlook could offer the stable backup that Aries needs to get there first. In return, Aries' methods could pull Capricorn out of the ordinary.

Turn-offs: Capricorn values the traditional, Aries the trendy. Aries can seem like a self-centered baby, while Capricorn can seem like an old fuddy-duddy. Capricorn's rules and structure can seem confining to Aries; while headstrong methods seem foolhardy to Capricorn.

Celebrity Couple: Capricorn Diane Keaton and Aries Warren Beatty.

Aries/Aquarius

Turn-ons: You're both visionaries who are turned on by the avant-garde—anything goes with you two. Aquarius will find Aries a willing and experimental partner who also loves surprises. Both freedom loving, you'll give each other plenty of space.

Turn-offs: Aries may resent being surrounded by Aquarius' squadron of friends and associates, unless they are united by common ideals and goals. A bossy Aries and a know-it-all Aquarius could clash. Aquarius' cool detachment could send Aries looking for attention elsewhere.

Celebrity Couples: Aquarius Farrah Fawcett and Aries Ryan O'Neal.

Aries/Pisces

Turn-ons: Pisces love to be swept off their feet—and Aries is happy to comply! Here is someone who appreciates Aries' dynamism and is not threatened by Aries' "go-power." Aries will be number one with Pisces, who'll have wonderful, romantic ideas to contribute. Aries tempts Pisces to swim in new waters, to follow that dream.

Turn-offs: Super-sensitive Pisces' feelings are a problem here. Pushy, bossy, or inconsiderate partners turn Pisces into martyrs or monsters who could rain on Aries' parade. Balancing positive and negative energies is the key—Aries needs brakes to slow down and consider the consequences, Pisces needs a charge to get up and running.

Celebrity Couple: Aries Jane Leeves and Pisces Kelsey Grammer of the TV sitcom "Frasier."

Taurus

Taurus/Taurus

Turn-ons: Loyalty and emotions run deep with these sign-mates. Here is the cozy, familiar, comfortable kind of love, spiced by strong sensuality. In this solid, secure relationship, you could be so contented, you never leave home!

Turn-offs: Disagreements, if they occur, can be devastating. You two lock horns and never let go. Or there's a permanent standoff. The other possibility is you'll bore—rather than gore—each other to death, or look for stimulation elsewhere.

Celebrity Couple: Daniel Day Lewis and Michelle Pfeiffer in the film *The Age of Innocence.*

Taurus/Gemini

Turn-ons: Next-door signs may be best friends as well as lovers. In this case, Gemini gets Taurus out of the house and into the social life, adding laughter to love. Taurus has a soothing, stabilizing quality that can make Gemini bloom.

Turn-offs: Homebody Taurus usually loves one-on-one relations, while social Gemini loves to flirt with a crowd. Gemini will have to curb roving eyes and bodies. Infidelity can be serious business with Taurus, but taken lightly by Gemini. The balance scales between freedom and license swing and sway here.

Celebrity Couple: Taurus Andre Agassi and Gemini Brooke Shields; Gemini Paula Abdul and Taurus Emilio Estevez; Taurus Natasha Richardson and Gemini Liam Neeson.

Taurus/Cancer

Turn-ons: In theory, this should be one of the best combinations. Taurus can't get too much affection and TLC, which Cancer provides. And Taurus protects Cancer from the cold world, with solid, secure assets. Both are homeloving, emotional, and sensual.

Turn-offs: Cancer's dark moods, plus Taurus' stubbornness, could create some muddy moments. Both partners should look for constructive ways to let off steam rather than brood and sulk over grievances.

Celebrity Couple: Cancer Anjelica Huston and Taurus Jack Nicolson; Cancer Ginger Rogers and Taurus Fred Astaire.

Taurus/Leo

Turn-ons: Leo passion meets Taurus sensuality and there's a volcanic physical attraction, as you test each other's strength. Both lovers of beauty and comfort, you also have high ideals, fidelity, and a love of good food and music going for you. Taurus money management could provide Leo with a royal lifestyle.

Turn-offs: Tensions between these two fixed signs are inevitable. Leo plays dangerous games here, such as denying each other affection or sex. Focus on building emotional security and avoiding no-win emotional showdowns. Leo's extravagance and Taurus' possessiveness could be bones of contention.

Celebrity Couple: Leo George Hamilton and his Taurus ex-wife and current talk show co-host, Alana Stewart.

Taurus/Virgo

Turn-ons: Taurus admires Virgo's analytical mind, while Virgo admires Taurean concentration and goal orientation and feels secure with predicable Taurus. You enjoy taking care of each other. Relaxed, soothing Taurus brings out Virgo's sensuality, while Virgo brings the world of ideas home to Taurus.

Turn-offs: Virgo's nagging can cause Taurus self-doubt, which can show up in bullheaded stubbornness. Taurus' slow pace and ideal of deep-rooted comfort could feel like constraint to Virgo, who needs the stimulation of diversity and lively communication.

Celebrity Couple: Taurus Roberto Rossellini and Virgo Ingrid Bergman; Taurus Audrey Hepburn and Virgo Mel Ferrer.

Taurus/Libra

Turn-ons: Both Venus-ruled signs are turned on by beauty and luxury, and they tend to indulge each other. Libra brings intellectual sparkle and social savvy to Taurus, while Taurus gives Libra financial stability and adoration. And Libra profits from Taurus' strong sense of direction and decisiveness.

Turn-offs: Taurus is possessive and enjoys staying at home, while Libra loves social life and flirting. Watch out for jealousy, Taurus, because Libra's flirtations are rarely serious. Libra can be extravagant, while Taurus sticks to a budget—another cause for resentment.

Celebrity Couple: Taurus Evita and Libra Juan Peron.

Taurus/Scorpio

Turn-ons: Many marriages happen when these opposites attract. Taurus has a calming effect on Scorpio's innate paranoia. And Taurus responds to Scorpio's intensity and fascinating air of mystery. Together, these signs have the perfect complement of sensuality and sexuality.

Turn-offs: Problems of control are inevitable when you both want to run the show. Avoid long and bitter battles or silent standoffs by drawing territorial lines from the start.

Celebrity Couple: Scorpio Bonnie Raitt and Taurus Michael O'Keefe; Taurus Candice Bergen and Scorpio director Louis Malle; Taurus Jessica Lange and Scorpio Sam Sheppard.

Taurus/Sagittarius

Turn-ons: Sagittarius energizes Taurus and gets this sign to take calculated risks. Dare to think big. Taurus provides the solid support and steady income to make Sagittarius ideas happen. Sagittarius will be challenged to produce, Taurus to stretch and grow.

Turn-offs: You are very different types who are not especially sympathetic to each other's needs. Taurus believes in hard work, Sagittarius in luck. Sagittarius is a rolling stone, while Taurus is a quiet meadow. Sagittarius appreciates freedom, but Taurus appreciates substance.

Celebrity Couple: Taurus Barbra Streisand and Sagittarius Don Johnson.

Taurus/Capricorn

Turn-ons: Your similar traditional values can make communication easy. This is a combination that works well on all levels. You find it easy to set goals and to organize and support each other. There's earthy passion and instinctive understanding.

Turn-offs: There may be too much "earth" here; the relationship can become too dutiful, practical, and unromantic. You both need to expand your horizons occasionally and may look for stimulation elsewhere. Taurus may resent Capricorn's devotion to career, since home and family are top priority.

Celebrity Couple: Capricorn Martin Luther King and Taurus Coretta King.

Taurus/Aquarius

Turn-ons: This is an uncomfortable but stimulating partnership between the conventional Taurus and the rule-breaking Aquarius. Taurus takes care of the practical, while Aquarius brings inspiration and shakes Taurus out of a rut.

Turn-offs: Resolution of conflicts can wear this one out. Taurus is predictable; Aquarius is unpredictable. Taurus loves privacy, while Aquarius is a people person. Taurus wants to settle down, but Aquarius needs space. Taurus is possessive; Aquarius is detached.

Celebrity Couple: Taurus President Harry Truman and Aquarius Bess Truman; Taurus Billy Joel and Aquarius Christy Brinkley.

Taurus/Pisces

Turn-ons: You both love the good things in life and can indulge each other sensually and sexually. Taurus' focus adds stability and direction to Pisces, while Piscean creativity is lovingly encouraged by Taurus.

Turn-offs: Taurus wants Pisces to produce, not just dream, and will try to corral the slippery fish. Pisces can't be bossed or caged, and may leave Taurus with the dotted line unsigned!

Celebrity Couple: Pisces poet Elizabeth Barrett Browning and Taurus poet Robert Browning; Dance partners Rudolf Nureyev (Pisces) and Margot Fonteyn (Taurus).

Gemini

Gemini/Gemini

Turn-ons: When Gemini twins find each other, you know you'll never be bored. Here is enough multifaceted mental activity, games, and delightful social ife to double your pleasure. You'll understand the complexities of your sign as only fellow Geminis can.

Turn-offs: When the realities of life hit, you may go off in five directions at once. The combination lacks focus and functions best in a light, creative atmosphere. Serious problems could split your personalities and send you running elsewhere for protection and guidance.

Celebrity Couple: Former President George Bush and Barbara Bush; Bob and Delores Hope.

Gemini/Cancer

Turn-ons: This is a very public pair with charisma to spare. Gemini charm sets off Leo's poise with the perfect light touch, while Leo adds substance and focus to Gemini. Like JFK and Jacqueline, you go places together.

Turn-offs: It's not easy for Gemini to deliver the total loyalty and attention Leo demands—there are too many other exciting options. Leo pride and Gemini restlessness could sink this one if you don't have strong mutual interest or projects.

Celebrity Couple: Cancer John Tesh and Gemini Connie Selleca; Cancer Tom Cruise and Gemini/Cancer cusp Nicole Kidman.

Gemini/Leo

Turn-ons: Gemini's good humor, ready wit, and social skills delight and complement Leo. Here is someone who can share the spotlight without trying to steal the show from the regal Lion. This is one of the most entertaining combinations. Steady Leo provides the focus Gemini often lacks and directs the twins toward achieving goals and status.

Turn-offs: Gemini loves to flirt and flit among many interests, romantic and otherwise, which is sure to irritate the Lion, who does one thing at a time and does it well. Gemini might be a bit bored with Leo's self-promotion and might poke fun at this sign's notorious vanity. The resulting feline roar will be no laughing matter.

Celebrity Couple: Gemini President John F. Kennedy and Leo Jacqueline Kennedy.

Gemini/Virgo

Turn-ons: Both Mercury-ruled, your deepest bond will be mental communication and appreciation of each other's intelligence. Virgo's Mercury is earthbound and analytical, while Gemini's Mercury is a jack-of-all-trades. Gemini shows Virgo the big picture; Virgo takes care of the details. Your combined talents make a stimulating partnership. Virgo becomes the administrator here, while Gemini is the idea person.

Turn-offs: Your different priorities can be irritating to each other. Virgo needs a sense of order, while Gemini needs to experiment and is forever the gadabout. An older Gemini who has slowed down somewhat makes the best partner here.

Celebrity Couple: Gemini Queen Victoria and Virgo Prince Albert.

Gemini/Libra

Turn-ons: Air signs Gemini and Libra have both mental and physical rapport. This is an outgoing combination, full of good talk. You'll never be bored. Libra's good looks and charm, as well as fine mind, could keep restless Gemini close to home.

Turn-offs: Both of you have a low tolerance for boredom and practical chores. The question of who will provide, do the chores, and clean up can be the subject of many a debate. There could be more talk than action here, leaving you turning elsewhere for substance.

Celebrity Couple: Gemini Paul McCartney and Libra Linda McCartney.

Gemini/Scorpio

Turn-ons: You're a fascinating mystery to each other. Gemini is immune from Scorpio paranoia, laughing away dark moods and matching wits in power games. Scorpio's intensity, focus, and sexual magnetism draws Gemini like a moth to a flame.

Turn-offs: Scorpio gets heavy, possessive, and jealous, which Gemini doesn't take seriously. To make this one last, Gemini needs to treat Scorpio like the one and only, while Scorpio must use a light touch and learn not to take Gemini's flirtations to heart.

Celebrity Couple: Gemini tycoon Donald Trump and Scorpio Marla Maples.

Gemini/Sagittarius

Turn-ons: These polar opposites shake each other up— happily. Sagittarius helps Gemini to see higher truths, to look beyond the life of the party and the art of the deal. Gemini adds mental challenge and flexibility to Sagittarius.

Turn-offs: Gemini pokes holes in Sagittarius' theories. Sagittarius can brand Gemini as a superficial party animal. Work toward developing non-threatening, non-judgmental communication. However, you can't talk away practical financial realities—you need a well-thought-out program to make things happen.

Celebrity Couple: Gemini Marilyn Monroe and Sagittarius Joe Dimaggio.

Gemini/Capricorn

Turn-ons: Capricorn benefits from Gemini's abstract point of view and lighthearted sense of fun. Gemini shows Capricorn how to enjoy the rewards of hard work. Support and structure are Capricorn's gifts to Gemini.

(Taking that literally, Capricorn Howard Hughes designed the famous bra that supported Gemini Jane Russell's physical assets.)

Turn-offs: Capricorn can be ultra-conservative and tight-fisted with money, which Gemini will not appreicate. Gemini will have to learn to take responsibility and to produce solid results.

Celebrity Couple: Gemini Johnny Depp and Capricorn model Kate Moss; Capricorn Kirstie Alley and Gemini Parker Stevenson.

Gemini/Aquarius

Turn-ons: In this open, spontaneous relationship, the pressure's off and two air signs have room to breathe freely. At the same time, you can count on each other for friendship, understanding, and mental stimulation, as well as highly original romantic ideas. You'll keep each other entertained and your love life fresh and stimulating.

Turn-offs: Be sure to leave time in your busy schedule for each other. If there is no commitment, you could both fly off, but sharing causes, projects, or careers could hold you together.

Celebrity Couple: Aquarius John Forsythe and Gemini Joan Collins in the "Dynasty" TV series.

Gemini/Pisces

Turn-ons: You are dual personalities in mutable, freedom-loving signs, who fascinate each other with ever-changing facets. You keep each other from straying by providing constant variety and new experiments to try together.

Turn-offs: At some point, you'll need a frame of reference for this relationship to hold together, but since neither likes structure, this could be a problem. Over-stimulation is another monster that can surface. Pisces' sensitive feelings and Gemini's hyperactive nerves could send each other searching for soothing, stabilizing alternatives.

Celebrity Couple: New York's Gemini tycoon Donald Trump and his Pisces former wife, Ivana; Gemini supermodel Linda Evangelista and Pisces Kyle Mac-Laughlin.

Cancer

Cancer/Cancer

Turn-ons: Ideally, here is someone who understands your moods, gives you the mothering care you crave, and protects you from the cold, cruel world. Your home can be a loving sanctuary for your extended family and a secure nest for each other.

Turn-offs: You both take slights so personally that disagreements can easily get blown out of proportion. And if you are both in a down mood at the same time, your relationship can self-destruct. You'll need some outside activities for balance and time away from each other to regain perspective. Creative expression can save the day here.

Celebrity Couple: Sylvester Stallone and Brigitte Neilson.

Cancer/Leo

Turn-ons: These neighboring signs come through for each other like good buddies. Cancer gives Leo total attention, backup support, and the VIP treatment the Lion craves. Here is someone who won't fight for the spotlight. Leo gives Cancer confidence and this sign's positive mental outlook is good medicine for Cancer moods.

Turn-offs: Cancer's blue moods and tendency to cling tenaciously can weigh Leo down, while Leo can steamroll sensitive Cancer feelings with high-handed behavior.

Celebrity Couple: Leo Mick Jagger and Cancer Jerry Hall; Cancer Sylvester Stallone and Leo Jennifer Flavin.

Cancer/Virgo

Turn-ons: You two vulnerable signs protect and nurture each other. Moody Cancer needs Virgo to refine and focus emotions creatively. Virgo gives Cancer protective care and valuable insight. Cancer's charming romantic tenderness nurtures the shy side of Virgo. You'll have good communication on a practical level, respecting each other's shrewd financial acumen.

Turn-offs: Cancer's extreme self-protection could arouse Virgo suspicion. Why must they be so secretive? Virgo's protectiveness could become smothering, making Cancer overly dependent. Virgo must learn to offer suggestions instead of criticism, to coddle Cancer's feelings at all times.

Celebrity Couple: Virgo Anne Bancroft and Cancer Mel Brooks.

Cancer/Libra

Turn-ons: You'll bring out each other's creativity, as Cancer sensitivity merges with Libra's balanced aesthetic sense. Libra's innate sense of harmony could create a serene, elegant atmosphere where Cancer flourishes. You'll create an especially beautiful and welcoming home together.

Turn-offs: Libra's detachment could be mistaken for rejection by Cancer, while Cancer's hypersensitivity could throw Libra's scales off balance. Emotions—and emotional confrontations—are territories Libra avoids, so Cancer may look elsewhere for sympathy and nurturing.

Celebrity Couple: Libra Heather Locklear and Cancer rocker Richie Sambora; Cancer Pamela Anderson of "Baywatch" and Libra rocker Tommy Lee.

Cancer/Scorpio

Turn-ons: Cancer actually enjoys Scorpio's intensity and possessiveness—it shows how much they care! And, like Prince Charles and Diana (or Camilla Parker Bowles) this pair cares deeply about those they love. Strong emotions are a great bond that can survive heavy storms.

Turn-offs: Scorpio's mysterious, melancholy moods can leave Cancer feeling isolated and insecure. And the more Cancer clings, the more Scorpio withdraws. Outside interests can lighten the mood—or provide a means of escape.

Celebrity Couple: Scorpio Prince Charles and either Cancer Princess Diana or Cancer Camilla Parker-Bowles.

Cancer/Sagittarius

Turn-ons: Sagittarius gets a sensual partner who will keep the home fires burning and the coffers full, while Cancer gets a strong dose of optimism that could banish the blues. Sagittarius' carefree, outgoing outdoor lifestyle expands Cancer's sometimes narrow point of view and gets that sign physically fit.

Turn-offs: This joyride could reach a dead end when Sagittarius shows little sympathy for Cancer's need for mothering or runs roughshod over sensitive feelings. Cancer could withdraw into a protective shell or use claws when Sagittarius exercises a free hand with the budget.

Celebrity Couple: Sagittarius actress Liv Ullman and Cancer director Ingmar Bergman.

Cancer/Capricorn

Turn-ons: A serious sense of duty, family pride, and a basically traditional outlook bring you together. The zodiac mother (Cancer) and father (Capricorn) establish a strong home base. Cancer's tender devotion could bring out Capricorn's earthy sensual side. This couple gets closer over the years.

Turn-offs: Melancholy moods could muddy this picture, so develop a strategy for coping if depression hits. Capricorn is a lone wolf who may isolate himself emotionally, or withdraw into work, or take on an overload of duties. Cancer could look elsewhere for comfort and consolation.

Celebrity Couple: Capricorn Marlene Dietrich and Cancer writer Ernest Hemingway.

Cancer/Aquarius

Turn-ons: The clue to this one of a kind couple is basic ideals. If you two share goals and values, there is no limit to how far you can go. Cancer is turned on by the security of a high position and offers Aquarius strong support and caring qualities that touch everyone's heart, the perfect counterpoint to Aquarius charisma. Former President Ronald Reagan and his wife, Nancy, are a case in point.

Turn-offs: Cancers are at their best one-on-one, while Aquarians love a crowd. Cancers have to learn to share their love with many, while Aquarians have to learn to show warmth and emotion rather than turn off Cancer moods.

Celebrity Couple: Aquarius Former President Ronald Reagan and Cancer Nancy Reagan.

Cancer/Pisces

Turn-ons: You both love to swim in emotional waters, where your communication flows easily. Cancer's protective attention and support help Pisces gain confidence and direction. Pisces gives Cancer dreamy romance and creative inspiration. A very meaningful relationship develops over time.

Turn-offs: You two emotionally vulnerable signs know where the soft spots are—and can really hurt each other. Pisces has a way of slipping through clingy Cancer's clutches, possibly to "dry out" after too much emotion. Learn to give each other space and find creative projects to diffuse negative moods and give you a sense of direction.

Celebrity Couple: Pisces James Taylor and Cancer Carly Simon.

Leo

Leo/Leo

Turn-ons: This mirror-image couple can be a mutual-admiration society. You'll love showing each other off, spotlighting each other's talents, and radiating confidence, warmth, and optimism. If you can get the right working dynamics, you'll move ahead together socially and professionally.

Turn-offs: You may be too dazzled to deal with practical realities. Popularity won't take the place of long-range goals and clear priorities. You could burn out from high living or eclipse each other if you don't learn to share the stage and take turns boosting each other.

Celebrity Couples: Delta Burke and Gerald McRaney; Kathie Lee Gifford and Frank Gifford; Antonio Banderas and Melanie Griffith.

Leo/Virgo

Turn-ons: Leo confidence, sales power, and optimism, as well as aristocratic presence, is a big Virgo draw. Virgo will have a ready-made job efficiently running the mechanical parts of Leo's life—which Leo is only too happy to delegate. And Leo's social poise brings Virgo into the public eye—and can help this shy sign bloom! Both are faithful and loyal signs who find much to admire in each other.

Turn-offs: You may not appreciate each other's point of view. Virgo is more likely to dole out well-meaning criticism and vitamins than the admiration and applause Leo craves. Virgo will also protest Leonine high-handedness with the budget. Virgo makes the house rules, but Leo is above them, a rule unto itself. Leo always looks at the big picture, Virgo at the nitty-gritty. You could dampen each other's spirits unless you find a way to work this out early in the relationship.

Celebrity Couple: Talk-show hosts Kathie Lee Gifford and Virgo Regis Philbin.

Leo/Libra

Turn-ons: Libra is the perfect audience for Leo theatrics—and this sign knows how to package Leo for stardom. You both love the best things in life, and you are intelligent, stylish, and social. Since you have similar priorities and stroke each other the right way, you could have a long-lasting relationship.

Turn-offs: Getting the financial area of your life under control could be a problem for these two big spenders. Since you both love to make an elegant impression, you may find yourself perennially living beyond your means. You are both flirts, which is easier for Libra to tolerate than Leo, who could unleash lethal jealousy.

Celebrity Couple: Leo Steve Martin and Libra Victoria Tennant.

Leo/Scorpio

Turn-ons: Scorpio's innate power and Leo's confidence and authority can make a fascinating, high-profile combination like Leo Arnold Schwarzenegger and Scorpio

Maria Shriver. There is great mutual respect and loyalty here, as well as sexual dynamite. You two magnetic, unconquerable heros offer each other enough challenges to keep the sparks flying.

Turn-offs: Scorpio's natural secretiveness and Leo's openness could conflict, especially if Scorpio reveals a powerful will and need for control from under a deceptively quiet facade. And Leo is often surprised by the sheer intensity of Scorpio's drive and willpower. Though Scorpio won't fight for the spotlight, they will often control behind the scenes. When these two intense, stubborn, demanding signs collide, it's a no-win situation.

Celebrity Couple: Leo Arnold Schwarzenegger and Scorpio Maria Shriver; Leo President Bill Clinton and Scorpio Hillary Rodham Clinton.

Leo/Sagittarius

Turn-ons: Under Sagittarius' optimism and good humor, Leo's luck soars. You both inspire each other and boost each other creatively. If you like the outdoor life, have a spirit of adventure, and love to travel, you're a winning combination that could feel fated to be together.

Turn-offs: Sagittarius is not one to pour on the flattery Leo loves, nor is this sign known for monogamy. When both your fiery tempers explode, Leo roars and Sagittarius heads for the door. Leo must tone down bossiness and give Sagittarius a very long leash, while Sag must learn to coddle the Leo ego and keep that blazing temper on hold.

Celebrity Couple: Leo Melanie Griffith and Sagittarius Don Johnson.

Leo/Capricorn

Turn-ons: Here's the perfect mix of business and pleasure. Dignified, refined Capricorn has energy and discipline to match Leo's. However, Leo comes to the rescue of this ambitious workaholic, adding confidence, poise, and joie de vivre. Capricorn reciprocates with the royal treatment.

Turn-offs: Capricorn prefers underplayed elegance to glitz and glamour; Leo may have to tone down the flamboyant style. Capricorn cuts off the cash flow when Leo becomes extravagant and may not pour out the megadoses of affection that Leo requires. Leo can't bear a partner who is stingy with love or money.

Celebrity Couples: Leo model Iman and Capricorn rock star David Bowie; Leo Connie Chung and Capricorn Maurey Povich.

Leo/Aquarius

Turn-ons: Love at first sight often happens between these magnetic zodiac opposites. You both flourish in the public eye and enjoy sharing your life with admiring fans. You enjoy taking on big projects and helping humanity together. Leo warmth is a social plus for Aquarius, and Aquarius vision tunes in to Leo's spiritual side.

Turn-offs: Detached Aquarius may not give Leos the devotion they demand, and may need to devote more time and attention to stroking Leo's ego. Aquarius likes an open relationship, with lots of freedom to roam—though not necessarily to stray. Leo will need to put this sign on a very long leash.

Celebrity Couple: Leo Whitney Houston and Aquarius Bobby Brown.

Leo/Pisces

Turn-ons: Highly sensitive Pisces admires Leo's radiant confidence and gains stability under his warm, encouraging protection. Leo will gain an adoring admirer who easily shows affection and satisfies Leo's constant craving for romance. This is a noncompetitive mutual admiration society where you promote each other enthusiastically.

Turn-offs: Pisces also loves to flirt, but unlike Leo is not basically monogamous. Sticklers for loyalty, Leo may try to keep the Pisces dancing attendance by strong-arm tactics. Pisces operates best in free-flowing waters, swimming off when this sign senses a hook.

Celebrity Couple: Princess Margaret and Anthony Armstrong-Jones.

Virgo

Virgo/Virgo

Turn-ons: There's a strong mental turn on as you both approach love in an analytical and rather clinical way. Two Virgo signmates have a mutual respect and intuitive communication that is hard to beat. You'll evolve a carefully ordered way of being together, which works especially well if you share outside projects or similar careers.

Turn-offs: Be careful of constantly testing or criticizing each other. You need to focus on positive values and not forever try to meet each other's standards or get bogged down in details. Bring a variety of friends into your life to add balance.

Celebrity Couple: Virgo model Claudia Schiffer and Virgo magician David Copperfield.

Virgo/Libra

Turn-ons: You are intelligent companions with refined tastes, perfectionists in different ways. Libra charm and elegant style works well with Virgo's clearheaded decision making.

Turn-offs: Libra responds to admiration and can turn off to criticism or too much negativity. Virgo will need to use diplomacy to keep Libran scales in balance. Virgo values function as well as form, and sticks to a well-thought-out budget; extravagant Libra spends for beauty alone, regardless of the pricetag.

Celebrity Couple: Virgo Peter Sellers and Libra Britt Eklund.

Virgo/Scorpio

Turn-ons: With Scorpio, Virgo encounters intense feelings too powerful to intellectualize or analyze. This could be a grand passion, especially when Scorpio is challenged to uncover Virgo's earthy, sensual side. Your penetrating minds are sympatico, and so is your dedication to meaningful work (here is a fellow healer). Virgo provides the stability and structure that keeps Scorpio on the right track.

Turn-offs: Virgo may cool off if Scorpio goes to extremes or plays manipulative games, while Scorpio could find Virgo's perfectionism irritating and approach to sex too limited.

Celebrity Couple: Scorpio Hedy Lamarr and Virgo Charles Boyer in the vintage film *Algeria*.

Virgo/Sagittarius

Turn-offs: Sagittarius inspires Virgo to take risks and win, bringing fun, laughter, and mental stimulation to Virgo's life. Virgo supplies a much-needed support system, organizing and following through on Sagittarius ideas. These two signs fulfill important needs for each other.

Turn-offs: Virgo won't relate to Sagittarius' happy-go-lucky financial philosophy and reluctance to make firm commitments. Sagittarius would rather deal with the big picture, and may resent Virgo's preoccupation with details. Sexual fidelity could be a key issue if this Sagittarius' casual approach to sex conflicts with Virgo's desire to have everything perfect.

Celebrity Couple: Virgo Amy Irving and Sagittarius Steven Speilberg.

Virgo/Capricorn

Turn-ons: This looks like a sure thing between two signs who have so much in common. You're good providers who have a strong sense of duty and respect for order, similar conservative tastes, and a basically traditional approach to relationships. You could accomplish much together.

Turn-offs: You may be too similar! Cary Grant (Capricorn) and Sophia Loren (Virgo) had strong chemistry but finally opted for other commitments. Romance needs challenges to keep the sparks flying.

Celebrity Couple: Virgo Shelley Long and Capricorn Ted Danson in "Cheers"; Virgo Lauren Bacall and Capricorn Humphey Bogart; Virgo Sophia Loren and Capricorn Cary Grant.

Virgo/Aquarius

Turn-ons: Aquarius inspires Virgo to get involved in problem solving on a large scale. You are both analytical and inquisitive, and can both be detached emotionally. You'll appeal to each other's idealistic side and fuel interest with good mental communication.

Turn-offs: Virgo has a basically traditional, conservative outlook, while Aquarius likes to stay open to all possibilities and can swing into spur-of-the-moment action. Virgo's nerves could be jangled by Aquarian unpredictability and constant need for company. Aquarius could feel confined by Virgo's structured, ordered approach and focus on details.

Celebrity Couple: Virgo Michael Jackson and Aquarius Lisa Marie Presley; Virgo Jeremy Irons and Aquarius Sinead Cusack.

Virgo/Pisces

Turn-ons: Virgo supplies what Pisces often needs most—clarity and order—while Pisces' creative imagination takes Virgo's life out of the ordinary. If you can reconcile your opposing points of view, you'll have much to gain from this relationship.

Turn-offs: There are many adjustments for both signs here. Virgo could feel in over your head with Pisces' emotions and seeming lack of control—and frustrated when makeover attempts fail, while Pisces could feel bogged down with Virgo worries and deflated by negative criticism. Try to support, not change, each other.

Celebrity Couple: Pisces Cindy Crawford and Virgo Richard Gere.

Libra

Libra/Libra

Turn-ons: Two Libras are a double dose of charm and sytle. You'll understand each other's need for beautiful, harmonious surroundings, and you'll be each other's perfect social escort. It's the light, lively, elegant kind of romance seen in Hollywood films in the 1940s.

Turn-offs: This couple is long on glamour, short on practicality. Someone has to make the decisions, balance the budget, and handle the chores. Discuss matters gracefully and objectively, then delegate fairly.

Celebrity Couple: Libra Tim Robbins and Libra Susan Sarandon.

Libra/Scorpio

Turn-ons: The interplay of Scorpio intensity and cool Libran objectivity makes an exciting cat-and-mouse game. Libran intellect and flair balances out Scorpio's powerful charisma, while Scorpio adds warmth and substance to Libra.

Turn-offs: Libras must learn to handle Scorpio's sensitive feelings with velvet gloves. When not taken seriously, Scorpio retaliates with a force that could send the Libran scales swinging off balance. On the other hand, Scorpio must give Libra room to exercise his/her mental and social skills.

Celebrity Couple: Libra Bryant Gumbel and Scorpio Jane Pauley, co-hosts for many years of "Today."

Libra/Sagittarius

Turn-ons: Libra's charm smooths over the rough spots, while Sagittarius provides lofty goals and a spirit of adventure. This can be a blazing romance, full of action and fun on the town together. Neither of you are stay-at-homes.

Turn-offs: Libra's vacillations and Sagittarius' wanderlust could keep you from making a firm commitment. You both need to find a solid launching pad (either mutual interest or career goals to give this relationship structure). Libra needs a partner, but Sagittarius, who travels fastest alone, resents being tied down in any way.

Celebrity Couple: Sagittarius Darryl Hannah and Libra Jackson Browne.

Libra/Capricorn

Turn-ons: Capricorn is quick to spot Libra's potential as a social asset as well as a romantic lead. Libra loves Capricorn's dignified demeanor and elegant taste. You can climb the heights together, helping each other get the lifestyle you want.

Turn-offs: Capricorn's a loner and a home lover, while Libra is a party person who likes to do things in tandem. Libra's expensive tastes could create tension with frugal Capricorn. Learn to look at the budget as well as the beauty.

Celebrity Couple: Libra Kirk Cameron and Sagittarius Chelsea Noble.

Libra/Aquarius

Turn-ons: Shared interests and common causes are the keys to keeping the romance on track. You'll have excellent communication that combines a sense of friendship with romantic chemistry. You both understand how to be there for each other without making demands and how to mix public with private life.

Turn-offs: Libra needs flattery and romance, which Aquarius may be too busy to provide. Remember to send Valentines to Libra! And don't forget birthdays, ever. Aquarius needs freedom (too much togetherness is confining. Remember to let this sign fly solo occasionally, Libra.

Celebrity Couple: Aquarius John Travolta and Libra Kelly Preston.

Libra/Pisces

Turn-ons: You're one of the most creative couples. Libra keeps the delicate Pisces' ego on keel, while Pisces provides the romance and attention Libra craves. You are ideal collaborators. Pisces appreciates Libra's aesthetic judgment, while Libra refines Pisces' ideas without dampening their creative spirit or deflating their ego.

Turn-offs: Pisces swims in the emotional waters where Libra gets seasick. Fluctuating moods rock the boat here, unless you find a way to give each other stability and support. Turn to calm reason, avoiding emotional scenes, to solve problems.

Celebrity Couple: Libra Sarah Ferguson (Fergie) and Pisces Prince Andrew.

Scorpio

Scorpio/Scorpio

Turn-ons: The list of legendary couples here reads like a historical who's who—from Abigail and John Adams and Marie and Pierre Curie, to Dale Evans and Roy Rogers. You'll match each other's intensity and commitment, and know instinctively where to tread with caution.

Turn-offs: Since you both like to be in control, power struggles are always on the menu. Share some of your secrets and air your grievances immediately, rather than letting them fester.

Celebrity Couple: Scorpios Julia Roberts and Lyle Lovett; Linda Evans and Yanni.

Scorpio/Sagittarius

Turn-ons: Sagittarius sees an erotic adventure in Scorpio, and doesn't mind playing with fire. Scorpio's impressed with Sagittarius' high ideals, energy, and competitive spirit. Sagittarian humor diffuses Scorpio intensity, while Scorpio provides the focus for Sagittarius to reach those goals.

Turn-offs: Scorpio sees through schemes and won't fall for a sales pitch unless it has substance. Sagittarius may object to Scorpio's drive for power rather than for higher goals, and will flee from Scorpio possessiveness or heavy-handed controlling tactics.

Celebrity Couple: Sagittarius Jane Fonda and Scorpio Ted Turner; Scorpio Marlo Thomas and Sagittarius Phil Donohue.

Scorpio/Capricorn

Turn-ons: Sexy Scorpio takes Capricorn's mind off business. Though you could get wrapped up in each other, you are also turned on by power and position, and you'll join forces to scale the heights.

Turn-offs: Capricorn has no patience for intrigue or hidden agendas. Scorpio will find this sign is going to be focused on his or her own goals and won't be easily diverted, even if this means leaving Scorpio's emotional needs—and ego—in the backseat.

Celebrity Couple: Capricorn Diane Sawyer and Scorpio director Mike Nichols.

Scorpio/Aquarius

Turn-ons: Both of you respect each other's uncompromising position and mental focus. You will probably have an unconventional relationship, spiced up by sexual experimentation and the element of surprise.

Turn-offs: Scorpio could feel that Aquarius is a loose cannon who is liable to sink the ship. Or both fixed signs could come to a stubborn standoff. Aquarius tunes out Scorpio possessiveness; Scorpio looks elsewhere for intimacy and intensity.

Celebrity Couple: Scorpio Sally Field and Aquarius Burt Reynolds.

Scorpio/Pisces

Turn-ons: When these two signs click, nothing gets in their way. Pisces' desire to merge completely with his beloved is just the all or nothing message Scorpio has been waiting for. These two will play it to the hilt, often shedding previous spouses or bucking public opinion (like Liz Taylor and Richard Burton did).

Turn-offs: Both signs are possessive, yet neither likes to be possessed. Scorpio could easily mistake Piscean vulnerability for weakness—a big mistake. Both signs fuel each other's escapist tendencies when dark moods hit. Learning to merge without submerging one's identity is an important lesson for this couple.

Celebrity Couple: Scorpio Demi Moore and Pisces Bruce Willis; Scorpio Goldie Hawn and Pisces Kurt Russell; Pisces Elizabeth Taylor and Scorpio Richard Burton.

Sagittarius

Sagittarius/Sagittarius

Turn-ons: This pair functions best on the road. You share each other's ideal and goals, and you are the greatest of traveling companions, never tying each other down.

Turn-offs: In the real world, your life together may be like a series of one-night stands—rarely are you in the same place for long, unless you arrange to travel together. You'll need to make an effort to establish a solid home base, and delegating financial matters to a disciplined, responsible third party. Otherwise, you could have no one to come home to.

Celebrity Couple: Darryl Hannah and John F. Kennedy, Jr., both Sagittarians.

Sagittarius/Capricorn

Turn-ons: Capricorn has a built-in job organizing Sagittarius, but the challenge of doing something for the greater good could bring Capricorn status and recognition. Sagittarius encourages Capricorn to elevate goals beyond the material and brings out both the spiritual side and the humor of this sign.

Turn-offs: Optimistic Sagittarian meets pessimistic Capricorn—and you cancel each other out! Ultimately, you can't play it for laughs—Capricorn pushes Sagittarius to produce and commit. And Sagittarius was off to do his or her own thing.

Celebrity Couple: Sagittarius Woody Allen and Capricorn Diane Keaton.

Sagittarius/Aquarius

Turn-ons: Aquarius' unpredictability and concern for humanitarian causes meshes well with Sagittarians' adventurous spirit and lofty ideals. You'll give each other plenty of freedom and probably invent a unique, unconventional lifestyle.

Turn-offs: Dealing with everyday realities could be problematic. This pair-up may not be able to get things done. There is lots of talk and a fiery debate, but little concrete action. Each may go your own way or look elsewhere for backup support.

Celebrity Couple: Sagittarius Woody Allen and Aquarius Mia Farrow.

Sagittarius/Pisces

Turn-ons: You spark each other creatively and romantically. Pisces imagination and Sagittarius innovation work well on all levels. Variety, mental stimulation, and spiritual understanding, plus an appreciation of exotic places, could draw and keep you together.

Turn-offs: Pisceans can turn from a gentle, tropical angel-fish to a vengeful shark, when Sagittarians disregard their tender feelings. Sagittarius goes for direct attacks and could feel self-protective Pisces hides truths far beneath the surface.

Celebrity Couple: Sagittarius Frank Sinatra and his Pisces wife, Barbara.

Capricorn

Capricorn/Capricorn

Turn-ons: You two mountain goats can climb to the top together. You'll share the same traditional values and appreciate each other's thrifty, practical ways and excellent organization. You'll bring out each other's dry sense of humor and earthy sensuality.

Turn-offs: Two much sameness could bury the romance. You both need the inspiration and stimulation of different energies to keep climbing. Otherwise, it's all work and no fun.

Celebrity Couple: Capricorns Mary Tyler Moore and Grant Tinker; Dyan Cannon and Cary Grant.

Capricorn/Aquarius

Turn-ons: When the Capricorn lone wolf and the Aquarius oddball team up, the romantic route takes an unpredictable detour. Aquarius discovers that Capricorn's know-how and organizational skills can make wild dreams come true, and Capricorn finds that an Aquarius shakeup can have productive results.

Turn-offs: After the initial fascination, these two signs may go off in opposite directions unless there are shared goals or a project to get done. Capricorn may push for a traditional relationship, while Aquarius follows a different drummer.

Celebrity Couple: Capricorn Ted Danson and Aquarius Mary Steenbergen.

Capricorn/Pisces

Turn-ons: Capricorn's organizational abilities and worldly know how impress Pisces and help them find a clear direction. Pisces' romance, tenderness, and knowledge of the art of love bring out the gypsy in Capricorn—a fair exchange.

Turn-offs: What spells security for Capricorn could look like a gilded cage to Pisces, who doesn't play by the same rules. If you can make allowances for radical differences, you'll find you can go far together. Caution: Don't try to make each other over!

Celebrity Couple: Pisces megastar Elizabeth Taylor and Capricorn construction worker Larry Fortensky.

Aquarius

Aquarius/Aquarius

Turn-ons: You're a charismatic pair, like Clark Gable and Lana Turner on the screen, who gravitate to the public eye. You turn each other on with original ideas and unpredictable romantic adventures. With your own sign, you'll feel the intimacy that comes from good communication and respect for each other's individuality. You're two rule breakers who enjoy a liberated partnership.

Turn-offs: Someone has to be the audience when you hold forth. Two know-it-alls can clash mightily or tune each other out. You could prefer to surround yourself with more admiring fans or someone who lets you have the spotlight.

Celebrity Couple: Aquarians Lana Turner and Clark Gable.

Aquarius/Pisces

Turn-ons: You two neighboring signs can be best buddies. You both need plenty of space and freedom, though in different ways. You'll have great tolerance for each other's eccentricities and can inspire each other to be original, unpredictable and romantic, exploring unknown waters together.

Turn-offs: Intense emotions feed the Pisces fish, but make Aquarians swim away. Aquarian detachments could cause Pisces to look for warmer seas. Pisces needs one-on-one intimacy and reassurance, while Aquarians are people who need people in groups. You'll both have to leave your element to make this work.

Celebrity Couple: Aquarius Paul Newman and Pisces Joanne Woodward; Aquarius Oprah Winfrey and Pisces Stedman Graham.

Pisces

Pisces/Pisces

Turn-ons: Who understands your inner complexity better than one of your own? Here's the psychic soulmate you've been waiting for. Finally, someone who's as sensitive and sensual as you are. You'll love the good life together and spark each other creatively.

Turn-offs: This romance can sink if you both get into a negative mood at the same time. There you are, caught in the undertow without a lifeguard! Avoid escaping into alcoholic binges. Plan a strategy to diffuse black moods with lighthearted friends and shared creative projects.

Celebrity Couple: Pisces Sally Jessy Raphael and her husband, Bert Soderlund.

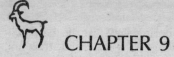

CHAPTER 9

Need a Reading?
Here's What to Expect

If you've been wondering about whether an astrological reading could give you the competitive edge in business, help you break through a personal dilemma, decide on the best day for a key event in your life, or help you make a career change, this may be the time to have a personal consultation. An astrologer might give you reassurance and validation at a turning point or crisis time in your life, or simply help you get where you want to go by maximizing the positive aspects in your chart.

Since there are more astrology services available than ever, those who are interested in a personal consultation are now faced with a mind-boggling array of possibilities, from standardized printouts by a computer service to customized written interpretations by a famous astrologer; from individual taped readings to one-on-one consultations with an astrologer who specializes in a specific area such as medical, financial, or family relationships. Then there are the 900-lines that promise amazing results at a fee calculated by the minute.

Your first priority should be to choose a qualified astrologer. Rather than relying on word of mouth or grandiose advertising claims, do this with the same care you would choose any trusted adviser such as a doctor, lawyer, or banker. Unfortunately, anyone can claim to be an astrologer—to date, there is no licensing of astrologers or established professional criteria. However, there are nationwide organizations of serious, committed astrologers that can help you in your search.

Good places to start your investigation are organizations such as the American Federation of Astrologers or the National Council for Geocosmic Research (NCGR), which offers a program of study and certification. If you live near a major city, there is sure to be an active NCGR chapter or astrology club in your area—many are listed in astrology magazines available at your local newsstand. In response to many requests for referrals, the NCGR has compiled a directory of professional astrologers, which includes a glossary of terms and an explanation of specialties within the astrological field. Contact the NCGR headquarters (see the resource list in Chapter 6) to order a copy.

As a potentially lucrative freelance business, astrology has always attracted self-styled experts who may not have the techniques or the counseling experience to give a helpful reading. These astrologers can range from the well-meaning amateur to the charlatan or street-corner gypsy who has for many years given astrology a bad name. Be very wary of astrologers who claim to have occult powers or who make pretentious claims of celebrated clients or miraculous achievements. You can often tell from the initial phone conversation if the astrologer is legitimate. He or she should ask for your birthdate, time, and place and conduct the conversation in a professional way. Any astrologer who gives a reading based only on your sun sign is highly suspect. Most astrologers will then enter this information into a computer, which will calculate your chart in seconds. From the resulting chart, the astrologer will do an interpretation. Some astrologers who do telephone consultations will call up your chart on their computer screen immediately and proceed with the reading. Others do more in-depth preparation prior to a consultation. This will be reflected in the cost of your reading.

If you don't know your exact birth time, you can usually find it filed at the bureau of vital statistics at the city hall or country seat of the state where you were born. If you have no success in getting your time of birth, some astrologers specialize in rectification, using past events of your life to estimate an approximate birth time.

If you are having a personal consultation, it should be conducted in a private, quiet place. The astrologer should be interested in your problems of the moment.

A good reading involves feedback on your part, so if the reading is not relating to your concerns, you should let the astrologer know. You should feel free to ask questions and get clarifications of technical terms. The reading should be an interaction between both parties, rather than a solo performance by the astrologer. The more you actively participate, rather than expecting the astrologer to carry the reading or come forth with oracular predictions, the more meanful your reading is likely to be. An astrologer should help you validate your current experience and be frank about possible negative happenings, but be helpful about directing you toward your most positive options.

In their approach to a reading, some astrologers may be more literal, others more intuitive. Those who have had counseling training may take a more psychological approach. Though some astorlogers may seem to have an almost psychic ability, extrasensory perception or another parapsycholocal talent is not necessary to be a good astrologer. A very accurate picture can be drawn from factual data as shown in your chart.

An astrologer may do several charts for each client—one for the time of birth, one for the current date, and a progressed chart showing the evolution from birth to the present time. According to your individual needs, there are many other possibilities, such as a chart for a differnt location, if you are contemplating a change of place. Relationships between any two people, things, or events can be interpreted with a synastry chart, which compares the chart of one birth date with the chart of another date. Another type of relationship chart is the composite chart, which uses the midpoint between planets in two individual charts to describe the relationship.

An astrologer will be particularly interested in transits—times when planets pass over the planets or sensitive points in your chart, which signal important times for you.

Another option is a taped reading—the astrologer will mail you a previously taped reading based on your birth chart. This type of reading is more personal than a computer printout and can give you valuable insights, but it is not equivalent to a live reading when you can have a dialogue with the astrologer and can address your specific interests and issues of the moment.

About Telephone Readings

Telephone readings come in two varieties. One is a dial-in taped forecast, usually by a well-known astrologer. The other is a live consultation with someone who is supposed to be an astrologer. The taped readings are general daily or weekly forecasts, applied to all members of your sign and charged by the minute. The quality depends on the astrologer. One caution: Be aware that these readings can run up quite a telephone bill, especially if you get into the habit of calling every day. Be sure that you are aware of the per-minute cost of each call. Live telephone readings also vary with the expertise of the person giving them. Since you have no way of checking credentials, you should remain objective about all that is said. Ideally, the astrologer enters your birth data into a computer and refers to that chart during the consultation. The advantage to this kind of a live telephone reading is that your individual chart is used and you can ask about a specific problem. However, before you invest in any reading, be sure that your astrologer is qualified and that you fully understand how much you will be charged.

About Computer Readings

Most of the companies that offer computer programs (such as ACS, Matrix, ASTROLABE) also offer a wide variety of computer-generated horoscope interpretations. These can be quite comprehensive, offering a beautiful printout of your chart plus many pages of information. A big plus is that these basic natal-chart interpretations can be an ideal way to learn more about your own chart, since most readings interpret all the details of the chart in a very understandable way. However, the interpretations will be general, since there is no input from you. Therefore, the reading may not cover your immediate, specific concerns and problems. Nor are these likely to be helpful in determining the most optimal timing for an activity. But they are still a good option for a first reading, especially since these printouts are much lower in cost than live consultations. You might consider them as either a supplement or a preparation for a living reading (study one before you have a live reading to familiarize yourself with your chart and plan specific questions) and they make a terrific gift for someone interested in astrology.

You'll find several companies that do computer readings listed in Chapter 6. Ask for their catalogues or call the ones with toll-free numbers to get an idea of the different possibilities and price ranges available.

CHAPTER 10

Where to Find that Pot of Gold in 1997

Predicting where pots of gold lie hidden has kept forecasters of every kind in business for centuries. Astrology can be a far more precise and reliable source of intelligence for predicting current growth trends, where your best opportunities lie, and what stage of the wheel of success you'll be passing through.

The Jupiter Factor

Good fortune and big money are always associated with Jupiter, the planet that embodies the principle of expansion. Jupiter has a 12-year cycle, staying in each sign for approximately one year. When Jupiter enters a sign, the fields governed by that sign seem new and profitable, and they usually provide excellent investment opportunities. Areas of speculation governed by the sign Jupiter is passing through will have the hottest market potential—they're the ones that currently arouse excitement and enthusiasm.

This year, Jupiter is traveling through Aquarius. Sun-sign Aquarians, or those with strong Aquarius influence in their horoscopes, will have the most growth opportunities. Those born under Leo, the sign opposite Aquarius, will need to make adjustments because the expansive atmosphere is opposed to their natural tendencies. For example, Aquarius prospers when identified with a group. Leo is a self-promoter. In a Jupiter in Aquarius period, when teamwork, good political relationships, and identification with a humanitarian causes are most fortunate, those who play the personality game could find themselves out of sync.

Jupiter-favored Growth Areas

This year, Aquarian-type fields are targeted for expansion. This should be an especially strong year for high-technology ventures because Uranus, ruler of high-tech and Aquarius, is now firmly established in its own sign, reinforcing the emphasis of Jupiter there. It's a double whammy that's sure to fill the pockets of those in the forefront of science and technology. Researchers, social workers and reformers, those who work for humanitarian organizations and at future-oriented jobs, people involved with aeronautics, television workers, and any worker whose job is connected with the use of electricity (Uranus-ruled) should prosper. Expect a new emphasis on independence in the workplace and much more reliance on computers. One big growth area that is expanding rapidly at this writing is the home-office worker, who communicates via computer. At the same time, there will be a new and different emphasis on teamwork and group effort within organizations.

In Your Personal Life

Find the house where Jupiter in Aquarius falls in your chart to indicate where you'll have the most expansive potential this year. Just look up your rising sign in the chart in this book on page 175 and check the following list.

Aquarius Rising—The Image that Sells

For most of this year, you hold the luckiest cards. With Jupiter energizing your ascendant, you look like a winner without even trying. Use this time to kick off the next 12-year cycle in the most advantageous way. Circulate among influential people, make personal contacts, sell yourself. Push yourself out in the public eye, even if you're the shy type. This is the time to be your most social self! One cautionary note: Jupiter means expansion—and this position rules your physical body—so watch your diet. You could put on weight.

Pisces Rising—Warmup for the Big Time

You've come to the end of a 12-year Jupiter cycle. Now you're in a period of gestation for a big push when Jupiter enters your sign next year. Use this time to review what you've learned in the last 12 years. This is also a time when things that happened during this cycle are brought to a close. You'll be completing tasks and working behind the scenes. It is also a time for quiet reflection, meditation, and getting centered spiritually so that you'll be able to use the opportunities coming up.

Aries Rising—the Big League

Jupiter brings you group connections this year. Others will be looking to you for inspiration. Since you can now get the support of the movers and shakers in your field and may be taking on group leadership, this is a time when you can put some of the ideas formulated in previous cycles into action. You'll have plenty of help from friends. It is not so much a time for solo creativity—instead, make the most of opportunities offered to you by groups. This is the time when you make the team, come to the aid of your party, or find a new audience for your talents.

Taurus Rising—Build your Prestige

It's a great time to enhance your reputation and to build up your image and career. This cycle favors public activities rather than domestic life. It's a great time to sell yourself or deal with those in power. You should be feeling superconfident. You may be starting a new career or making a stronger commitment to the one you're in.

Gemini Rising—Aim High!

This is a time when you may expand your way of thinking on a large scale. This is the ideal time to get higher education, develop your philosophy of life, formulate new directions for your life. This is the time to aim high and to look at the big overall picture. It is an excellent time for publishing or getting advanced education or travel abroad. You may feel like changing your life around and trying something completely new. The ideas you get now or the people you meet can make your reputations in the future.

Cancer Rising—Watch the Cash Flow!

Until November 10, you'll have rare opportunities to use credit and to deal with banks, loan companies, and the IRS. Be very careful with your credit cards during this period. There could be a strong temptation to over-extend. You may find others more than willing to lend you money at high interest. If you're a risk taker, you may have to keep a strict eye on expenditures—Jupiter encourages gambling! You might also find yourself managing money for others, and getting involved in joint ventures.

Leo Rising—Making Commitments

Those with whom you have committed relationships can be fortunate for you. Many people marry at this time. However, this is not a good time for solo ventures—you are best off working in tandem and letting your partner take the spotlight. You may have to submerge your own personality for a while in order to take full advantage of this period. So think "togetherness." You can use others to your advantage, but don't try to take over. Since this is the area of open enemies, you could learn much about your adversaries and gain the advantage in the future.

Virgo Rising—Details, Details!

This is the time when you may seem bogged down in details, in learning the operation of the company from the ground up, or in taking care of the mundane aspects that made a business operate efficiently. But remember, it is only through creating a smooth working operation that fortunes can be made in the long haul. You have only to read the financial section of your newspaper to see how many promising companies get swept away by poor management. This is also an excellent time to take care of yourself—set up a diet and exercise regime and get your body in good shape.

Libra Rising—a Creative Bonanza

For anyone involved in creative fields, this is bonanza time—the inspiration flows! Put some fun into your life and help others to do so for profit. Your best ideas will come when you play at your job (don't they always?), finding more creative ways to get the work done. The only danger here is too much fun—you may be more interested in pleasure than profit. Love affairs, fun times, and recreation can impose on work time. You may find it difficult to stick to any routines. Since this placement also rules children, you may find yourself involved with them in some way—or you may become a parent.

Scorpio Rising—Luck begins at Home

Your success potential is tied in to your domestic life. This is often a time of moving or relocating, when you arrange your personal lifestyle for the next 12 years. This is the time to establish your personal space, strengthen family ties, and give yourself a solid base of operations. You can now create the much-needed balance between your private life and the outside world that will shore you up for the next 12 years. Aim for greater family harmony and inner strength.

Sagittarius Rising—Communications

You will overflow with ideas that you should record for future reference. This is a time when you can write up a storm and when opportunities abound at your doorstep. You may take up a course of study that will pay off in the future. Your social life is buzzing as the phone rings off the hook. New contacts in your local area can pay off. You may also find a lucky financial venture that involves your friends or siblings.

Capricorn Rising—Increase Your Security

Now is the time to use those contacts you made last year to consolidate your financial security. You may find that your cash flow increases as there is generally more money available. However, you could also be a big spender, so it is important to use this time of opportunity to give yourself backup funds for the future. This is a time to develop good money management habits as well.

CHAPTER 11

The Key to Your Chart—
Your Rising Sign

At the moment you were born, announcing your presence in the world with a lusty cry, your horoscope was set in motion by the sign passing over the eastern horizon: This is called the rising sign or ascendant. Like your personal advertisement, this sign shows how you present yourself to the world.

The ascendant is one of the most important factors in your chart because it shows not only how we appear outwardly, but it sets up the path we are to follow. After the rising sign is determined, each area of our chart is governed by the signs following in sequence. It gives the planets a specific context, an area of life where they will operate. Without a valid rising sign, your collection of planets would have no home. Once the rising sign is established, it becomes possible to analyze a chart accurately. That is why many astrologers insist on knowing the exact time of a client's birth before they analyze a chart.

Some ascendants will complement the sun sign; others hide the sun under a totally different mask, as if playing an entirely different role, so it is often difficult to guess the person's sun sign from outer appearances. A Leo with a conservative Capricorn ascendant would come across as much less flamboyant than a Leo with an Aries or Sagittarius ascedant. If the sun sign is reinforced by other planets in the same sign, it can also assert its personality much more strongly. A Leo with Venus and Jupiter also in Leo might counteract the conservative image of the Capricorn ascendant in the above example.

However, it is usually the ascendant that is reflected in the first impression.

Rising signs change every two hours with the earth's rotation. Those born early in the morning, when the sun is on the horizon, will be most likely to project the image of the sun sign. These people are often called a "double Aries" or a "double Virgo," because the same sun sign and ascendant reinforce each other.

In a horoscope, the other signs follow the rising signs in sequence, rotating counter-clockwise. Therefore, the rising sign sets up the pathway of your chart. It rules the first house, which is your physical body, and your appearance; it also influences your style, tastes, health, and physical environment, showing where you are most comfortable working and living.

Look up your rising sign on the chart at the end of this chapter. Since rising signs change rapidly, it is important to know your birth time as close to the minute as possible. Even a few minutes difference could change the rising sign and the setup of your chart. If you are unsure about the exact time, but know within a few hours, check the following descriptions to see which is most like the personality you project.

Aries Rising—Fiery Emotions

You are the most aggressive version of your sun sign, with boundless energy that can be used productively. Watch a tendency to overreact emotionally and blow your top. You come across as openly competitive, a positive asset in business or sports. Be on guard against impatience, which could lead to head injuries. Your walk and bearing could have the telltale head-forward Aries posture. You may wear more bright colors, especially red, than others of your sign. You may also have a tendency to drive your car faster.

Taurus Rising—The Earth Mother

You'll exude a protective, nurturing quality, even if you're male, which draws those in need of TLC and support. You're slow moving, with a beautiful or distinctive speaking or singing voice that can be especially soothing or melodious.

You probably surround yourself with comfort, good food, luxurious surroundings, and sensual pleasures, and you prefer welcoming others into your home to adding about. You may have a talent for business, especially in trading, appraising, or real estate. This ascendant gives a well-padded physique that gains weight easily.

Gemini Rising—Expressive Talents

You have an airier, lighter, more ethereal look than others of your sign, especially if you're female. You love to be with people and express feelings easily. You may have writing or speaking talent. You need variety and a constantly changing scenario, with many different characters, though you may relate at a deeper level than might be suspected and you will be far more sympathetic and caring than you might project. You will probably travel widely and change partners and jobs several times—or juggle two at once. Physically, you should try to cultivate tranquility and create a calmer atmosphere, because your nerves are quite sensitive.

Cancer Rising—Sensitive Antenna

You easily pick up others' needs and feelings, a great gift in business, the arts, and personal relationships. But guard against overreacting or taking things too personally, especially during full moon periods. Find creative outlets for your natural nurturing gifts, such as helping the less fortunate, particularly children. Your insights would be useful in psychology; your desire to feed and care for others welcome in the restaurant, hotel, or childcare industry. You may be especially fond of wearing romantic old clothes, collecting antiques, and, of course, good food. Since your body will retain fluids, you should pay attention to your diet. Escape to places near water for relaxation.

Leo Rising—Scene Player

You may come across as more poised than you really feel; however, you play it to the hilt, projecting a commanding royal presence. This ascendant gives you a natural flair for drama that masks your sensitive interior. You'll also project a much more outgoing, optimistic, sunny personality than others of your sign. You take care to please your public by always projecting your best star quality, probably tossing a luxuriant mane of hair or, if you're female, dazzling with a spectacular jewelry collection. Since you may have a strong parental nature, you could well be the regal family matriarch or patriarch.

Virgo Rising—Cool and Calculating

Virgo rising masks your inner nature with a practical, analytical outer image. You seem very neat, orderly, and more particular, than others of your sign. Others in your life may feel they must live up to your high standards. Though at times you may be openly critical, this masks a well-meaning desire to have only the best for loved ones. Your sharp eye for details could be used in the financial world, or your literary skills could draw you to teaching or publishing. The healing arts, health care, and service-oriented professions attract many with this Virgo emphasis in their chart. Physically, you have a very sensitive digestive system.

Libra Rising—The Charmer

Libra rising makes you appear as a charmer, more of a social, public person than others of your sign. Your private life will extend beyond your home and family to include an active social life. You may tend to avoid confrontations in relationships, preferring to smooth the way or negotiate diplomatically than give in to an emotional reaction. Because you are interested in all aspects of a situation, you may be slow to reach decisions. Physically, you'll have good proportions and pleasing symmetry. You're likely to have pleasing, if not beautiful, facial features. You move gracefully. You have a winning smile and good taste in your clothes and home decor. Legal, diplomatic, or public relations professions could draw your interest.

Scorpio Rising—Magnetic Power

You project an intriguing air of mystery when Scorpio's secretiveness and sense of underlying power combines with your sign. You are a master manipulator who can move in the world of power. You come across as more intense and controlled, with a direct and penetrating gaze. But you'll never reveal your private agenda. Watch a tendency toward paranoia. You may have secret love affairs. You often wear black and are happiest near water.

Sagittarius Rising—The Wanderer

You travel with this ascendant. You may also be a more outdoor, sportive type, with an athletic, casual, outgoing air. Your moods are camouflaged with cheerful optimism or a philosophical attitude. You'll laugh at your troubles or crack a joke more easily than others of your sign. This ascendant can also draw you to the field of higher education or to spiritual life. You'll seem to have less attachment to things and people and may travel widely. Your strong, fast legs are a physical bonus.

Capricorn Rising—Serious Business

This rising sign makes you come across as serious, goal oriented, disciplined, and careful with cash. You are not one of the zodiac's big spenders, though you might splurge occasionally on times with good investment value. You're the traditional, conservative type in dress and environment, and you might come across as quite formal and businesslike. You'll function well in a structured or corporate environment where you can climb to the top—you are always aware of who's the boss. In your personal life, you could be a loner or a single parent who is both father and mother to your children.

Aquarius Rising—One of a Kind

You come across as less concerned about what others think and could even be a bit eccentric. You're more at ease with groups of people than others of your sign, and may be attracted to public life. Your appearance may be unique and unconventional—or it may be unimportant to you. Those with the sun in a water sign (Cancer, Scorpio, Pisces) may exercise your nurturing qualities with a large group, an extended family, or a day-care or community center.

Pisces Rising—Romantic Roles

Your creative, nurturing talents are heightened, and so is your ability to project emotional drama. And your dreamy eyes and poetic air bring out the protective instinct in others. You could be attracted to the arts, especially theater, dance, film, or photography; or to psychology, spiritual, or charity work. Since you are vulnerable to up-and-down mood swings, it is especially important for you to find interesting, creative work where you can express your talents and boost your self-esteem. Accentuate the positive and be wary of escapist tendencies, particularly involving alcohol or drugs, to which you are super-sensitive.

	1 AM	2 AM	3 AM	4 AM	5 AM	6 AM	7 AM	8 AM	9 AM	10 AM	11 AM	12 NOON
Jan 1	Lib	Sc	Sc	Sc	Sag	Sag	Cap	Cap	Aq	Aq	Pis	Ar
Jan 9	Lib	Sc	Sc	Sag	Sag	Sag	Cap	Cap	Aq	Aq	Pis	Ar	Tau
Jan 17	Sc	Sc	Sc	Sag	Sag	Cap	Cap	Aq	Aq	Pis	Ar	Tau
Jan 25	Sc	Sc	Sag	Sag	Sag	Cap	Cap	Aq	Pis	Ar	Tau	Tau
Feb 2	Sc	Sc	Sag	Sag	Cap	Cap	Aq	Pis	Pis	Ar	Tau	Gem
Feb 10	Sc	Sag	Sag	Sag	Cap	Cap	Aq	Pis	Ar	Tau	Tau	Gem
Feb 18	Sc	Sag	Sag	Cap	Cap	Aq	Pis	Pis	Ar	Tau	Gem	Gem
Feb 26	Sag	Sag	Sag	Cap	Aq	Aq	Pis	Ar	Tau	Tau	Gem	Gem
Mar 6	Sag	Sag	Cap	Cap	Aq	Pis	Pis	Ar	Tau	Gem	Gem	Cap
Mar 14	Sag	Cap	Cap	Aq	Aq	Pis	Ar	Tau	Tau	Gem	Gem	Can
Mar 22	Sag	Cap	Cap	Aq	Pis	Ar	Ar	Tau	Gem	Gem	Can	Can
Mar 30	Cap	Cap	Aq	Pis	Pis	Ar	Tau	Tau	Gem	Can	Can	Can
Apr 7	Cap	Cap	Aq	Pis	Ar	Ar	Tau	Gem	Gem	Can	Can	Leo
Apr 14	Cap	Aq	Aq	Pis	Ar	Tau	Tau	Gem	Gem	Can	Can	Leo
Apr 22	Cap	Aq	Pis	Ar	Ar	Tau	Gem	Gem	Gem	Can	Leo	Leo
Apr 30	Aq	Aq	Pis	Ar	Tau	Tau	Gem	Can	Can	Can	Leo	Leo
May 8	Aq	Pis	Ar	Ar	Tau	Gem	Gem	Can	Can	Leo	Leo	Leo
May 16	Aq	Pis	Ar	Tau	Gem	Gem	Can	Can	Can	Leo	Leo	Vir
May 24	Pis	Ar	Ar	Tau	Gem	Gem	Can	Can	Leo	Leo	Leo	Vir
June 1	Pis	Ar	Tau	Gem	Gem	Can	Can	Can	Leo	Leo	Vir	Vir
June 9	Ar	Ar	Tau	Gem	Gem	Can	Can	Leo	Leo	Leo	Vir	Vir
June 17	Ar	Tau	Gem	Gem	Can	Can	Can	Leo	Leo	Vir	Vir	Vir
June 25	Tau	Tau	Gem	Gem	Can	Can	Leo	Leo	Leo	Vir	Vir	Lib
July 3	Tau	Gem	Gem	Can	Can	Can	Leo	Leo	Vir	Vir	Vir	Lib
July 11	Tau	Gem	Gem	Can	Can	Leo	Leo	Leo	Vir	Vir	Lib	Lib
July 18	Gem	Gem	Can	Can	Can	Leo	Leo	Vir	Vir	Vir	Lib	Lib
July 26	Gem	Gem	Can	Can	Leo	Leo	Vir	Vir	Vir	Lib	Lib	Sc
Aug 3	Gem	Can	Can	Can	Leo	Leo	Vir	Vir	Vir	Lib	Lib	Sc
Aug 11	Gem	Can	Can	Leo	Leo	Leo	Vir	Vir	Lib	Lib	Lib	Sc
Aug 18	Can	Can	Can	Leo	Leo	Vir	Vir	Vir	Lib	Lib	Sc	Sc
Aug 27	Can	Can	Leo	Leo	Leo	Vir	Vir	Lib	Lib	Lib	Sc	Sc
Sept 4	Can	Can	Leo	Leo	Vir	Vir	Vir	Lib	Lib	Lib	Sc	Sc
Sept 12	Can	Leo	Leo	Leo	Vir	Vir	Lib	Lib	Lib	Sc	Sc	Sag
Sept 20	Leo	Leo	Leo	Vir	Vir	Vir	Lib	Lib	Sc	Sc	Sc	Sag
Sept 28	Leo	Leo	Leo	Vir	Vir	Lib	Lib	Lib	Sc	Sc	Sag	Sag
Oct 6	Leo	Leo	Vir	Vir	Vir	Lib	Lib	Sc	Sc	Sc	Sag	Sag
Oct 14	Leo	Vir	Vir	Vir	Lib	Lib	Lib	Sc	Sc	Sag	Sag	Cap
Oct 22	Leo	Vir	Vir	Lib	Lib	Lib	Sc	Sc	Sc	Sag	Sag	Cap
Oct 30	Vir	Vir	Vir	Lib	Lib	Sc	Sc	Sc	Sag	Sag	Cap	Cap
Nov 7	Vir	Vir	Lib	Lib	Lib	Sc	Sc	Sc	Sag	Sag	Cap	Cap
Nov 15	Vir	Vir	Lib	Lib	Sc	Sc	Sc	Sag	Sag	Cap	Cap	Aq
Nov 23	Vir	Lib	Lib	Lib	Sc	Sc	Sag	Sag	Sag	Cap	Cap	Aq
Dec 1	Vir	Lib	Lib	Sc	Sc	Sc	Sag	Sag	Cap	Cap	Aq	Aq
Dec 9	Lib	Lib	Lib	Sc	Sc	Sag	Sag	Sag	Cap	Cap	Aq	Pis
Dec 18	Lib	Lib	Sc	Sc	Sc	Sag	Sag	Cap	Cap	Aq	Aq	Pis
Dec 28	Lib	Lib	Sc	Sc	Sag	Sag	Sag	Cap	Aq	Aq	Pis	Ar

RISING SIGNS—P.M. BIRTHS

	1 PM	2 PM	3 PM	4 PM	5 PM	6 PM	7 PM	8 PM	9 PM	10 PM	11 PM	12 MIDNIGHT
Jan 1	Tau	Gem	Gem	Can	Can	Can	Leo	Leo	Vir	Vir	Vir	Lib
Jan 9	Tau	Gem	Gem	Can	Can	Leo	Leo	Leo	Vir	Vir	Vir	Lib
Jan 17	Gem	Gem	Can	Can	Can	Leo	Leo	Vir	Vir	Vir	Lib	Lib
Jan 25	Gem	Gem	Can	Can	Leo	Leo	Leo	Vir	Vir	Lib	Lib	Lib
Feb 2	Gem	Can	Can	Can	Leo	Leo	Vir	Vir	Lib	Lib	Lib	Sc
Feb 10	Gem	Can	Can	Leo	Leo	Leo	Vir	Vir	Lib	Lib	Lib	Sc
Feb 18	Can	Can	Can	Leo	Leo	Vir	Vir	Vir	Lib	Lib	Sc	Sc
Feb 26	Can	Can	Leo	Leo	Leo	Vir	Vir	Lib	Lib	Lib	Sc	Sc
Mar 6	Can	Leo	Leo	Leo	Vir	Vir	Vir	Lib	Lib	Sc	Sc	Sc
Mar 14	Can	Leo	Leo	Vir	Vir	Vir	Lib	Lib	Lib	Sc	Sc	Sag
Mar 22	Leo	Leo	Leo	Vir	Vir	Lib	Lib	Lib	Sc	Sc	Sc	Sag
Mar 30	Leo	Leo	Vir	Vir	Vir	Lib	Lib	Sc	Sc	Sc	Sag	Sag
Apr 7	Leo	Leo	Vir	Vir	Lib	Lib	Lib	Sc	Sc	Sc	Sag	Sag
Apr 14	Leo	Vir	Vir	Vir	Lib	Lib	Sc	Sc	Sc	Sag	Sag	Cap
Apr 22	Leo	Vir	Vir	Lib	Lib	Lib	Sc	Sc	Sc	Sag	Sag	Cap
Apr 30	Vir	Vir	Vir	Lib	Lib	Sc	Sc	Sc	Sag	Sag	Cap	Cap
May 8	Vir	Vir	Lib	Lib	Lib	Sc	Sc	Sag	Sag	Sag	Cap	Cap
May 16	Vir	Vir	Lib	Lib	Sc	Sc	Sc	Sag	Sag	Cap	Cap	Aq
May 24	Vir	Lib	Lib	Lib	Sc	Sc	Sag	Sag	Cap	Cap	Aq	Aq
June 1	Vir	Lib	Lib	Sc	Sc	Sc	Sag	Sag	Cap	Cap	Aq	Aq
June 9	Lib	Lib	Lib	Sc	Sc	Sag	Sag	Sag	Cap	Cap	Aq	Pis
June 17	Lib	Lib	Sc	Sc	Sc	Sag	Sag	Cap	Cap	Aq	Aq	Pis
June 25	Lib	Lib	Sc	Sc	Sag	Sag	Sag	Cap	Cap	Aq	Pis	Ar
July 3	Lib	Sc	Sc	Sc	Sag	Sag	Cap	Cap	Aq	Aq	Pis	Ar
July 11	Lib	Sc	Sc	Sag	Sag	Sag	Cap	Cap	Aq	Pis	Ar	Tau
July 18	Sc	Sc	Sc	Sag	Sag	Cap	Cap	Aq	Aq	Pis	Ar	Tau
July 26	Sc	Sc	Sag	Sag	Sag	Cap	Cap	Aq	Pis	Ar	Tau	Tau
Aug 3	Sc	Sc	Sag	Sag	Cap	Cap	Aq	Aq	Pis	Ar	Tau	Gem
Aug 11	Sc	Sag	Sag	Sag	Cap	Cap	Aq	Pis	Ar	Tau	Tau	Gem
Aug 18	Sc	Sag	Sag	Cap	Cap	Aq	Pis	Pis	Ar	Tau	Gem	Gem
Aug 27	Sag	Sag	Sag	Cap	Cap	Aq	Pis	Ar	Tau	Tau	Gem	Gem
Sept 4	Sag	Sag	Cap	Cap	Aq	Pis	Pis	Ar	Tau	Gem	Gem	Can
Sept 12	Sag	Sag	Cap	Aq	Aq	Pis	Ar	Tau	Tau	Gem	Gem	Can
Sept 20	Sag	Cap	Cap	Aq	Pis	Pis	Ar	Tau	Gem	Gem	Can	Can
Sept 28	Cap	Cap	Aq	Aq	Pis	Ar	Tau	Tau	Gem	Gem	Can	Can
Oct 6	Cap	Cap	Aq	Pis	Ar	Ar	Tau	Gem	Gem	Can	Can	Leo
Oct 14	Cap	Aq	Aq	Pis	Ar	Tau	Tau	Gem	Gem	Can	Can	Leo
Oct 22	Cap	Aq	Pis	Ar	Ar	Tau	Gem	Gem	Can	Can	Leo	Leo
Oct 30	Aq	Aq	Pis	Ar	Tau	Tau	Gem	Can	Can	Can	Leo	Leo
Nov 7	Aq	Aq	Pis	Ar	Tau	Tau	Gem	Can	Can	Can	Leo	Leo
Nov 15	Aq	Pis	Ar	Tau	Gem	Gem	Can	Can	Can	Leo	Leo	Vir
Nov 23	Pis	Ar	Ar	Tau	Gem	Gem	Can	Can	Leo	Leo	Leo	Vir
Dec 1	Pis	Ar	Tau	Gem	Gem	Can	Can	Can	Leo	Leo	Vir	Vir
Dec 9	Ar	Tau	Tau	Gem	Gem	Can	Can	Leo	Leo	Leo	Vir	Vir
Dec 18	Ar	Tau	Gem	Gem	Can	Can	Can	Leo	Leo	Leo	Vir	Vir
Dec 28	Tau	Tau	Gem	Gem	Can	Can	Leo	Leo	Vir	Vir	Vir	Lib

CHAPTER 12

The Capricorn Man and Woman

The Capricorn Man

The Capricorn man is usually the traditional macho man of the zodiac. You are an ambitious achiever, a hard, methodical worker who is most comfortable in a male-run world. Sometimes, when Capricorn is a young man, you may appear to be a drifter; however, this is usually just a phase where you are learning from experience about how the world works and setting serious goals. Later in life, the dignified Capricorn manner takes over, and, like Cary Grant, Robert Stack, or Humphrey Bogart, you'll embody the elegant tough guy, wise in the ways of the world.

Since you are most concerned with rising to the top, you may discount anything or anyone who is not related to your goals. Many of you embody the term workaholic. Your personal life is usually second to your pursuit of success, at least in the early part of your career. Persistence and tolerance of difficult working conditions are two of your great assets. You can overcome great obstacles as long as there is a clear vision of where you're heading. Therefore, it is essential that you see the top of the mountain before you embark on any venture. Once established, you may decide to make up for lost time and enjoy the fruits of your labors, allowing your hidden romantic, dreamy side to be revealed.

The Capricorn man has an earthy, rather chauvinistic view of women. In the early stages of a relationship, you are usually most interested in the physical side of a relationship and may dismiss women as serious companions or competitors. A woman who can help you in your career or create the right public image is most likely to appeal to you. Though you may experiment sexually with women of a lower class, your wife is usually chosen for her ability to elevate your position in some way.

The Capricorn man usually ages very well and becomes more appealing after forty, when your natural dignity and dry sense of humor shine through. The natural physical signs of aging, especially gray hair, add a distinguished touch of sex appeal. By this time, you're likely to have have established yourself financially and feel freer to indulge in the pleasures of life, which adds to your attractiveness to the opposite sex. (Cary Grant and Humphrey Bogart portrayed the sexy middle-aged Capricorn, the tough guy with a heart and a dry sense of humor.)

As a family man, you also improve as you get older, especially when you become the family's rock of Gibraltar, a source of paternal help and wisdom. Since family security means a great deal to you, you're likely to create a traditional family structure when you finally settle down.

As a Husband

The Capricorn man's way of showing love is to share your goals with your mate—and you'll expect that she do everything in her power to help you achieve them. Career comes first; therefore, your wife will be expected to adjust to your plans, not vice versa. You won't commit to anyone who doesn't support your goals. Often you'll marry someone who can help you up the mountain with position or good contacts, or someone whose talents support yours. You usually don't go for the more independent type of career woman, because you prefer to be the strong figure, so it is no surprise that there is often a considerable May–September (or even December) generation gap between the Capricorn man and his wife. This works especially well when the older Capricorn becomes a mentor to his younger, ambitious wife.

The plus with a Capricorn is that you get better as you get older. Many of these older man–younger woman relationships last because Capricorn mellows and becomes more fun-loving with age.

The Capricorn Woman

Capricorn women seem to be born competent and well-organized, even though you may appear fragile as flowers—the term "steel magnolia" was surely used to describe a Capricorn woman. Elegantly dressed, beautifully groomed in classic feminine clothes, the typical Capricorn, such as Diane Sawyer, presents a cool, calm image, with everything under control. You give the impression of someone who takes life very seriously. Even those who run counter to type, such as Dolly Parton, are, underneath the glitter, highly competent businesswomen who understand the commercial value of their facade. One of your biggest assets is your natural self-discipline. You are able to focus on your goal, mobilize your forces, and get the job done more effectively than most other signs of the zodiac.

Many Capricorns have followed a rocky road through life, yet with enormous self-discipline you can muster all your resources for the road ahead and overcome many obstacles to reach a high position. Your focus on the path upward puts great value on quality, power, and prestige—and those who have it. But though you'll carefully cultivate contacts with VIPs, you'll stay loyal to anyone who helps you and always repays favors in full.

You are most fulfilled when you are using your energy to manage someone or something. You also understand how to use the talents of others, which makes you an excellent business manager or stage mother. If you feel that you cannot accomplish goals on your own, you may do it vicariously, through others in your life, which can cause problems with rebellious independent types, those who have different values, or those who may have a less ambitious agenda. However, with a willing pupil, you can be a very good mentor and wise counselor.

Family relationships mean a great deal to Capricorn women. You are especially caring and solicitous of elders, often taking personal care of older relatives. You are proud of your family background and will make special efforts to maintain appearances and keep up family traditions. You can always be counted on to attend important family-related events and ceremonies.

Strongly goal-oriented, you are a wonderful worker who'll be first to arrive on the job and last to leave, always delivering what you promise. Your clear sense of priorities helps you work more effectively than others who may not have your drive and direction. As long as there is a possibility for promotion, you're likely to be happy in your job. Though you might have many time conflicts between work and family, you'll juggle your schedule expertly, to assure that your family is well provided for.

As a Wife

In marriage, Capricorn often works out a very complex relationship with her father and lives out her desire for personal power through a man. She rarely marries impulsively for grand passion. If her husband produces the expected lifestyle, she'll fulfill her responsibilities. Once she acquires self-confidence, she makes a wise, realistic, and helpful mate. As she matures, she may indulge more in affairs of the heart, allowing herself more spontaneous pleasure as her earthy, sensual side finally emerges. But she will not commit herself until she feels totally secure inside, or until she has established herself at the top of her profession. Once they have a successful career, many Capricorn women then marry a much younger husband—and keep up with him easily.

CHAPTER 13

Capricorn Family Values

The Capricorn Parent

Your sign is considered the natural father of the zodiac, while your opposite sign, Cancer, is considered the natural mother. Even female Capricorns have the paternal, responsible, dutiful outlook of the family provider. An ambitious, hard worker yourself, you'll want your children to rise to the top in life; therefore, you'll try to provide them with the best tools possible. That includes education, good manners, and the knowledge of how to handle money. Your children will probably be given an allowance at an early age, with instructions in how to budget. You will provide your children with steady support, never spoiling or indulging them, and an appreciation of tradition. Since even the more flamboyant Capricorns are solidly rooted in family values, you'll impart this sense of lineage to your children. To the artistic child, who may lack a sense of focus and have difficulty getting organized, you'll provide a sense of direction and a strong dose of reality. You are especially good at teaching your children the perseverance and organizational skills they'll need to achieve their goals.

The Capricorn Stepparent

Establishing an atmosphere of trust over a period of time should be your priority as a stepparent. Your realistic expectations and methodical step-by-step approach can work wonders in creating respect and reestablishing a stable family structure with rules to be followed and lines of authority clarified. Though you may seem cool and calculating to your stepchildren at first, they will come to respect your boundaries and appreciate your gradual approach to intimacy. Later they will come to trust you as a mentor and adviser—you are the one who knows what works. Let your stepchildren see your creative side, too, and your delightful dry sense of humor. You're not all work, no play! As they get to know you, they'll grow to appreciate your realistic outlook and your sincere support.

The Capricorn Grandparent

Capricorn is the sign we all envy, as you seem to have the anti-aging formula. You lighten up and warm up as you grow older, putting the workaholic days far behind. As a grandparent, you'll kick up your heels, enjoying your grandchildren, playing with them, and probably expressing more affection than with your own children. You're in great shape and looking terrific—silver hair is sensational on you. You are the grandparent who goes out dancing, often with a much younger mate. You love to be surrounded by younger friends, reveling in their youthful energy; you are more relaxed and free now that you have reached the top of the mountain where the air is clear and rarified.

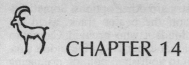

CHAPTER 14

Capricorn Professional Life

Capricorn is the serious, super-achiever of the zodiac. You know how to use every situation to your advantage. Each job must pay off in some way and be a concrete step upward toward your ultimate goal. You were dealt the perfect hand for success, with iron discipline and great concentration, plus focused ambition. However, you are not a risk taker. You prefer a career that has a clear-cut route to the top, with few detours for diversified scenery and experience. You will probably map out your goals well in advance and take a very disciplined, organized approach. There is a cool lack of emotion in everything you do—watch out for others who are very suspicious of being used and who may set up roadblocks. You'll progress faster if you learn to show more of your natural warmth and caring along the way.

Capricorn Careers

You are attracted to power positions, or to places where there is definite leadership potential. Big traditional organizations, learning institutions, banks, publishing houses, and museums attract you. Your refined, rather conservative tastes make you excellent at creating status environments for others as an interior designer, art collector, or antique dealer. Working with an auction house, with fine woods or leather could give vent to your creative instincts. Capricorn would have a natural affinity for working with the elderly, which could make your fortune in the years ahead, since the elderly population is growing rapidly. Working in a distinguished position as a counselor or professor, in orthopedic or chiropractic healing arts, or in dentistry are other options. Sometimes your ambitions can go off the beaten track, as in the case of the Mayflower Madam who brought Capricorn efficiency and organizational expertise to the oldest profession. Capricorns seem to flourish in politics, producing such diversified public figures as Martin Luther King, Richard Nixon, Barry Goldwater, Helmut Schmidt, and Walter Mondale.

Capricorn as Boss

The Capricorn boss is a no-nonsense leader who knows exactly how to use the talents of others. You're a master delegator who sets very definite roles for everyone to follow. But your inflexibility could freeze out some of the more creative types who tend to be free spirits. Opting for the sure thing every time, you're not one to risk the company's money on an untried product or mode of operations. You play by the rules, enforcing a very strict budget with minimum company perks—no long lunch hours for you. It may pay off to allow a bit more leeway with your rules—a tight ship can be a prison!

Capricorn as Coworker

The Capricorn worker will very rarely bring your personal life to the job. You are all business, aiming to fulfill the company's expectations to the letter. You will be very creative in devising the best way to get the job done, present the correct image, and find the most economical methods. Very decisive and determined, you will move mountains, a stone at a time, if necessary. You'll happily take advantage of any courses the company offers, or invest in self-improvement to boost your chances of success. And you are one employee who will never abuse expense account privileges.

Your Best Business Partner

Choose someone who can appreciate your disciplined approach and who can really contribute to your goals.

Oddly, the creative, rather romantic Pisces could be just the complement you need. You'll recognize their enormous talent and creativity and give them the benefit of your organizational ability. They'll encourage you to take a few risks and brighten your life. And since you like control of the organizational setup, they'll never challenge or compete with you.

Be A Capricorn Winner

Play Up for Success: Organizational ability, intelligence, perception, efficiency, decisiveness, good planning, understanding of power structures, and good taste.

Play Down: Inflexibility, an overdisciplined attitude, a too-serious nature, too much structure, insecurity with any risk taking, negative moods, and preoccupation with routine.

CHAPTER 15

Capricorn Style and Flair

Your Hero and Heroine of Style: Cary Grant and Lady Mendl.

The Capricorn Environment

Your style heroine, Lady Mendl, was a true Capricorn icon who reached her peak in later years. Though never considered a beauty, she had the last word in fashion and virtually invented the profession of interior decorator. With her silver-blue hair, well-maintained figure, and revolutionary sense of style, Elsie de Wolfe, Lady Mendl, became the toast of European society at an age when most women would be peacefully retired. This dowager of design threw out the trend for heavy Victorian furniture and cultivated our taste for fine French antiques, light-colored walls, animal prints, and uncluttered settings. Read some of the biographies of this remarkable lady who defined Capricorn style.

Lady Mendl's key word, "suitability," at once reveals the down-to-earth principles of your sun sign. Her interiors had to be as practical as they were stunning. If a room didn't work, it didn't matter how beautiful it was. The same goes for every Capricorn room. "Form follows function" could be your best decorating guideline.

Most Capricorns have innate good taste, based on your natural sense of restraint and your traditional values. You are happiest in a tasteful, rather conservative environment, with high ceilings, beautiful dark woods, and the look of old money. Monograms, crests, heraldic motifs, fine antiques, oriental rugs, and rich colors suit you. Capricorns from the South like columns in front of their house and a country club look. Even Elvis Presley, a more flamboyant type of Capricorn, returned to his Southern roots in choosing the plantation theme for his home, Graceland. Yankee Capricorns prefer the traditional look of Ivy League gothic. If the decor is modern, it should still feature fine woods and a solid structured look. Since many of you take work home, space should be set aside for a home office, complete with the latest technology discreetly hidden in oak cabinets.

Capricorn Music

Capricorn has eclectic musical tastes: You like classical music, string quartets, and medieval sounds. But the earthy country and western sounds of Dolly Parton and Barbara Mandrell also appeal. You are especially attracted to the music of people who have worked their way through hardship to reach the top. You kick up your heels to rockers Rod Stewart and David Bowie. But it is the Latin sound of flamenco guitars and tangos that really lights your fire.

Capricorn Flowers

Geraniums, daisies, and all climbing flowers and espaliered fruit trees are for you.

Capricorn Places

Capricorn likes clubby places with organized social life and superb service. You're an expert at mixing business with pleasure, where the rich and famous congregate, like Southhampton, Long Island, or Palm Beach. But South America and Spain speak to your wild side, and could just lure you away from business. India, Afghanistan, and, closer to home, Iowa, Georgia, and Utah, are soul spots.

Capricorn Colors

Black and white, sparked with bright red, are your special colors. Or try rich, deep earth and tapestry tones.

Capricorn Fashion Tips

You take a no-nonsense approach to fashion. Your clothes have to work for your job or social requirements. Capricorn males are especially fussy about their clothing, with good reason. They understand how important it is to project the right image. Cary Grant never looked sloppy, even in blue jeans. And who could forget Humphrey Bogart's beautifully cut, immaculate white dinner jacket in *Casablanca?* You rarely make a fashion mistake with your eye for quality and taste for conservative, classic styles. Take a tip from Cary and invest in well-cut, high-quality clothing that never goes out of style. Choose fabrics that span the seasons. Stretch your wardrobe with separates in a few colors that combine well together, so you'll always look pulled together. Then add some special effects—antique jewelry, a serious fur coat, and elegant shoes—to make your statement. Use your hairstyle and makeup to play up your strong bone structure, and keep your beauty tools organized in a compartmented carryall.

CHAPTER 16

Capricorn Care and Maintenance

The good news for Capricorn is that you are often called the sign of longevity. You're the ones we all envy. Just think of the film stars of the thirties and forties, whose careers lasted much longer than others—like Jane Wyman, Cary Grant, Marlene Dietrich, Loretta Young—who became role models for attractive, sexy, healthy elders. But such optimum health is usually the payoff of years of disciplined diet and regular exercise. You'll probably jog, and play golf or tennis regularly once you fit these activities into your schedule. A well-organized, structured program with definite goals is the key to the success of any Capricorn program. Joining a club or gym is incentive to go there often and make use of the facilities. Take advantage of any perks your company provides, such as fitness classes or office gyms, where you can take an exercise break.

All Capricorns should take special care of your knees, especially if you are a runner or jogger. These Capricorn weak spots—knees, joints, bones—may show early signs of arthritis, so be sure your calcium intake is right for your age.

Remember to exercise for fun as well as results! Grim determination can be counter-productive, especially if your goal is to relieve tension. Take up a sport to enjoy for itself, not necessarily to become a champion. Then you'll be more likely to make exercise a part of your life after you've achieved your fitness goals. Many Capricorns choose the more solitary sports such as skiing, mountain-climbing, or running, where they can commune with nature. Sports that get you out into the fresh mountain air are ideal choices.

Capricorn workaholics may find it difficult to wind down or get away from it all. But it is particularly necessary for you to do so. Not only will you get fresh and potentially profitable ideas, but you often need to spend more time strengthening your personal relationships and being with those you love. And playing! Young Capricorns are often so engrossed in their climb to the top, or in pushing their spouses ahead, that they forget to smell the roses. In later life, however, many Capricorns make up for lost time by kicking up their heels, becoming much more sociable and fun-loving.

Because work is so important to you, any injuries to your ego at work, such as being passed over for an important position, really strike hard. You are so goal oriented that it is very difficult for you to distance yourself emotionally from your work. That is why it is very important for you to balance your life by cultivating outside interests.

Another stressful point is the spending of your hard-earned cash. To put it mildly, you are often tight fisted. Learn to enjoy the fruits of your labor and share them with others. Generosity does not come easy to Capricorn, particularly in youth.

You need to take time to reflect, relax, and get away from it all. Don't wait until your old age! Build in good times with your family now. Take the necessary time to show affection to your loved ones; listen to their problems.

Capricorn should look to their earth element for the ideal places to relax—in the country or near mountains. Get off by yourself and read poetry. Get a hobby that has nothing to do with work, like drawing, carpentry, aviation or art collecting—something that puts you in an unpressured environment. Music, particularly country and western or flamenco guitar music, soothes you.

Capricorns often forget that their work environment can sabotage their health. Good lighting and air quality are often neglected in offices and can easily aggravate stress. Avoid smoke-filled rooms, or bring along an ionizer. You may actually prefer a small, cozy office to a large, impressive one. Be sure you have a comfortable, back-supporting chair. And walk around the office as much as possible to improve your circulation.

The Healthy Capricorn Vacation

It's a temptation for Capricorn to use the vacation to get ideas for work or, even worse, take work with them. Instead, why not try to get away from it all completely? You naturally gravitate to status places where powerful people congregate, such as the Hamptons on Long Island. But Spain and South America also exert a powerful attraction. So do India and Afghanistan, and the states of Iowa, Georgia, and Utah. As mentioned before, any place with mountains is Capricorn territory. A fantasy castle-hotel in the mountains of Spain or South America, a hiking vacation in the Great Smokies or the Rocky Mountains could put your life in the proper perspective.

CHAPTER 17

Capricorn Astro-Outlook for 1997

This is a good financial and business year for you, as Jupiter enters Aquarius in January and will remain in your money house the rest of the year. With Uranus also in your second house, there will be many new money-making opportunities presenting themselves this year, particularly just before and after February 16, when these major planets attain a momentous conjunction.

Changes that are taking place in the national and world economy will not throw you. Rather, they tend to play into your hands.

With Saturn moving through your fourth house this year, you can stabilize domestic, property, real estate, and ownership matters. Gains and profits in this zone will crystallize over the summer for you. Properties and ownership ideas can be consolidated successfully and it will be less difficult to secure family agreement here.

Local travel is under pressure early in March, when a change in routines and schedules may be in the offing. Give relatives and neighbors the benefit of every doubt over March, and keep close tabs on changes in your career. With Mars erratic over February, March, and up until April 28, be cautious with accumulations of money and remain alert, since there will be an increase in accident-producing potential.

Your love life is dynamically stimulated over late April and early May—it's a good period for eligibles to meet their heart's desire.

Health, diet, and nutritional needs can be served well over early June, while late June is good for completing important projects. You can cash in on them later this year. Money making is favored during the second half of August, while love and romance are once again activated in mid-November.

With Neptune dominating your Sign all year, your spiritual life is stimulated. Long-delayed rewards and awards can also materialize. You gain from having kept your own counsel in the past, from honoring secrets and confidences, and at the same time keeping your weather ear to the ground, so that you can do more than just suspect what has been happening behind the scenes.

The presence of Pluto, the force of awareness and transformation, in Sagittarius is a powerful indication that your intuition is serving you in security interests, savings, investments, and anything related to accumulations.

The lunar north Node in your ninth house constitutes a guarantee of success when you deal in long-range and long-distance matters.

Your 1997 is a different year, a more promising year, one in which your Daily Guides are assuming great importance, for each day is a unit unto itself.

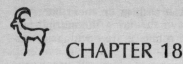

CHAPTER 18

Eighteen Months of Day-by-Day Predictions—July 1996 to December 1997

JULY 1996

Monday, July 1 (Moon in Capricorn) The full moon is in your sign and illuminates personal matters, aspirations, and ambitions. You know how to use your personality and character assets and how to tone down any possible liabilities. In your lunar cycle high, you can face difficult challenges and win big. Lemon is your color. Your lucky number is 8.

Tuesday July 2 (Moon in Capricorn to Aquarius 8:05 a.m.) Health and work pick up steam. While you are still in your lunar cycle high, you can lead, direct, produce, and hold the initiative. Stand tall. Look rich and royal, and the mantle of leadership will fall on your shoulders naturally. Stake claims. Buy and sell. Pink is in. Your lucky number is 1.

Wednesday, July 3 (Moon in Aquarius) Aquarius is the one who knows how to crowd all your work and play into the day. Fine trends exist in earning power, in acquiring new possessions, and in a possible new source of investment capital. Violet is your color. Lucky lottery numbers: 3, 12, 21, 30, 39, 48.

Thursday, July 4 (Moon in Aquarius to Pisces 8:07 a.m.)   Spend some part of the day with kindred spirits who know what you are all about. Leo and Aries can be in the picture. Aquarius will impact your thinking and doing. You could hear about a promising investment and a source of additional income. Read financial newspapers and magazines. Your lucky number is 5.

Friday, July 5 (Moon in Pisces)   Pisces understands what you're doing. Today's accent falls on immediate and pressing matters, everyday routines, communications, and transportation interests. Discuss some of your plans with a relative or sympathetic neighbor. Your ideal color is beige. Hot combination numbers: 7 and 3.

Saturday, July 6 (Moon in Pisces to Aries 10:42 a.m.) Scorpio and Cancer have key roles. Studies, hobbies, your learning processes are all stimulated in the right direction. Progress can be made with good ideas available to you. The day reveals much beauty in gardens, parks, and in the minds and hearts of children. Mauve is your color. Lucky lottery numbers: 6, 9, 18, 27, 36, 45.

Sunday, July 7 (Moon in Aries)   Aries intends to persuade you. Domestic, residential, and property matters are activated. The family stands together, but does not want to play together. It may be next to impossible to get seniors and juniors to accept the plans of the managerial generation. Your winning color is electric blue. Number 2 is your best bet.

Monday, July 8 (Moon in Aries to Taurus 4:43 p.m.)   There is much talk about increased property taxes, while the cost of home, lawn, and vehicle maintenance is on the rise. The community wonders where its financial base is coming from. Still, there is a willingness to share greater burdens, if the problem is presented to others in the right way. Play number 6 to win.

Tuesday, July 9 (Moon in Taurus)   Taurus brings charm and charisma to the scene. Romance will find you today. Courtship does well, and lovemaking soars to ecstasy. Be cautious, if you are contributing to the jealousy of a child, who may want more attention. Crimson and white are your colors. Your lucky number is 8.

Wednesday, July 10 (Moon in Taurus) Parties and entertainment will do well. Fine trends exist for talks with parents and children. Spontaneous activities do best under prevailing aspects. The desire to socialize is particularly strong. Consult another Capricorn or a Virgo on important matters. Chestnut is your color. Lucky lottery numbers: 1, 10, 19, 28, 37, 46.

Thursday, July 11 (Moon in Taurus to Gemini 1:52 a.m.) Gemini has the right word for it. Health maintenance is featured with new medical information available to you. The job that has to be done today can be boring, and you may wish you could just walk out. You are vitally interested in more creative and original assignments. Hot combination numbers: 3 and 9.

Friday, July 12 (Moon in Gemini) Express yourself clearly, so that nothing is left to the imagination. Some danger of being misquoted by kids exists also. You welcome the late afternoon and the promise of a more exciting evening. A weekend traveling high up in the air would do much to clear away the cobwebs. Rust is your color. Number 5 is a winner.

Saturday, July 13 (Moon in Gemini to Cancer 1:08 p.m.) Watch what you eat and drink. Summer complaints can catch up with busy teenagers. Foods left in the sun or automobile too long can upset the stomach. Aquarius has something to say about health and nutrition, business and independence. Winning colors are navy and copper. Lucky lottery numbers: 5, 7, 16, 25, 34, 43.

Sunday, July 14 (Moon in Cancer) Pisces and Cancer can impact your day. There is much togetherness and unity. Share, cooperate, consult your mate and other partners before making any hard-and-fast decision. Public relations demand that you dress up and put your best foot forward. Wonderment is evident. Your lucky number is 9.

Monday, July 15 (Moon in Cancer)   The new moon illuminates your marriage, other partnerships, the fine art of sharing and cooperating, and all public relations measures that you may undertake now. You may discover new ways to make your marriage more interesting and secure. Sapphire and azure are your colors. Your lucky number is 4.

Tuesday, July 16 (Moon in Cancer to Leo 1:31 a.m.)   The matters of Leo and those ruled by Leo are dominant. All security needs and changes can be stepped up. The urge to improve and correct is strong in Capricorn. Fine aspects exist for holding conferences and interviews. Do children have more clout in your home than is wise? Hot combination numbers: 6 and 1.

Wednesday, July 17 (Moon in Leo)   A fine day for paying bills, collecting what is owed you, and making your home and place of business more secure. Don't park your vehicle in lonely, deserted, darkened areas, just to escape a parking fee. You are strongly conscious of the cost and standard of living. Flame is your color. Lucky lottery numbers: 2, 8, 17, 26, 35, 44.

Thursday, July 18 (Moon in Leo to Virgo 2:17 p.m.)   Take changes in stride. Do what you can to help loved ones adjust. A feuding couple may tell you too much of their private business; try to avoid this, for the sake of future relationships. Use caution if you're out in the sun. White is your color. Your lucky number is 1.

Friday, July 19 (Moon in Virgo)   Virgo and Taurus can impact your day. You will want time off now, to get away from the daily grind, but the beach is not the answer. Drive into the country and buy local farm products. You want to get back to basics and to the days when people made what they required. Hot combination numbers: 3 and 9.

Saturday, July 20 (Moon in Virgo)   Fine aspects for travel, away from the familiar and the usual. You are impressed with the determined, persevering types you meet under these aspects. There can be a strong field of magnetic attraction between you and a stranger you meet in a rural setting. You relax well this evening. Pearl gray is your color. Lucky lottery numbers: 5, 14, 23, 32, 41, 50.

Sunday, July 21 (Moon in Virgo to Libra 2:14 a.m.) Trust Libra to investigate and explain. Your mind is busy with thoughts of your career, social and economic status, and what you can do with the prestige you already have won. Where are you headed? Can you surmise the amount of potential you have to utilize? Milky white is your color. Your lucky number is 7.

Monday, July 22 (Moon in Libra) Push your career potential for all it is worth. Let employers and supervisors know what you are doing and what you hope to get out of total effort in their behalf. Conferences, discussions, and interviews will go well. Fairness, honesty, and loyalty marks the day. Cardinal red is your color. Your lucky number is 2.

Tuesday, July 23 (Moon in Libra to Scorpio 11:43 a.m.) Leo and Aries have front seats. Coworkers can aggravate a work situation. You could encounter some jealousy on the job. You can cash in now on the goodwill you have been spreading on the job and also in your own neighborhood. Your earned reputation runs interference for you. Number 4 is a winner.

Wednesday, July 24 (Moon in Scorpio) Scorpio and Cancer are in your corner. Excellent trends in friendships, the social side of your job, group activities, and all church and club participation. You could run into someone you haven't seen in a long time, and discover that there are still embers from an old physical attraction. Lucky lottery numbers: 6, 15, 24, 33, 42, 51.

Thursday, July 25 (Moon in Scorpio to Sagittarius 5:24 p.m.) Seek out genuine kindred spirits who boost your morale today. Avoid people who tend to be critical and envious of you. Seize happiness when you identify it. Reveal your aspirations and hopes for the future.

You'll also be at home with those who share your hobby. Hot combination numbers: 8 and 2.

Friday, July 26 (Moon in Sagittarius)   Sagittarius will help you catch up on any work that may have been ignored earlier. A good day for dealing with important executives and large organizations. Give your mate or another partner the benefit of the doubt and say as little as possible about something that's bothering you. Cherry is your color. Hot combination numbers: 1 and 4.

Saturday, July 27 (Moon in Sagittarius to Capricorn 7:17 p.m.)   Aries and Leo may have the information you require. Fine aspects for catching up, finishing a no-win project, and opening the door to new interests. You may have your own ideas about what parents and children should be saying, doing, and thinking, but you could be wrong. Lucky lottery numbers: 3, 12, 21, 30, 39, 48.

Sunday, July 28 (Moon in Capricorn)   In your lunar cycle high, you can shift emotional gears and do what you can to regain the confidence of a difficult person. Seize and hold the initiative. Lead the big parade and don't let a relative detract you from what you know should be done. Colors are mauve and old rose. Your lucky number is 5.

Monday, July 29 (Moon in Capricorn to Aquarius 6:47 p.m.)   The day is yours for competing, contesting, challenging, and doing very well. Another Capricorn and a Virgo are on your side. Air your aspirations, be completely honest as to what you want from your current job and from your career. Where others know, they can be of assistance. Wear plaid today. Play number 9 to win.

Tuesday, July 30 (Moon in Aquarius)   The full moon illuminates earning power, income, the value of what you own, and uncovers possible sources of additional income. Aquarius and Leo have key roles. This is a fine day for a special sale and for advertising something you want to sell. A neighbor may express interest in what you want to dispose of now. Ultramarine is your color. Hot combination numbers: 2 and 6.

Wednesday, July 31 (Moon in Aquarius to Pisces 6 p.m.)   You could come across an idea or pointer that can put you on the road to higher income. Someone who is very independent may express an interest in what you are doing or planning to do. You gain today in communications with someone very different from yourself. Lavender is your color. Lucky lottery numbers: 4, 13, 22, 31, 40, 49.

AUGUST 1996

Thursday, August 1 (Moon in Pisces)   A quiet day which favors local, immediate, and pressing matters, studies, hobbies, communications and transportation. Pisces and Virgo figure prominently. Know what those closest to you are thinking. There is much talk about school as the day advances. Winning colors are plum and sand. Your lucky number is 3.

Friday, August 2 (Moon in Pisces to Aries 7:05 p.m.)   Scorpio and Cancer have key roles. What is happening behind the scenes can be more important than what you are observing. People aren't telling all. Instructions and directions leave much to be desired. Hold off making any important decision, until you have all the facts. Raspberry is your color. Your lucky number is 5.

Saturday, August 3 (Moon in Aries)   Aries and domesticity are in the picture. The accent falls on what you own and what you don't own. Real estate, community, residential, and family matters top your agenda. A fine day for deciding what painting you want done, inside and outside your home, including inspecting gutters. Old rose is your color. Lucky lottery numbers: 3, 7, 16, 25, 34, 43.

Sunday, August 4 (Moon in Aries to Taurus 11:33 p.m.)   Stick to what your family wants and expects from you. There are changes taking place in your community, which have people talking negatively. Isn't it time to admit that everything in the world is changing? In all these changes, you may find a more beneficial and happier lifestyle in a developing paradise. Lime and lemon are your colors. Your lucky number is 9.

Monday, August 5 (Moon in Taurus) Taurus and Virgo have key roles. This is a fine day for socializing, hosting a party for a group in which you hold a membership, or just getting together with your favorite relatives and friends. Bonding with children gets top grades. The bedroom beckons to you and your beloved. Your lucky number is 4.

Tuesday, August 6 (Moon in Taurus) It's another good day for partying, spending leisure time with happy types, enjoying chats with children, and issuing or receiving social invitations. If you want to see people, just phone spontaneously and either visit or open your home to them. Your lucky number is 6.

Wednesday, August 7 (Moon in Taurus to Gemini 7:49 a.m.) Gemini means exciting conversation during which you will learn much that can be applied to overall well-being and/or the work that has to be done. Fine aspects for starting new preventative medicine routines. An excellent day for gaining the confidence of a kindred spirit. Amber is your color. Lucky lottery numbers: 2, 8, 17, 26, 35, 44.

Thursday, August 8 (Moon in Gemini) Be careful what you eat and drink today. Careless habits have found their way into kitchens, slaughterhouses, and all food preparation, packaging, and preservation methods. Throw away anything left unrefrigerated too long. Plum is your color. Your number is 1.

Friday, August 9 (Moon in Gemini to Cancer 6:57 p.m.) Libra and Aquarius can impact your day. Work has a way of getting ignored under existing aspects. Also, it is a day of many pleasant distractions and interruptions. You may find yourself daydreaming about the upcoming weekend and of all that you might expect from it. Maroon is your color. Hot combination numbers: 3 and 6.

Saturday, August 10 (Moon in Cancer)　　There are fine aspects for beach and water activities. Cancer and Pisces can impact your day. Marriage, other partnerships, and public relations get green lights. You do well when sharing joy and delight with your beloved. Winning colors are champagne and mauve. Lucky lottery numbers: 5, 14, 23, 32, 41, 50.

Sunday, August 11 (Moon in Cancer)　　Again, the beach and water can beckon strongly. A family picnic is favored under these aspects. Excellent rays for joint decisions and joint investment of time, energy, and money. Families do well together in a lively setting. Don't expose senior citizens to too much sun. Magenta is your color. Number 7 is a winner.

Monday, August 12 (Moon in Cancer to Leo 7:29 a.m.)　　Leo will add spice to your day. Fine trends exist in security matters, saving, preserving, conserving, budgeting, and investing. This is a good day for definite improvements and corrections. Winning colors are brown and coral. You lucky number is 2.

Tuesday, August 13 (Moon in Leo)　　Amending, reinterpreting, and changing are important trends. You could feel the need to further explain plans to a relative or to help someone investigate peculiar happenings in their home or locality. It's a good day for following the leader. Your winning colors are olive and taupe. Your best number is 4.

Wednesday, August 14 (Moon in Leo to Virgo 8 p.m.)　　The new moon in Leo illuminates the changes you have been contemplating. There is enlightenment in ways to increase your personal and family security. Many members of your sign will be wondering whether to buy firearms due to an increase in crime. Lucky lottery numbers: 6, 15, 24, 33, 42, 51.

Thursday, August 15 (Moon in Virgo)   Virgo and another Capricorn have parts to play. Travel, changing your scene, remembering an enjoyable trip you took in the past, and handling long-range and long-distance matters are favored. You extend your thinking and look beyond the obvious and evident. Beige is your color. Number 8 is the winner.

Friday, August 16 (Moon in Virgo)   Try to get away from the familiar, the usual, and the possibly boring, even if only for the weekend. Some good work can be done as a preface to travel. The beach and water are not what you need now; rather, it would be advisable to visit a historic rural town. Beige is your color. Your lucky number is 1.

Saturday, August 17 (Moon in Virgo to Libra 7:55 a.m.)   In any question about career or employment, consult a Libra. It's a good day to cash in on your earned reputation. No unconventional behavior under these aspects, please! You may suddenly be excited by some tidbit of information that comes to you. Tawny brown and pea green are winning colors. Lucky lottery numbers: 3, 12, 21, 30, 39, 48.

Sunday, August 18 (Moon in Libra)   Isolate yourself from people this morning; contemplate your career and what you might do to liven it up a bit. What responsibility could you undertake in order to draw your boss's attention to your willingness, loyalty, and persistence? Orange is your color. Your lucky number is 5.

Monday, August 19 (Moon in Libra to Scorpio 5:50 p.m.)   Pitch in to duties, responsibilities, and obligations. Talks with your boss can prove helpful, and you may receive some valuable pointers about how to increase your job potential. Some honors and awards can be shaping up behind the scenes. Orchid and lilac are your colors. Number 9 is a winner.

Tuesday, August 20 (Moon in Scorpio)   An excellent day for checking up on people you haven't seen since the beginning of summer. Isn't it amazing how this can happen when groups in which you are active decide to recess for summer? You might bring coworkers and supervisors together by arranging a picnic or beach celebration. Hot combination numbers: 2 and 4.

Wednesday, August 21 (Moon in Scorpio) Let Scorpio in on your good news. Friendships, the social side of your job and of your hobby are favored. Group activities will do well. Church and club membership and participation get top billing. Phone or write friendly letters. Yellow is your color. Lucky lottery numbers: 4, 13, 22, 31, 40, 49.

Thursday, August 22 (Moon in Scorpio to Sagittarius 12:48 a.m.) Sagittarius can see the light at the end of the dark tunnel. A fine day for completing annoying tasks. An excellent day for spending time outdoors, enjoying the summer scene. Beach and water activities do well. Fine aspects for watching an athletic event. Your winning colors are magenta and amber. Hot combination numbers: 6 and 1.

Friday, August 23 (Moon in Sagittarius) Aries and Leo can impact your day. As summer wanes, it would be a good idea to get away, at least for the weekend. There are things you want to do at a resort that you intended to do before this late date. You deal well with powerful people and organizations. Blue and green are your colors. Try number 8.

Saturday, August 24 (Moon in Sagittarius to Capricorn 4:22 a.m.) Hurrah! You are now in your lunar cycle high and can correct, improve, redirect, maneuver successfully, and generally change things for the better. Hold the initiative and keep leading, rather than following. Khaki is your color. Lucky lottery numbers: 1, 10, 19, 28, 37, 46.

Sunday, August 25 (Moon in Capricorn) It's good that you have a free day to win others over to your point of view. Keep up the pressure where you want to air your aspirations and your goals for the future, hoping to get sympathetic listeners. It's a day when self-confidence and self-reliance will pay off. Your lucky number is 3.

Monday, August 26 (Moon in Capricorn to Aquarius 5:10 a.m.)   Push your earning power and income. Aquarius won't stand in your way, even though the big differences between you were never more visible. You take the practical approach: Aquarius tends to believe that time and money take care of themselves. You could decide that there is special money waiting for you. Number 7 is best.

Tuesday, August 27 (Moon in Aquarius)   Leo tends to dramatize your feelings. You are conscious of what you own and of the value of your possessions. Special sales and wise shopping can bring gains and profits. Fine aspects for buying ledgers and text that will help you with more visible budgeting. Those in power intrigue you. Number 9 is a good bet.

Wednesday, August 28 (Moon in Aquarius to Pisces 4:49 a.m.)   The full moon illuminates your local scene. You will receive enlightenment through special studies, hobbies, and discussions with businesspeople. Communications and transportation are at their best. Relatives and neighbors are with you in spirit. Rust and chestnut are your colors. Lucky lottery numbers: 2, 11, 20, 29, 38, 47.

Thursday, August 29 (Moon in Pisces)   Let Pisces in on your secret. You may be overly concerned about a local matter, while children can be discontented with school. It may be difficult to assess what is taking place behind the scenes in your neighborhood. Winning colors are rainbow and emerald. Your lucky number is 4.

Friday, August 30 (Moon in Pisces to Aries 5:16 a.m.)   Aries has some interesting suggestions for you. There may be an important invitation involved. You could be interested in new housing developments and apartments that claim to be the latest thing in what you need and in what you no longer require. Are living rooms passé? Turquoise is your color. Hot combination numbers: 6 and 1.

Saturday, August 31 (Moon in Aries)   Fine aspects for household chores, gardening, and cleaning up debris. You can win a great deal of satisfaction for yourself and your family by what you do to spruce things up. Your attic and garage should be given some attention. What will a little wallpaper do for that dull room? Lucky lottery numbers: 2, 8, 17, 26, 35, 44.

SEPTEMBER 1996

Sunday, September 1 (Moon in Aries to Taurus 8:19 a.m.)   Aries has directions or instructions you may not wish to honor. Family, residential, community, property, and ownership matters are high on your agenda. You are strongly aware of the passing of summer and of the changes you would like to implement in your home. Lapis lazuli is your color. Your lucky number is 7.

Monday, September 2 (Moon in Taurus)   Taurus and Scorpio have key roles. You are in a pleasant interval, where love, romance, socializing on a grand scale, relationships with parents and children are all favored. You may be a little annoyed at the way social activities cost, the price of license fees and dues are increasing. Your lucky number is 2.

Tuesday, September 3 (Moon in Taurus to Gemini 3:08 p.m.)   Virgo and another Capricorn are in your corner. Make love, be romantic, deal in lovely adventurous and investigative prologues and epilogues to love. Spontaneous entertaining gets the green light. You excel at making both older and younger people happy. Hot combination numbers: 4 and 7.

Wednesday, September 4 (Moon in Gemini)   Your career could be sluggish today. You may retire early under these health aspects. Work that is repetitive can depress you, but there may be good reasons why some work has to be redone. Refrain from placing blame, on a day when you could be wrong. Talks with older people will be helpful tonight. Lucky lottery numbers: 6, 15, 24, 33, 42, 51.

Thursday, September 5 (Moon in Gemini)   Your career is still sluggish today. Libra and Gemini have key roles. It would be easy to experience some fatigue and not really want to give your all to your job under prevailing aspects. You can slow your pace without anyone noticing it. Your colors are rust and mocha. Your lucky number is 8.

Friday, September 6 (Moon in Gemini to Cancer 1:29 a.m.)   Cancer and Scorpio will have the information you need. It's a good day for partnerships, for sharing, making joint decisions, and dealing in joint endeavors. Your mate has ideas that you can put to good use. Public relations work will get results. Yellow and khaki are your color. Your lucky number is 1.

Saturday, September 7 (Moon in Cancer)   Marital relations can be improved under existing aspects. Also, you can draw closer to an in-law you once didn't trust completely. Don't make changes that affect your beloved without due consultation. There are times when it's better not to mention another's faults. Lucky lottery numbers: 3, 12, 21, 30, 39, 48.

Sunday, September 8 (Moon in Cancer to Leo 1:54 p.m.)   Two can do everything better than one. There is no sense in going off by yourself today. Stay the course. Listen, when you realize that another knows what he or she is talking about. We cannot know everything, and we can't have it all. Be self-disciplined for best results. Number 5 is your best bet.

Monday, September 9 (Moon in Leo)   Leo may not have better ways of doing it than you, but Leo's gains will be more visible. Nor will Leo take a backseat, just to be courteous and well-mannered, which you certainly will under existing aspects. Friends may wish that you would stand up for yourself more. Your lucky number is 9.

Tuesday, September 10 (Moon in Leo)   Aries and Sagittarius can impact your day. Good trends exist where you are preserving and conserving, economizing, and improving budgets, especially household and kitchen expenses. Security is the word to be applied to these aspects. Honor the saving graces. Hot combination numbers: 2 and 6.

Wednesday, September 11 (Moon in Leo to Virgo 2:28 a.m.)   Virgo has practical ideas, and will present them with powerful determination. Travel gets green lights, and budget vacations are in style. You handle long-range and long-distance decisions well. Cousins and people at or from a distance can impact your day in a lucky way. Lucky lottery numbers: 4, 13, 22, 31, 40, 49.

Thursday, September 12 (Moon in Virgo)   The new moon in Virgo illuminates what you have perking for yourself at a distance. What is happening behind the scenes can impact your day. It may be difficult to get clues about what others are thinking. Olive and beige are your colors. Hot combination numbers: 6 and 4.

Friday, September 13 (Moon in Virgo to Libra 1:51 p.m.)   Avoid listening to, or acting on any superstitions about this day. Travel is sluggish and information may not arrive when you expect it. It can be difficult to determine what another is thinking, and you are inclined to think the worst. Beige and rust are your colors. Your lucky number is 8.

Saturday, September 14 (Moon in Libra)   Libra has good ideas that you may be able to use on the job and while working for career advancement. Protect your good reputation now, by avoiding any behavior that could be termed unconventional. Be kind, considerate, and tolerant for best results. Your lucky color is beige. Lucky lottery numbers: 1, 10, 19, 28, 37, 46.

Sunday, September 15 (Moon in Libra to Scorpio 11:20 p.m.)   Use a few hours to prepare for the work you will be doing during the week ahead. Make sure you have all information and forms available. The late afternoon is favorable for inviting a few kindred spirits in for tea and dessert. The approval, appreciation, and affection you receive will do wonders for your ego and morale. Your lucky number is 3.

Monday, September 16 (Moon in Scorpio) Scorpio has much to say that you should hear. People who have your best interests at heart may have to lower the boom, when you are all work and no play. Group activities will add to your peace of mind. Organization matters may require more than perusal. Your lucky number is 7.

Tuesday, September 17 (Moon in Scorpio) Fine trends exist for entertaining in your home, mixing dear friends and coworkers and neighbors. You will enjoy a chance to strut your stuff and to show off your possessions. Church and club involvements can be annoying you. Light blues are in. Your lucky number is 9.

Wednesday, September 18 (Moon in Scorpio to Sagittarius 6:31 a.m.) Sagittarius excels in knowing when a job or project should be finalized. Discuss the finished product with Sagittarius. Present suggestions along with work to those in power. A conference or interview will give you a marvelous pulpit for stating facts. Lucky lottery numbers: 2, 11, 20, 29, 38, 47.

Thursday, September 19 (Moon in Sagittarius) You deal well with large organizations and institutions under existing aspects. You can pick up some clues on what may be happening behind the scenes. Good opinions, suggestions, and implications can work wonders for you. Order what you need by phone. Hot combination numbers: 4 and 7.

Friday, September 20 (Moon in Sagittarius to Capricorn 11:12 a.m.) Listen to Aries and Leo. You may be able to add up the facts and decide on eliminating a no-win project. Spend some time outdoors as autumn shows up. Gather some of the more colorful leaves. You are glad to be alive today. Salmon and maroon are your colors. Number 6 is a winner.

Saturday, September 21 (Moon in Capricorn) You are now in your lunar cycle high, when you can take precedence over others. You know what to say and what to do, in order to come out a winner. But it's vital that you hold the initiative, stand tall, and speak your mind, so that others know what you want. Lucky lottery numbers: 2, 8, 17, 26, 35, 44.

Sunday, September 22 (Moon in Capricorn to Aquarius 1:39 p.m.) Push highly personalized ambitions. Stick to what you want to do and don't let others bring distractions to your work place. Let the world see you at your best, all dressed up, every hair in place, the symbol of the dedicated and elegant worker. Gold is your color. Your lucky number is 1.

Monday, September 23 (Moon in Aquarius) Aquarius and Libra show up. You have wonderful money-making ideas and systems now. Push your earning power, discuss the possibility of new assignments and greater responsibilities. Your job qualifications and duties may have to be rewritten, before you can expect a raise in pay. Your lucky number is 5.

Tuesday, September 24 (Moon in Aquarius to Pisces 2:43 p.m.) Fine aspects for talks with your banker and broker. Good trends where you are seeking better financial and economic information. Subscribe to a financially oriented magazine. Gather the information you need for a big push, and then present your findings to superiors. Hot combination numbers: 7 and 3.

Wednesday, September 25 (Moon in Pisces) Pisces may be leaning on you. The accent falls on what you *must* do, more than on what you *can* do. Locality, communications, and transportation are well-aspected. You could decide that it would be wise to shop out of your neighborhood, in order to get more bargains. Purple is your color. Lucky lottery numbers: 6, 9, 18, 27, 36, 45.

Thursday, September 26 (Moon in Pisces to Aries 3:46 p.m.) Protect all domestic flanks, as eclipse patterns form in Aries. Avoid overspending, buying what you don't need, and making sure your home is fireproof. Speak quietly to your children, and do what you can to keep their hackles from rising, when you want to teach them self-discipline. Your lucky number is 2.

Friday, September 27 (Moon in Aries) The total eclipse of the moon can bring depression within your family and home. There can be realistic fears about crime in your community and a strong demand that immediate steps be taken to make things better. You could feel pressured in residential matters. Your property needs better protection. Number 4 is your best bet.

Saturday, September 28 (Moon in Aries to Taurus 6:24 p.m.) Unplanned movement in the wake of yesterday's eclipse is not recommended—stay put. Keep close tabs on much older and much younger loved ones. Don't push impossible changes upon yourself or others. Wear cheerful colors to spice up the environment. Lucky lottery numbers: 6, 15, 24, 33, 43, 51.

Sunday, September 29 (Moon in Taurus) Check things out with Taurus, on a day when your love life is dynamically stimulated. You want to be utterly possessed by love. It's easy for you to make allowances for some of your beloved's shortcomings in other areas, as long as love remains complete and ecstatic. Your lucky number is 8.

Monday, September 30 (Moon in Taurus) Another auspicious day for making love and bonding even more closely with your beloved. Fine aspects for spontaneous parties and entertainment. Look your best under all circumstances, on a day when you are one of the big stars. Wear a little gold, along with immaculate white. Your lucky number is 3.

OCTOBER 1996

Tuesday, October 1 (Moon in Taurus to Gemini 12:01 a.m.) Gemini knows a lot about new medical, health, dietary, and nutrition findings and recommendations.

You will enjoy an in-depth conversation about health, making work less stressful, and newer ways of relaxation. Certainly, some attention to herbal medicines should be encouraged. Auburn is your color. Your lucky number is 3.

Wednesday, October 2 (Moon in Gemini) Pace yourself in the work you have to do, so that you don't tire easily under these aspects. Numerous interruptions and work done amidst constant distractions will prove of no avail. Aquarius has good financial advice for you. Your lucky colors are burgundy and dark reds. Lucky lottery numbers: 5, 14, 23, 32, 41, 50.

Thursday, October 3 (Moon in Gemini to Cancer 9:14 a.m.) Direct your questions to a Libra. Work can pile up today, and assistance is not top-flight. There are many complaints from coworkers and criticism from bosses. You relate to this time of year and will enjoy a walk about downtown areas, strolling in and out of parks and squares. Roast chestnuts. Your color is pinecone. Hot combination numbers: 7 and 3.

Friday, October 4 (Moon in Cancer) Virgo and Cancer have key roles. Partnerships and the joys of working with someone who understands you are strongly represented. Knowing your own community well is half the battle. Be willing to take a smaller cut of the financial and business pie, in order to create goodwill for the future. Number 9 is a winner.

Saturday, October 5 (Moon in Cancer to Leo 9:12 a.m.) Favorable aspects for closer bonding with your beloved, and for marital and business partnerships. Stick to contracts, agreements, and all regulations and rules. Teach children to share and to enjoy each other's company. Information may not arrive on time. Mauve and beige are your colors. Lucky lottery numbers: 2, 11, 20, 29, 38, 47.

Sunday, October 6 (Moon in Leo) Work on a new, more realistic budget. Write checks, so that bills due on the first can be paid now. You will notice that the costs of dues and license fees are rising. Tax matters can be somewhat disappointing. Know how much money you have on hand. Maroon and crimson are your colors. Your lucky number is 4.

Monday, October 7 (Moon in Leo)   Leo will be pushing you today, but you know what your pace should be. Remember, you are Earth and can extinguish Leo fire when you want to. You are strongly conscious of what you can and cannot afford to do. The complaints of others have a way of annoying you. Pumpkin is your color. Number 8 is your best bet.

Tuesday, October 8 (Moon in Leo to Virgo 9:49 a.m.)   A favorable day to collect what is due you and work on financial improvements and corrections. Personal, family, and home security matters can be pursued successfully. Aries and Sagittarius are in the winner's circle. Reddish-orange is your color. Hot combination numbers: 1 and 4.

Wednesday, October 9 (Moon in Virgo)   Virgo and Libra will impact your day. You program and plan effectively. Looking ahead, you can determine the day's needs and preferences. Any travel you do now is likely to put more money in the bank ultimately. Combine business with pleasure. Lucky lottery numbers: 3, 12, 21, 30, 39, 48.

Thursday, October 10 (Moon in Virgo to Libra 9 p.m.)   What is happening at a distance will impact your day. People who are determined to make their presence felt can find favor with you under these aspects. You respect endurance, perseverance, and persistence. The work gets done all right, but you could be very tired this evening. Ivory is your color. Number 5 is a winner.

Friday, October 11 (Moon in Libra)   You tend to step up the pace in order to complete a job that you want out of the way before the weekend. Libra has questions for you. Discussions about your future career will go well and leave you with the feeling that some sacrifice of ambition may be demanded of you. Your lucky number is 7.

Saturday, October 12 (Moon in Libra) The solar eclipse can pressure you in career, professional, authority, prestige, and status matters. Authorities say there are fewer genuine careers now; it's just a job which can change tomorrow. So we serve the shop's routines and schedules without the old guarantees. Still, you make good adjustments to new conditions. Lucky lottery numbers: 6, 9, 18, 27, 36, 45.

Sunday, October 13 (Moon in Libra to Scorpio 5:46 a.m.) Avoid quarrels, ultimatums, and showdowns in the wake of yesterday's eclipse. Scorpio will succeed in clearing the atmosphere of uncertainties and recriminations. Friends never were more important, and it would be wise to get away from the crowd, so that you and kindred spirits can talk. Number 2 is a good bet.

Monday, October 14 (Moon in Scorpio) The social side of your job can do much to keep you alert and happy. See each coworker as a person, a human being, and not just as a cog in the big wheel you turn so well. It's difficult for you to tolerate the inefficient and the whiners and complainers, but try. Emerald is your color. Number 6 is a winner.

Tuesday, October 15 (Moon in Scorpio to Sagittarius 12:07 p.m.) The group is the thing, and in unity there is great strength. Companionship with Cancer or Pisces can make your day. Ask questions, rather than run the risk of making errors. You will enjoy being outdoors, tracing the advance of autumn. Melon is your color. Hot combination numbers: 8 and 2.

Wednesday, October 16 (Moon in Sagittarius) Sagittarius arrives. What is rooted in the past can be counted on as you make decisions. What you learned more than seven years ago is back once again to serve you. You make good progress in dealings with corporations and government. Rust is your color. Lucky lottery numbers: 1, 10, 19, 28, 37, 46.

Thursday, October 17 (Moon in Sagittarius to Capricorn 4:37 p.m.)   Fine trends exist for completing jobs, closing one door so that a new one can be opened, and helping your mate with routine work. You adjust well now and can show more flexibility than your critics believed you had. White and pinecone are your colors. Your lucky number is 3.

Friday, October 18 (Moon in Capricorn)   Now you are in your lunar cycle high, and can make things go your way. Seize and hold the initiative, demonstrate the highest in self-confidence and self-reliance, and don't be too proud or humble to announce your aspirations for the future. Stick with the job, when others slow down. Your lucky number is 5.

Saturday, October 19 (Moon in Capricorn to Aquarius 7:51 p.m.)   Arise early and pounce on opportunities and advantages. You can make a difference. Encourage members of your family to help you as you keep your eyes on the prize. Get important shopping out of the way before noon. It's a fine day for fixing things, clearing away debris and misunderstandings. Lucky lottery numbers: 3, 7, 16, 25, 34, 43.

Sunday, October 20 (Moon in Aquarius)   Aquarius makes a good financial adviser today. You can see your way clear now to take a great leap forward in earning power and income. Are there items you want to dispose of now that can bring a good price? Money comes from odd jobs. Your lucky number is 9.

Monday, October 21 (Moon in Aquarius to Pisces 10:22 p.m.)   Financial and business transactions will do well today. Dress up and look affluent for best results. No cheapskates or others will try to take advantage of you. Gemini and Libra are in the picture. Avoid those steel traps that the wrong words can put you in. Salt and pepper are your colors. Number 4 is the winner.

Tuesday, October 22 (Moon in Pisces)   Pisces can impact your day. You narrow your sights now and give due attention to what is surrounding you. Your environment is all-important, together with neighbors and siblings. You communicate well, and any possible problem with transportation can be handled brilliantly. Off-white is your color. Number 6 is a good bet.

Wednesday, October 23 (Moon in Pisces)   A quiet, cool approach will work well for you. Ideally, the spiritual side of your nature is dominant. You want to do the right thing, and with you, the desire tends to win out. Scorpio and Cancer have good advice. Turquoise and sapphire are your colors. Lucky lottery numbers: 2, 8, 17, 26, 35, 44.

Thursday, October 24 (Moon in Pisces to Aries 12:50 a.m.)   Aries won't let you off the hook, but you are grateful for all this interest. Domestic, residential, ownership, and property matters top your agenda. You can reestablish a good relationship with a much older relative and with other kin who live far away. Champagne is your color. Hot combination numbers: 1 and 7.

Friday, October 25 (Moon in Aries)   What repairs could your home use before the colder weather sets in? You give prompt attention to the wishes of loved ones. It's not too early to consider plans for late November and December holidays. With a great deal of love, you consider relatives. Hot combination numbers: 3 and 6.

Saturday, October 26 (Moon in Aries to Taurus 4:11 a.m.)   The full moon illuminates your love life, the needs of your beloved, and the type of social program you should be putting together before the end of the month. Taurus and another Capricorn are in the picture. You see all the romance and adventure potential of this time of year. Yellow is right. Lucky lottery numbers: 5, 14, 23, 32, 41, 50.

Sunday, October 27 (Moon in Taurus, End of Daylight Saving Time)   A social program is stepped up, possibly due to your friends' wishes and needs. You approve, show warm affection, and let them know how much you appreciate them. This can be an exceptionally happy day. Spruce up your personal appearance. Silver is your color. Number 7 is a winner.

Monday, October 28 (Moon in Taurus to Gemini 8:35 a.m. EST)   Make love today. Celebrations, spontaneous entertainment, parties, and annual get-togethers bring happiness today. There is a special harmony between you and your beloved. Parent-child bonding is supported. Virgo can explain the serious side of the job. Ultramarine is your color. Your lucky number is 2.

Tuesday, October 29 (Moon in Gemini)   Gemini enters, with new directions and suggestions. Fine trends exist for hearing or reading about new medical findings. It's comforting to know that if you exercise, lose a little weight, and avoid salt, sugar, and fat, you can live to a ripe old age. Longevity can be serviced. Your lucky number is 4.

Wednesday, October 30 (Moon in Gemini to Cancer 4:56 p.m.)   Reorganize whatever you think needs attention. You do well where you make things simpler and quicker. Keep abreast of tools, appliances, methodologies, and technologies that can make your work more efficient and more accurate. Libra brings balance to the day. Lucky lottery numbers: 6, 15, 24, 33, 42, 51.

Thursday, October 31 (Moon in Cancer)   Fine trends for cooperative efforts with your beloved and a business partner. Discussions will be productive under these aspects. Cancer and Scorpio will deliver the goods. Know when your partner is on firmer ground than you may be. In-laws can be helpful. Apricot is your color. Your lucky number is 8.

NOVEMBER 1996

Friday, November 1 (Moon in Cancer)   A water sign person (Pisces, Scorpio, or Cancer) will make this a good day for you. Partnerships get top billing. Fine aspects for pillow talk with your spouse and serious talk with business contacts. Order what you need via mail or phone. Winning color is wheat. Your lucky number is 7.

Saturday, November 2 (Moon in Cancer to Leo 4:16 a.m.) Trust what Leo is telling you. Fine trends in security matters, including budgeting, savings, and investments. This is a good day for inaugurating a new household budget and for figuring out where to find bargains when you are shopping. The problem is you might have to shop in many places. Lucky lottery numbers: 6, 9, 18, 27, 36, 45.

Sunday, November 3 (Moon in Leo) Aries has some interesting suggestions but refuses to be pushed in any direction that doesn't make sense to you. Fine aspects for inaugurating and implementing improvements and corrections. You are strongly aware of what has not been done to the best of your ability. Champagne is your color. Your lucky number is 2.

Monday, November 4 (Moon in Leo to Virgo 4:57 p.m.) This is a fine day for making adjustments that will make upcoming holidays less stressful. Plan, make lists, resolve to keep a few steps ahead of the scheduled routines. Younger people are in the picture. Your lucky number is 6.

Tuesday, November 5 (Moon in Virgo) If you want to get away for a few days, so that you can be at home on Thanksgiving Day, this is the right time to take off like a big bird. Stick to your plans. Surface travel is better than air and will go much faster under prevailing aspects. Virgo is helpful. Hot combination numbers: 8 and 2.

Wednesday, November 6 (Moon in Virgo) At home or away from home, you distinguish yourself by your patience, cool attitude, quiet determination, and perseverance. You win the admiration of another Capricorn and a Taurus. Long-range and long-distance interests get strong support. Your colors are beige and bay green. Lucky lottery numbers: 1, 10, 19, 28, 37, 46.

Thursday, November 7 (Moon in Virgo to Libra 4:29 a.m.)   Libra comes calling and has some interesting suggestions about your career and professional interests. You gain much from the shrewd way in which you use the authority granted you. You can enhance your reputation by what you say and do under these aspects. Cardinal red and melon are winning colors. Number 3 is a winner.

Friday, November 8 (Moon in Libra)   Gemini has much to say on a subject you thought was closed. Talks with supervisors can help clear the air of misunderstandings. Keep a steady pace in work today, rather than pushing hard and then taking it easy. Sapphire and flame are winning colors. Number 5 is a good bet.

Saturday, November 9 (Moon in Libra to Scorpio 1:02 p.m.)   Work that you have been postponing can get done this morning. An excellent day for clearing away debris from your lawn and backyard. What do your trees and plants require in the way of fall attention? Harvest chores, and preserving fruit and vegetables will go well. Lucky lottery numbers: 3, 7, 16, 25, 34, 43.

Sunday, November 10 (Moon in Scorpio)   Scorpio takes a strong, definite stand. Friendships do wonders for your ego and morale. Involvements with church and club can produce peace of mind. The social side of your job can help you improve on-the-job relations with superiors and coworkers. Electric blue is your color. Number 9 is a winner.

Monday, November 11 (Moon in Scorpio to Sagittarius 6:27 p.m.)   The new moon in Scorpio illuminates your social and public life. There is a great deal of dèjá vu accented wherever you go and whatever you hear. You and a dear friend are on the same wavelength and can communicate despite the miles between. Cobalt is your color. You lucky number is 4.

Tuesday, November 12 (Moon in Sagittarius)   Sagittarius and Leo figure prominently. Fine trends exist for completing chores and long-range projects, dealing with executives and corporations. Help your beloved with chores that are not to your liking and which you seldom do. Your colors are old rose and carmine. Your lucky number is 6.

Wednesday, November 13 (Moon in Sagittarius to Capricorn 9:44 p.m.)   Clear the deck for more important actions tomorrow. Summarize, file away, present work for approval, close one door so that a new one can be opened, and deal with City Hall and the utility companies. Magenta and turquoise are winning colors. Lucky lottery numbers: 2, 8, 17, 26, 35, 44.

Thursday, November 14 (Moon in Capricorn)   Now in your lunar cycle high, you can catch up with the competition and breeze far ahead of the opposition. You are the winner because of your strong demonstration of self-confidence and self-reliance. Hold the initiative all day, lead, and invite good luck. Champagne is your color. Number 1 is a good bet.

Friday, November 15 (Moon in Capricorn)   Push hard so that highly personal aspirations can be realized. Where others might have objected a few days ago, they will remain silent now. Be courageous, self-confident, and stand up for your own rights. You can gain from your well-known patience and perseverance. Hot combination numbers: 3 and 6.

Saturday, November 16 (Moon in Capricorn to Aquarius 12:14 a.m.)   Aquarius and Leo are in your corner. You can locate some money that is earmarked for you. Sales and bargains are there waiting for you. There are fine trends for buying up-to-date, time-saving items. Good rays exist for shedding inhibitions. Your color is sand. Lucky lottery numbers: 5, 14, 23, 32, 41, 50.

Sunday, November 17 (Moon in Aquarius)   Take a more independent approach toward earning and spending. You could resent criticism from an older person. The acceptance you desire is based upon your endurance, self-disciplined ways, and perseverance in the face of problems and interference. Auburn is your color. Your lucky number is 7.

Monday, November 18 (Moon in Aquarius to Pisces 3 a.m.) Trust Pisces to know what is going on behind the scenes. Local interests can be given a good airing. Studies, hobbies, and your learning processes are activated as a new and promising week begins. Communicate clearly, so that others know what you are really saying. Taupe is your color. Your lucky number is 2.

Tuesday, November 19 (Moon in Pisces) Cancer and Scorpio have choice seats and make you feel very much watched and observed. Everyday interests get strong support, as do usual routines and schedules. Neighbors and siblings know the score. Travel in your own town can reveal much. Beige is your color. Hot combination numbers: 4 and 7.

Wednesday, November 20 (Moon in Pisces to Aries 6:34 a.m.) The fire signs (Aries, Leo, and Sagittarius) will impact your day. Domestic, real estate, property, and ownership matters can be pushed toward a speedy success. You can be called upon to do some community work before the year ends. Rust and brown are your colors. Lucky lottery numbers: 6, 15, 24, 33, 42, 51.

Thursday, November 21 (Moon in Aries) Family matters top your agenda. What odd jobs do you want to do around your home before next month's holidays? A fine day to discuss plans with your beloved and other members of the clan. Community betterment programs may require a little help. Kelly green and pumpkin are winning colors. Your lucky number is 8.

Friday, November 22 (Moon in Aries to Taurus 11:12 a.m.) Sagittarius and Aries will show you how to recoup anything you may have lost or misplaced. Residential improvements get high grades. The property you would like to own can be tempting you. Copper and bronze are winning colors. Hot combination numbers: 1 and 4.

Saturday, November 23 (Moon in Taurus)   Taurus is charming and charismatic. Your love life is strengthened by the dominant aspects. It's a romantic time of the year for you. Some window-shopping and mall-walking will do you proud; buy items that will help you entertain in your own home. Brown and blue are winners. Lucky lottery numbers: 3, 12, 21, 30, 39, 48.

Sunday, November 24 (Moon in Taurus to Gemini 5:20 p.m.)   You will be very much at home with the earth signs (Taurus, Virgo, and another Capricorn). It's a good day for getting your beloved away from others and enjoying some pillow-talk epilogue to lovemaking. You can improve relationships with in-laws. Your lucky number is 5.

Monday, November 25 (Moon in Gemini)   Today's full moon illuminates your health and the work you wish you didn't have to do. There is enlightenment via what you read about overall physical well-being. The nutritional and dietary experiences of dear friends can be somewhat helpful to you now. Don't burn your candle at both ends. Your lucky number is 9.

Tuesday, November 26 (Moon in Gemini)   Gemini and Aquarius have key roles. If the weather or any other element is hard on your body, try to take time off and stay in bed for a few additional hours. You can nip a health problem in the bud under these aspects. There are viruses in the air. Your color is flesh. Your lucky number is 2.

Wednesday, November 27 (Moon in Gemini to Cancer 1:37 a.m.)   Cancer and Pisces are in the picture. Marriage, other partnerships are stimulated. You can enter into new experiences by sharing and cooperating. Encourage a dear friend to accompany you to a place of interest. Lucky lottery numbers: 4, 13, 22, 31, 40, 49.

Thursday, November 28 (Moon in Cancer)   You're a member of the team. Don't go off on your own, even if you want to make some important point. Stick with the group, helping your partner or spouse. You can bridge the various generation gaps successfully. Your colors are melon and rust. Hot combination numbers: 6 and 4.

Friday, November 29 (Moon in Cancer to Leo 12:30 p.m.) Fine aspects for teamwork, sharing, cooperative efforts, and joint investments. Spouse, business partners, more experienced people are front and center with questions for you. Though you feel that you are being driven too much, keep objections to a minimum. Pumpkin is your color. Your lucky number is 8.

Saturday, November 30 (Moon in Leo) Leo arrives full of news, and it's your job to listen. Before the month ends, there are changes, improvements, and corrections to be made. Security arrangements achieve top billing. Talks center around money, savings, expenses, and the increased cost of living. Lucky lottery numbers: 1, 10, 19, 28, 37, 46.

DECEMBER 1996

Sunday, December 1 (Moon in Leo) You do well to contemplate the probable expenses you are going to have this month. Leo and Sagittarius may have advice on these matters. Money and time are the major considerations—will you have enough? Your color is ruby. Your lucky number is 1.

Monday, December 2 (Moon in Leo to Virgo 1:11 a.m.) If there is any short trip you feel you should make this month, this is a good day for taking off. It's also a favorable interval for dealing in long-range projects and any matter at a distance. Virgo and another Capricorn can make things go smoothly. Your lucky number is 5.

Tuesday, December 3 (Moon in Virgo) A fine day for handling what you have perking for yourself at a distance. Good trends for living up to duties, responsibilities, and obligations. Taurus may have something important to say under these aspects. If domestic matters have been sluggish, there is forward movement now. Your lucky number is 7.

Wednesday, December 4 (Moon in Virgo to Libra 1:23 p.m.)   Information and research will do well, especially away from home. Get greeting cards for out-of-town acquaintances into the mail today. Arrangements that have been put together haphazardly can be straightened out. News from a distance tends to cheer you up. Emerald is your color. Lucky lottery numbers: 6, 9, 18, 27, 36, 45.

Thursday, December 5 (Moon in Libra)   Another Capricorn and a Libra have front seats, as you dig deeply into your career. Breeze ahead of the competition and get the month really organized, so that neither public nor private matters will be shortchanged. Lists are very helpful. Amber is your color. Number 2 is a winner.

Friday, December 6 (Moon in Libra to Scorpio 10:39 p.m.)   Push your career, authority, earned reputation, status, and prestige matters. Deal with top-flight supervisors who can give you a good tip. Know what has to be done this month before you devote part of your effort to the domestic and the social. Is there too much volunteering? Cherry is your color. Hot combination numbers: 4 and 7.

Saturday, December 7 (Moon in Scorpio)   Address greeting cards, shop with a friend who has good suggestions, and keep abreast of the social demand on your time over the rest of the month. Church and club membership and participation demand some of your attention now. Salmon is your color. Lucky lottery numbers: 6, 15, 24, 33, 42, 51.

Sunday, December 8 (Moon in Scorpio)   Scorpio has the vitality you admire. Friends are in the picture, together with new demands on your leisure time. Make no social promises without checking you calendar. Aunts and uncles are likely to expect some special consideration. Fuchsia is your color. Your lucky number is 8.

Monday, December 9 (Moon in Scorpio to Sagittarius 3:59 a.m.) An excellent day for completing projects, delivering items to charitable collections, engaging in humanitarian efforts, and dealing with large organizations and institutions. The homeless are now in your thoughts. Sagittarius and Aries can impact your day. Wear a little white. Your lucky number is 3.

Tuesday, December 10 (Moon in Sagittarius) The new moon in Sagittarius illuminates secret trends, the past, times for traditions to be honored and other times when they must bow to circumstance. Your mate or partner may expect more consideration from you. Silver is your color. Hot combination numbers: 5 and 2.

Wednesday, December 11 (Moon in Sagittarius to Capricorn 6:15 a.m.) You move into your lunar cycle high, when the unlikely suddenly becomes possible. You can mount your high horse, and, more or less, get your own way. Self-discipline, reasonableness, perseverance, and persistence are all working in your favor. Consult another Capricorn or a Taurus. Lucky lottery numbers: 3, 7, 16, 25, 34, 43.

Thursday, December 12 (Moon in Capricorn) Push hard, on a day when you can win! Lead, issue orders, look like a boss, and refuse to surrender the initiative so that much more work can be done. You can win the admiration of a difficult senior citizen because of what you do now. Magenta is your color. Your lucky number is 9.

Friday, December 13 (Moon in Capricorn to Aquarius 7:14 a.m.) Don't permit superstition to get in the way of the real progress that can be made. Stick to your guns, stand tall, and explain why things must be done your way. Some may say you are too organized and bossy, but in their hearts, they know that you are right. Forest green is your color. Your lucky number is 2.

Saturday, December 14 (Moon in Aquarius) This is a good money day, with fine aspects for spending some of what you earn. Be lavish in selecting gifts for your beloved. You will enjoy looking at new-model vehicles and some of the brand-new computer hardware and software. You are strongly conscious of value, worth, and cost. Lucky lottery numbers: 4, 13, 22, 31, 40, 49.

Sunday, December 15 (Moon in Aquarius to Pisces 8:44 a.m.)   There are fine aspects for engaging in seasonal, annual, special, volunteer, charitable, and humanitarian endeavors. Be generous with your time, if you can't contribute as much as you would like. The cost of living is getting in the way of charitable contributions. Pastels will relieve the more somber look. Number 6 is a good bet.

Monday, December 16 (Moon in Pisces)   You can make good headway in the usual, familiar, everyday matters. Attend to immediate and pressing demands. Siblings and neighbors have plenty to say and do. Studies and hobbies can demand some of your attention. Marigold is your color. Your lucky number is 1.

Tuesday, December 17 (Moon in Pisces to Aries 11:55 a.m.)   Sagittarius and Pisces come front and center. What has to be done will be achieved. Duties, responsibilities, and obligations push more relaxing and enjoyable activities out of the way. There are projects connected with the holiday that have to be finished. Your family may be finding fault. Hot combination numbers: 3 and 6.

Wednesday, December 18 (Moon in Aries)   Give almost total attention to your family, residence, community, property, ownership, and real estate interests. Help children with their gift purchasing and giving. Older loved ones will demand their share of your attention also. Your winning colors are champagne and yellow. Lucky lottery numbers: 5, 14, 23, 32, 41, 50.

Thursday, December 19 (Moon in Aries to Taurus 5:10 p.m.)   Household chores will be easier and more satisfying if you let youngsters do their share. It's a fine day for teaching youngsters how to be better people and better citizens. An Aries will have much to say on this subject. Your winning colors are aquamarine and Wallis blue. Hot combination numbers: 7 and 5.

Friday, December 20 (Moon in Taurus) Excellent trends for entertaining in your home. Combine the old traditions with the very new. Relatives, friends, coworkers, and neighbors will do well in this big mix. Be lavish in your decorations, and most assuredly include beautiful pastel flowers. Hot combination numbers: 9 and 3.

Saturday, December 21 (Moon in Taurus) It's another wonderful day for parties, entertainment, making love, relating well to parents and children, and seeing the romance and adventure potential in the season itself. Taurus and Virgo figure prominently. Your winning colors are cherry and kelly green. Lucky lottery numbers: 2, 11, 20, 29, 38, 47.

Sunday, December 22 (Moon in Taurus to Gemini 12:17 a.m.) Gemini will cheer you up. Fine trends exist for getting that bit of sleep, rest, and genuine relaxation before the festivities begin. Health maintenance and quiet household chores top your agenda. Keep close tabs on how the hectic pace of the season may be affecting the health of the very young and the very old. Your lucky number is 4.

Monday, December 23 (Moon in Gemini) There are things that aren't going to get done; so be it! A tendency to do more than is necessary is there, but you can expect much opposition, interference, and surprise involvements. Libra and Aquarius can bring problems connected with your career and expense account. Celery is your color. Your lucky number is 8.

Tuesday, December 24 (Moon in Gemini to Cancer 9:14 a.m.) Personal involvements are sluggish. It's time to sit back and enjoy the scenery. Let others do the worrying; you are taking things in stride. It's a day when too many cooks certainly spoil things, and too many assistants in the living room may cause freak accidents. Listen to one authority: a sun-in-Cancer person. Play number 1 to win.

Wednesday, December 25 (Moon in Cancer) Your beloved becomes the center of attention, and this is how you want it. Listen to what your mate and a business confidant may have to say. Your mind is very agile now, really involved in the thought processes, but actions come in a few days. This is a fine time to make decisions regarding business and your public image. Scarlet and the lighter greens are in. Lucky lottery numbers: 3, 12, 21, 30, 39, 48.

Thursday, December 26 (Moon in Cancer to Leo 8:09 p.m.) The family still is number one in what you are thinking and doing. Marriage, joint endeavors, and joint investments are favored. There are fine aspects for bargain hunting, making joint decisions, and opening up new lines of communication. Information arrives, which will cheer you up. Cerulean blue is your color. Your lucky number is 5.

Friday, December 27 (Moon in Leo) Leo and Aries have key roles. Something valuable can be protected and saved. Hold discussions with your lawyer, banker, and broker, so that whatever financial changes you should be making before the end of this tax year can be implemented. Newer investments are favored. Strawberry is your color. Your lucky number is 7.

Saturday, December 28 (Moon in Leo) Push savings, your personal war on waste, and work on a more realistic budget for home and car. Your cost of living is on the rise, and it would be advisable to see what lifestyle adjustments you can make that might result in savings. Discuss budgets with loved ones. Lucky lottery numbers: 3, 9, 18, 27, 36, 45.

Sunday, December 29 (Moon in Leo to Virgo 8:45 a.m.) If you have been considering some travel, perhaps connected with the holidays, today would be a good day to get going. But plan to stay off the crowded highways on New Year's Eve. Sagittarius and Virgo can impact your day. Your colors are magenta and claret. Your lucky number is 2.

Monday, December 30 (Moon in Virgo)   A good day to be away from home, attending to love, devotion, loyalty, and business. Taurus and another Capricorn can make your day. Since you can see clearly into the upcoming weeks, good decisions can be made. You are getting ready for what must be done early next month. Your lucky number is 6.

Tuesday, December 31 (Moon in Virgo)   A quiet New Year's Eve is recommended. Stay put, wherever you are. Show patience, perseverance, and honor the old traditions. You are warming the cockles of many a heart by what you say and do at this time. All the dependability of which you can boast is evident. Your lucky number is 8.

JANUARY 1997

Wednesday, January 1 (Moon in Libra)   The year begins with your career strongly stimulated. One of your resolutions should be to improve assignments and to come to grips with whatever you can do to advance in your public life. Seek more authority now, relying on advice from a Libra or Gemini. Old rose is your color. Lucky lottery: 5, 14, 23, 32, 41, 50.

Thursday, January 2 (Moon in Libra)   Continue yesterday's routines and schedules in career and professional matters. An Aquarius may have good suggestions about increasing your earning power and income. Talks with those in charge will produce for you. Orange and tangerine are your colors; hot combination numbers are 7 and 3.

Friday, January 3 (Moon in Libra to Scorpio 8:02 a.m.)   You're still on a career roll as the day begins. Look your best, because you are most likely being observed on the job. Today is fine for getting more help. Writing, record keeping, and finding the right and proper way of doing things are in this picture. Emerald is your color; your lucky number is 9.

Saturday, January 4 (Moon in Scorpio) — Today is fine for socializing, group activities, and church and club responsibilities. There is volunteer work that could bring a small financial stipend now and then. A Scorpio and a Taurus are represented in the day's scenario. Beige is your color. Lucky lottery: 2, 11, 20, 29, 38, 47.

Sunday, January 5 (Moon in Scorpio to Sagittarius 2:27 p.m.) — Warm up to the work you will be doing during the week ahead. Give due thought to what those in power expect you to do with an assignment. Gather materials and information, and perhaps even discuss the work with supervisors or underlings. It's a good day for preparation work. Your lucky number is 4.

Monday, January 6 (Moon in Sagittarius) — Fine trends exist for completing preparation work associated with one assignment and presenting another one for approval. You do well keeping things moving on schedule today. Past experiences are wonderful instructors under existing aspects. Raven is your color; your lucky number is 8.

Tuesday, January 7 (Moon in Sagittarius to Capricorn 4:55 p.m.) — Sagittarius will listen to your explanations and suggestions. What is transpiring behind the scenes will impact the way today turns out. You are adept at extracting additional gains from a matter rooted in the past. Cerulean blue is your color. A little jewelry increases your confidence. Your lucky number is 1.

Wednesday, January 8 (Moon in Capricorn) — Now in your lunar-cycle high, you can change things to suit yourself. You invite improvements, corrections, and changes for the better when you hold the initiative and take the lead. Let others know how you feel about the work that is being done. Another Capricorn can be helpful. Lucky lottery: 3, 12, 21, 30, 39, 48.

Thursday, January 9 (Moon in Capricorn to Aquarius 4:22 a.m.) — Take full advantage of your marvelous personality and character assets to get ahead. These are your patience, perseverance, endurance, and survival tactics, which are second to none. Your self-discipline is the stuff of winners. Check things out with a Virgo. Hot combination numbers: 5 and 2.

Friday, January 10 (Moon in Aquarius)   You can increase earning power and income under prevailing aspects. Aquarius and Libra are on your side. This is a fine day for funding special projects, improving your work by using the newest state-of-the-art apparatus and software. Hot combination numbers: 7 and 3.

Saturday, January 11 (Moon in Aquarius to Pisces 4:51 p.m.)   Money can be earned in unusual ways, such as special sales, by being paid back money you loaned much earlier, or through the discovery of funds that are due you for some other reason. Fuchsia is your color. You can find some good bargains in the larger outlet stores and this, too, is money in the bank. Lucky lottery: 9, 18, 27, 36, 45, 6.

Sunday, January 12 (Moon in Pisces)   Tackle the simple little details of special projects. Write letters, make phone calls, communicate with self-confidence. The vehicle can prove more important than your destination under these trends. The usual, expected, and familiar are favored. Purple is your color; your lucky number is 2.

Monday, January 13 (Moon in Pisces to Aries 6:22 p.m.)   All highly personalized interests are picking up steam, as Mercury resumes direct movement in your sign. You do well where you communicate and move about, seeing people and discussing pertinent subjects. Studies and hobbies pay off. Siblings are helpful. Reddish browns are right; your lucky number is 6.

Tuesday, January 14 (Moon in Aries)   Domestic, residential, and community interests get top billing, and property and ownership matters deserve your attention. Aries-ruled matters apply fully under prevailing aspects. You accept changes with grace and show some daring qualities that please younger people. Iron gray is your color; your number is 8.

Wednesday, January 15 (Moon in Aries to Taurus 10:40 p.m.) Don't rush things today and pay attention to any loved one who is seemingly ultra-aggressive. Inside, this person may be more insecure than you would have believed. Fine trends exist for polite behavior and the appreciation you evoke from others. Lucky lottery: 1, 10, 19, 28, 37, 46.

Thursday, January 16 (Moon in Taurus) Taurus brings joy, delight, and instant happiness into your life. There's plenty of affection and approval coming your way. Spontaneous entertaining and socializing will pay off. You can come into a deeper understanding of younger relatives, including your offspring. Saffron is your color. Hot combination numbers: 3 and 9.

Friday, January 17 (Moon in Taurus) Make love on a day when romantic feelings permeate your being. You want to be with people, to socialize in a spontaneous way, to seize opportunities and press your advantages. Weather can serve your purposes. Umber is your color. You are being noticed and observed. Your lucky number is 5.

Saturday, January 18 (Moon in Taurus to Gemini 5:53 a.m.) Gemini and Aquarius make their presence felt—and heard. Dress appropriately. Be aware that weather changes can be quite severe. There is plenty of work to be done around your home, with garage and basement especially in need of reorganization of wall space. Lavender and deep purple are your colors. Lucky lottery: 7, 16, 25, 34, 43, 3.

Sunday, January 19 (Moon in Gemini) You could hear many health complaints under these aspects. Also, people are dissatisfied with their jobs and complain about not being able to make ends meet. You help when you speak of preservation and conservation and of preventative-medicine routines that you have found to be wise. Bay is your color; your lucky number is 9.

Monday, January 20 (Moon in Gemini to Cancer 3:29 p.m.) Things are looking up in earning power and income matters. Both employer and employees are getting along with each other. In peace and stability, there can be important production gains. Each part of a big project must be given its due, if the finished article is to be all it can be under these aspects. Your number is 4.

Tuesday, January 21 (Moon in Cancer)   It's an excellent day for bonding more closely with your mate and also with business partners, and fine also for signing new contracts and agreements. Share, cooperate, and listen to what the other person is saying, and the results will be good. Somebody who generally is cheerful could come through today as edgy. Be sympathetic. Your lucky number is 6.

Wednesday, January 22 (Moon in Cancer)   A Scorpio and a Cancer can impact your day. Your marital state has a lot to do with your reception of a romantic overture. If you are eligible, the foundations of a new and promising relationship could be formed today. You want to be closer to people you love under prevailing aspects. Encourage partners. Lucky lottery: 8, 17, 26, 35, 44, 1.

Thursday, January 23 (Moon in Cancer to Leo 2:50 a.m.)   Today's full moon enlightens you in security matters and illuminates the changes you are making in your lifestyle. Savings, budgeting, insurance, tax, and investment matters get a good airing. This is a fine day for completing your income tax reports. A Pisces is in the picture. Mint leaf is your color; your lucky number is 1.

Friday, January 24 (Moon in Leo)   Leo has the information and the know-how to lead, inspire, and guide. You see the big picture in family and residential security now. If you have been contemplating putting in a security system, this would be a good day to make the decision. The month is taking on more financial promise. Your number is 3.

Saturday, January 25 (Moon in Leo to Virgo 3:26 p.m.)   Aries and Sagittarius will help you with new beginnings and with the completion of odd jobs. You could be tempted to make a change in the way you travel to work and could get in a dry-run today. There is still some waste in your kitchen and automobile expenses. Bright red is your color. Lucky lottery: 5, 14, 23, 32, 41, 50.

Sunday, January 26 (Moon in Virgo)   You are determined, precise, and very earthy under these aspects. You know what you want and how to get it. It's a fine day for buying items that will help the appearance of your lawn, backyard, and driveways. What is happening far away can impact your thinking. Amber and canary are your colors; your number is 7.

Monday, January 27 (Moon in Virgo)   Virgo can give you good directions and instructions today. You could hear from someone at a distance and the news can be encouraging. Long-range and long-distance interests are perking favorably. You conserve well. You find drains in your new budget that can be corrected. Your number is 2.

Tuesday, January 28 (Moon in Virgo to Libra 4:21 a.m.)   You can take a great leap forward in your career, professional, and authority matters. Your willingness to embrace responsibilities is rewarded. Your Saturn-engineered patience and emotional stability is admired by those in charge. Taupe is your color. Hot combination numbers: 4 and 7.

Wednesday, January 29 (Moon in Libra)   Whatever is just, acceptable, and admirable should be pursued under these aspects. A Gemini has much to say on the subject. Interviews, conferences, and striking up a meaningful conversation with an executive can all impact your day favorably. Red is your color. Lucky lottery: 6, 15, 24, 33, 42, 51.

Thursday, January 30 (Moon in Libra to Scorpio 3:48 p.m.)   Give your best shot to career projects and to working in harmony with business partners and others. Organizational matters can take more time than you

234

planned. Married couples are your best bet in socializing this evening. There are good trends for ordering items by phone. Hot combination numbers: 8 and 2.

Friday, January 31 (Moon in Scorpio)   Scorpio comes aboard with a big smile and will show you how to allocate your leisure time. Fine trends exist in friendships, companionship, intimate conversation, traveling in a group, and asking questions and insisting on reasonable answers. Your colors are mauve and orchid; your lucky number is 1.

FEBRUARY 1997

Saturday, February 1 (Moon in Scorpio to Sagittarius 11:51 p.m.)   Trust Scorpio's explanations and suggestions and keep a big smile on your face. It's a fine day for leisure activities and it's a good day for being part of a group working on an interesting project, and for enjoying talks with kindred spirits. Your winning colors are red and yellow. Lucky lottery: 9, 18, 27, 36, 45, 3.

Sunday, February 2 (Moon in Sagittarius)   Sagittarius and Gemini have key roles. Fine trends exist for completing assignments or special projects. What is happening behind the scenes may be revealed to you today. Some interests rooted in the distant past seem to be recycling themselves. Wear a little silver with pink. Your lucky number is 2.

Monday, February 3 (Moon in Sagittarius to Capricorn 3:45 a.m.)   It may be difficult to get into anything new today because last week's incidents, work, and involvements are back in the picture. You may feel that the month is moving slowly. There's money showing up and it's a day when you can work out some good investments for your ultimate retirement. Your number is 6.

Tuesday, February 4 (Moon in Capricorn)   Now in your lunar-cycle high, you can have things your own way. Step lively this morning and schedule meetings. Let the world see you at your best. Hold the initiative and be the leader for best results. New government legislation should be studied for its impact on your affairs. Your number is 8.

Wednesday, February 5 (Moon in Capricorn to Aquarius 4:21 a.m.)   Push for approval and appreciation under today's aspects. Your patience, perseverance, persistence, and endurance are respected and honored. You feel very much in control of things and others get out of your way when you are hurrying to complete a chore. The angry reds are your colors. Lucky lottery: 1, 10, 19, 28, 37, 46.

Thursday, February 6 (Moon in Aquarius)   Excellent aspects exist in earning power, income, and overall wealth production. Today is fine for financial and business conferences and interviews. An Aquarius and a Gemini have much to offer. Funding for embryonic projects can get off to a good start. Your winning colors are deep blues and reds. Hot combination numbers: 3 and 9.

Friday, February 7 (Moon in Aquarius)   Today's new moon illuminates earning power and income and enlightens you on how to stabilize these vital matters. This is a good day for buying and selling and for making sensible decisions regarding saving more of what you earn. Discuss these matters with a Libra. Ecru is your color; your lucky number is 5.

Saturday, February 8 (Moon in Aquarius to Pisces 3:34 a.m.)   Narrow your sights and concentrate on what you want to begin and finish today. Everyday routines and schedules get green lights. Studies, hobbies, siblings, and neighborhood matters are accented. Discussions produce good results. Pisces and a Cancer are helpful. Lucky lottery: 7, 16, 25, 34, 43, 3.

Sunday, February 9 (Moon in Pisces)   Studies, hobbies, and relaxing activities are all favored. Discussions produce good results. Move about in your own neighborhood, enjoying the company of people you see almost every day. There is an intellectual trend permeating the afternoon and evening. Canary is your color; your lucky number is 9.

Monday, February 10 (Moon in Pisces to Aries 3:29 a.m.) A relative can seem unduly aggressive under these aspects. You can have the feeling that loved ones expect quicker and more definite decisions from you. Property and ownership matters are irksome, but only for the present. Don't forget your Valentine. Your winning colors are the angry reds; your lucky number is 4.

Tuesday, February 11 (Moon in Aries) Aries has definite, sharp ideas about what you should be doing. Domestic, community and real estate interests are favored. Do what you can to discourage virulent anger in a younger person. There are straws that finally break the camel's back. Cherry is your color. Hot combination numbers: 6 and 1.

Wednesday, February 12 (Moon in Aries to Taurus 5:56 a.m.) You are loving, cheerful, kind, and considerate, and you aim to please your beloved. Taurus and another Capricorn make a good team. Encourage youngsters to be more positive and optimistic. As you spread goodwill, you will find former critics moving into your corner. Amber is your color. Lucky lottery: 8, 17, 26, 35, 44, 2.

Thursday, February 13 (Moon in Taurus) You're cheerful, optimistic, loving, romantic, and anxious to please. You are favored when you and your beloved spend quality time together. Fine trends exist for entertaining in your own home, giving a Valentine party, helping small children to have their schoolmates in for fun. Your lucky number is 1.

Friday, February 14 (Moon in Taurus to Gemini 11:53 a.m.) It's a good day for parties and entertainments. Children will listen closely to what you are saying. Your good mood is contagious and others will appreciate you in the role of catalyst. Scarlet and crimson are your colors. A Virgo is helpful with the arrangements. Your lucky number is 3.

Saturday, February 15 (Moon in Gemini)   Gemini talks about health, new medical discoveries, nutrition, dietary matters, and the right exercise regimen for busy working people. Health improvements generally begin with each person. No doctor will ever know your body as well as you know it. Dress appropriately for sudden weather changes. Lucky lottery: 5, 14, 23, 32, 41, 50.

Sunday, February 16 (Moon in Gemini to Cancer 9:13 p.m.)   Discussions hit the target under the prevailing aspects. Today is fine for inviting a few friends to drop in for a chat and a big pot of black Ceylon or Darjeeling tea. Talk and tea will solve any problem on a day like this. Your winning colors are white, cream, and snow; your lucky number is 7.

Monday, February 17 (Moon in Cancer)   Fine trends exist for working out new contracts and agreements, and for opening a new checking or charge account. Legal matters can get a good airing. Partnerships tend to profit from the day's trends. Cooperation will pay off, as well as sharing and joint endeavors. Auburn is your color; your lucky number is 2.

Tuesday, February 18 (Moon in Cancer)   Listen to what the water sign people (Cancer, Scorpio, and Pisces) have to say. Talks with your mate and financial partners will produce more than you anticipated. The day is also favorable for signing new contracts and improving your relationships with in-laws and the friends of your beloved. Your lucky number is 4.

Wednesday, February 19 (Moon in Cancer to Leo 8:52 a.m.)   Teamwork is better than lone effort. Collaboration on a creative project will produce success. You tend to see the finished product in your mind's eye before putting pen to paper or canvas. Aunts and uncles can be helpful. Winning colors are beige and taupe. Lucky lottery: 6, 15, 24, 33, 42, 51.

Thursday, February 20 (Moon in Leo)   Let Leo lead. Excellent trends exist in security matters, more savings, less waste, an improved budget, and wiser investments.

The day moves along swiftly and it would be wise to ward off distractions, no matter how pleasant. Today is fine for working on improvements in the work you are doing. Hot combination numbers: 8 and 1.

Friday, February 21 (Moon in Leo to Virgo 9:38 p.m.) An appointment with an insurance salesman may please you. Accumulations of money and a surfeit of energy walk hand in hand to greater profits. You could put a hobby or avocation on a money-making basis today. Winning colors are fuchsia and magenta. Questions get answers. Hot combination numbers: 1 and 7.

Saturday, February 22 (Moon in Virgo) The full moon illuminates travel plans, as well as long-range and long-distance matters. You are going to do a lot of deep thinking about your future and what you have going for yourself at a distance. You could receive some good leads in new money-making ventures. Cherry is your color. Lucky lottery: 3, 12, 21, 30, 39, 48.

Sunday, February 23 (Moon in Virgo) It's an excellent day for taking care of work in your suspense file. The miniscule things of life seem to matter more under these aspects. You gain from paying more attention to the details in larger projects. There is a tendency to see things as bigger and more important than they are. Your lucky number is 5.

Monday, February 24 (Moon in Virgo to Libra 10:23 a.m.) You can run facts to the ground today. Information is flowing freely. Distance seems to matter less under prevailing aspects. You could travel mentally without leaving your favorite chair. Distant relatives might figure in the scenario, as well as ancestors and the long-departed. Olive is your color; your number is 9.

Tuesday, February 25 (Moon in Libra) You can make steady and impressive progress in your career. Be professional and use authority wisely. You can milk new gains from your long-established reputation for good work. There are honors and dignities looming on your horizon. Your cheerfulness will make a big difference. Your lucky number is 2.

Wednesday, February 26 (Moon in Libra to Scorpio 9:57 p.m.)   Let Libra have the floor. Talks with executives can clear up some mysteries on the work scene. Gossip and rumors will do a lot of damage if not nipped in the bud. A former coworker may be interested in returning. Watch any tendency to be too judgmental. Lucky lottery: 4, 13, 22, 31, 40, 49.

Thursday, February 27 (Moon in Scorpio)   Gold is your winning color. Your social agenda is accented, as friendships put you on the top of the world. Group activities are to your liking and do much to turn on an often drab neutral month. By dressing fashionably, you invite admiration. Hot combination numbers: 6 and 1.

Friday, February 28 (Moon in Scorpio)   Close the month with a lot of positive thinking. Spread goodwill. New friendships can be cemented today; you may learn that the friends of your friend want to know you better. Scorpio and Pisces are on your side. Your lucky colors are indigo and cerulean. Hot combination numbers: 8 and 2.

MARCH 1997

Saturday, March 1 (Moon in Scorpio to Sagittarius 5:01 a.m.)   Good trends exist in leisure activities, friendships, group interests, and figuring out some charitable and humanitarian effort that in time could be self-supporting. A Scorpio and a Cancer have key roles. Your winning colors are mauve and champagne. Lucky lottery: 1, 10, 19, 28, 37, 46.

Sunday, March 2 (Moon in Sagittarius)   Today is excellent for outdoor activities, stadium and arena events, and completing some household chore that has been hanging fire too long. Figure out what is transpiring behind the scenes. A Sagittarius and a Leo can impact your day. Be diplomatic and tactful for the best social results. Your lucky number is 3.

Monday, March 3 (Moon in Sagittarius to Capricorn 12:39 p.m.) Work to complete tasks that should have been gotten out of the way before this month began. Excellent trends exist where you are tracking the upcoming change of season. Pay attention to local, immediate, and pressing matters before next week's eclipse. Studies and hobbies are on your plate. Your lucky number is 7.

Tuesday, March 4 (Moon in Capricorn) Now in your lunar high cycle, you are getting better opportunities and you are more aware of your advantages. You can show enormous self-confidence and hold the initiative. Speak up for what you know to be your own interest. Ruby is your color; your number is 9.

Wednesday, March 5 (Moon in Capricorn to Aquarius 2:55 p.m.) While you have a strong sense of control, protect all educational, travel, and business discussion flanks, which may be pressured from now on to right after the total eclipse of the 9th. You have to take each day at a time and not as merely part of a week or month. Lucky lottery: 2, 11, 20, 29, 38, 47.

Thursday, March 6 (Moon in Aquarius) You can do well in a financial and business sense today, even where you sense some opposition to your ideas. It may be difficult to get a positive report on a request for funding, however. Aquarius and Libra have front seats. You may sense that the cost of living is inching up. Hot combination numbers: 4 and 3.

Friday, March 7 (Moon in Aquarius to Pisces 2:57 p.m.) Watch expenses. A youngster may have a lot to learn about warring on waste and saving for upcoming expenses. All around you, there is evidence of feasts followed by famines; high earning power creates higher expenditures for luxuries. Bright blue is your color; your lucky number is 6.

Saturday, March 8 (Moon in Pisces)   Pisces has something to tell you. Concentrate and ward off distractions if your work is to be up to par. There is a nuisance-type of person in this picture. Siblings and neighbors may have favors to ask at a time when you feel edgy about the future. Lucky lottery: 8, 17, 26, 35, 44, 2.

Sunday, March 9 (Moon in Pisces to Aries 2:33 p.m.)   A total solar eclipse can pressure your usual routines and schedules. People and things are not where you would expect to find them. Communications and transportation can break down under unusual circumstances. Beware of pity, for it can involve you with the wrong person. White and ebony are your colors; your number is 1.

Monday, March 10 (Moon in Aries)   There can be problems with water and flooding in the wake of this eclipse. Nautical accident-prone potential is higher. Decisions that ordinarily are quick can be slow in coming today. A Scorpio and a Cancer could help you accept annoyances connected with yesterday's eclipse. Your number is 5.

Tuesday, March 11 (Moon in Aries to Taurus 3:37 p.m.)   Aries tends to cope well with pressures and to invite improvements. Domestic, residential, real estate, property, and ownership matters may be sluggish. Your persistence does you proud. You can encounter challenging people and situations. Your winning colors are sky blue and reddish purple; your lucky number is 7.

Wednesday, March 12 (Moon in Taurus)   Taurus lights up your world. Your romantic nature is stimulated and a sense of adventure takes over. You can bond more closely with your beloved. It's a day for expressing affection, and for giving compliments and doing favors. People are happy to see you arriving. All the colors of the rainbow are yours. Lucky lottery: 9, 18, 27, 36, 45, 6.

Thursday, March 13 (Moon in Taurus to Gemini 7:48 p.m.)   The urge to love physically and mentally is activated in your chart. You see romance where others may fail to see it; while they complain, you remain cheerful and pleased with the way things are going. You party and entertain spontaneously and bond more closely with your mate and children. Your lucky number is 2.

Friday, March 14 (Moon in Gemini)   Cooperation with a Gemini or a Libra will produce good results. It would be well to be a little more cautious in your choice of foods and liquids under the prevailing aspects. Also, be cautious while lifting anything and don't attempt any heavy work alone. Saffron is your color; your lucky number is 4.

Saturday, March 15 (Moon in Gemini)   If you have been over-doing lately, an early fatigue can catch up with you now. A good, long, hot soak can be helpful under these aspects. Increase your allottment of leisure hours today. Youngsters will keep after you to join them in their roughhousing, but you are better off escaping into a good novel. Lucky lottery: 6, 15, 24, 33, 42, 51.

Sunday, March 16 (Moon in Gemini to Cancer 3:51 a.m.)   A Cancer and a Scorpio figure prominently. Sharing, cooperating, and honoring good teamwork are what's needed to get through this day successfully. Discussions with your mate and business partners are recommended, along with flexibility and the will to compromise. Amber and gold are your colors; your number is 8.

Monday, March 17 (Moon in Cancer)   Know what executives and coworkers have in mind when your cooperation is required. There is a trend of omission and misinterpretation permeating this day. An observer might feel that partners are working at cross-purposes. The week may seem slow in getting started. Your color is beige; your lucky number is 3.

Tuesday, March 18 (Moon in Cancer to Leo 3:08 p.m.)   Domestic happenings are fast and furious as winter runs down and you are surrounded by scenes of regeneration and refurbishment. You may have some fantasies about going off by yourself and letting the maddening throngs shift for themselves. Your family needs to call you back to earth. Your color is tan; your lucky number is 5.

Wednesday, March 19 (Moon in Leo)   As spring makes many dramatic announcements, it could seem the right time to revamp your budgets; give income tax returns a final review before getting them off; and making changes, improvements, and corrections in your financial dealings. You are aiming for a more complete security. Lucky lottery: 7, 16, 25, 34, 43, 3.

Thursday, March 20 (Moon in Leo)   Leo brings light, color, and promise. Talks with your banker and broker can produce good results. Your urge to improve investments is strong, and there can be some dissatisfaction with their payoffs, which is goading you on. It would be a good idea to read for the knowledge you seek. Off-white is your color. Hot combination numbers: 9 and 6.

Friday, March 21 (Moon in Leo to Virgo 3:59 a.m.)   It's a wonderful day for travel, seeing the sights, and moving about a park and dining outside. You want to track the coming of spring, which tends to bring on a lot of sentimental reminiscing. There's a temptation to rush the season and wear pastels. Hot combination numbers: 2 and 6.

Saturday, March 22 (Moon in Virgo)   It's a very earthy day with a Virgo and a Taurus accenting physical strength, assurance, determination, and self-reliance. You feel up to licking your weight in tigers. You keep on the go, travel about, and consider long-distance sightseeing. Work on long-range projects. Lucky lottery: 4, 13, 22, 31, 40, 49.

Sunday, March 23 (Moon in Virgo to Libra 4:35 p.m.)   As lunar eclipse patterns form, it would be well to stay put, avoid travel in unsafe areas, and make certain that you are living up to all career duties, responsibilities, and obligations. There are pressures in your workplace and some unfairness is represented. Your lucky number is 6.

Monday. March 24 (Moon in Libra)   The lunar eclipse in your tenth house pressures career, as well as your approach and response to authority, and it can reveal lacks in professionalism. No chastising of assistants or underlings in public, please! Decisions you hear about may seem wrong to you. Flame is your color; your lucky number is 1.

Tuesday, March 25 (Moon in Libra)   Protect your good reputation. It's one of those days when you could say the wrong thing in the wrong place to the wrong person. Gossip and rumors are making their rounds of the workplace. All this shall pass away, and by evening you are ready to socialize with more interesting people. Your number is 3.

Wednesday, March 26 (Moon in Libra to Scorpio 3:42 a.m.)   Scorpio makes a wonderful friend and companion for you; today is no exception to this rule. You want your leisure to be quality time and the trend is one of serious, enjoyable discussions. You may encounter a good lead on money to which you may be entitled. Lucky lottery: 5, 14, 23, 32, 41, 50.

Thursday, March 27 (Moon in Scorpio)   Group activities, church/club membership and participation matters, and socializing on the grand scale with a water sign person (Cancer, Scorpio, and/or Pisces) are indicated. You have a yen to be with people throughout the day and evening. Invite, attract, and court. Primrose is your color; your number is 7.

Friday, March 28 (Moon in Scorpio to Sagittarius 12:40 p.m.)   Springtime means longer days and lots of evening plans. The theater, movie houses, library, and art galleries are all beckoning you. Dining out in an unusual setting will appeal to you and your kindred spirits under these aspects. Tan, mocha, and cocoa are your colors; your lucky number is 9.

Saturday, March 29 (Moon in Sagittarius)   Sagittarius will remember the past events that intrigue you so much. Fine trends exist for completing projects connected with your lawn, backyard, garage, and basement. You are anxious to welcome spring and can discuss this productively with your local hardware or seed and feed store clerk. Lucky lottery: 2, 11, 20, 29, 38, 47.

Sunday, March 30 (Moon in Sagittarius)   Spend as much time as possible in the great outdoors, welcoming the seasonal changes you observe. You do well now to clear the deck for future action that deals in prologues to coming events. Raspberry is your winning color. Your plans are jelling well. Your lucky number is 4.

Monday, March 31 (Moon in Sagittarius to Capricorn 7:07 p.m.)   Now in your lunar-cycle high, you can win the approval and appreciation of others. Push your Capricorn personality and character assets: your sagacity, endurance, perseverance, patience, and self-discipline. Another Capricorn will be helpful. You begin the week with enormous self-confidence. Your lucky number is 8.

APRIL 1997

Tuesday, April 1 (Moon in Capricorn)   You are still in a lunar high cycle and can turn the day to good account. Air your aspirations and ambitions and be sure assistants know what you expect from them. Talks with executives can make some work a little easier and more inspired. Amber is your color. Hot combination numbers: 7 and 3.

Wednesday, April 2 (Moon in Capricorn to Aquarius 10:59 p.m.)   This is an excellent day for increasing your earning power and income. Go to the source with your questions—to the front office, to the one who can change things for the better. You may feel freer to express your desires, as others give you a wide latitude for doing so. Lucky lottery: 9, 18, 27, 36, 45, 6.

Thursday, April 3 (Moon in Aquarius)   Push financial and business matters with self-confidence. Good trends exist for explanations, investigation, and examination. You could meet a rather extreme person under these aspects, but you'd better say as little as necessary. Auburn is your color. Hot combination numbers: 2 and 4.

Friday, April 4 (Moon in Aquarius to Pisces 1:42 a.m.) Good trends exist in everyday routines and schedules in the usual, familiar, and expected. It's a day for taking in some new facts of life and work. Studies, hobbies, communications, and short-distance travel get green lights and high marks. A Pisces and a Cancer figure prominently. Your number is 4.

Saturday, April 5 (Moon in Pisces) Everyday matters can be given a big boost through your efforts. Siblings and neighbors are in accord with you. Conversation tends to produce good results. Short-distance travel gets green lights and high grades. A Scorpio and a Cancer make their contributions. Lucky lottery: 6, 15, 24, 33, 42, 51.

Sunday, April 6 (Moon in Pisces to Aries 2:19 a.m.) Listen to Aries. Domestic, property, and ownership matters get a good airing. Play some role in community projects that seem to interest so many of your friends. It's an excellent day for walking about and getting the lay of the land. Gray and ivory are winning colors; your lucky number is 8.

Monday, April 7 (Moon in Aries) Today's new moon illuminates domestic, household maintenance, family budgets, and what your parents and other seniors expect from you. You manage projects well, but your children may expect more tolerance of their pranks and shortcomings. Peach is your color; your lucky number is 3.

Tuesday, April 8 (Moon in Aries to Taurus 3:20 a.m.) It's a day for renewal, regeneration, and passionate responses to the romantic overtures of your beloved. There is a sense of adventure in the day's aspects and you accent your creativity and feeling for beauty. Today is fine for buying china—the more fragile, the better. Your number is 5.

Wednesday, April 9 (Moon in Taurus) Make love today when your world is bright, romantic, and adventurous. Courtship makes amazing progress. Single Capricorns can encounter their heart's desire. It's an excellent time for parties, entertainments, and spontaneous invitations. Parent–offspring understanding can also be improved. Lucky lottery: 7, 16, 25, 34, 43, 5.

Thursday, April 10 (Moon in Taurus to Gemini 6:28 a.m.)   Gemini conveys joy and excitement. The mind is in charge of the body and your location is therapeutic for you. You belong—you are sure of yourself on and off the job. Self-reliance pays off in the marketplaces of life. Bright blues are your winning colors. Hot combination numbers: 9 and 6.

Friday, April 11 (Moon in Gemini)   Fine trends exist for your annual physical and for discussing health matters with your doctor. You could decide on a new diet and exercise regimen under these aspects. You may wonder today if there is enough work for you and your coworkers to keep busy all week. Hot combination numbers: 2 and 4.

Saturday, April 12 (Moon in Gemini to Cancer 1:03 p.m.)   Libra and Aquarius will have something to say. Good trends exist for working around your house and grounds. A discussion about your lawn and backyard could produce fine results. Good trends exist for putting in seeds and seedlings. Neighbors will have differing ideas. Cherry is your color. Lucky lottery: 4, 13, 22, 31, 40, 49.

Sunday, April 13 (Moon in Cancer)   Heart-to-heart rather than brain-to-brain talks are wiser when the moon is in your seventh house. You are called on to be flexible in partnerships, willing to compromise now and then. The day favors contracts, agreements, and sticking to your word. Reddish-orange is your color; your lucky number is 6.

Monday, April 14 (Moon in Cancer to Leo 11:22 p.m.)   A Cancer and a Pisces have key roles. Your desire to get along with your in-laws and the spouses of your business partners may not be enough on a day when your patience is sorely pressured. Always know when to retreat from tactlessness under these aspects. Marigold is your color; your lucky number is 1.

Tuesday, April 15 (Moon in Leo)   Curtail spontaneous socializing for the time being. Be frank with children where money, expenses, and cost of living are concerned. Protect accumulated funds and long-term investments. Consider finding a secondary source of income or a part-time job between now and summer. Kelly green is your color; your number is 3.

Wednesday, April 16 (Moon in Leo)   A financial and business discussion with a Leo or an Aries would produce good results. Often investment capital can be raised on a long-term insurance policy or through a credit union loan. Your banker and broker may get into this act under the prevailing aspects. Lucky lottery: 5, 14, 23, 32, 41, 50.

Thursday, April 17 (Moon in Leo to Virgo 12 p.m.)   This is a good day for implementing changes, improvements, and corrections. Gold is your color. Spruce up your personal appearance, banishing a few wrinkles and years, for the moon is stimulating your zone of savings as it protects and fends off the marks of aging. Ask questions rather than risk error. Hot combination numbers: 7 and 3.

Friday, April 18 (Moon in Virgo)   Virgo will give helpful advice on the flower and vegetable garden you are about to put in. You may be interested in running down some plants and shrubs from distant places, which are said to do well where you live. You are anxious to improve the appearance of your property. Your color is azure; your number is 9.

Saturday, April 19 (Moon in Virgo)   Excellent trends exist for moving about, beginning a trip, and getting control of long-range plans. What is happening at a distance can impact your thinking. It would be a good idea to write and acquire more recent news of what is transpiring. Lucky lottery: 2, 11, 20, 29, 38, 47.

Sunday, April 20 (Moon in Virgo to Libra 12:36 a.m.) The sun enters Taurus and warms your emotions. The moon at the top of your chart accents career, professional, authority, honor, dignity, and reputation. Fine trends exist for taking pride in your appearance and accomplishments. You are capable of top-flight work. Your lucky number is 4.

Monday, April 21 (Moon in Libra) You will be able to push career efforts in better and more effective ways than was possible earlier this month. Now is the time to strike up a conversation with higher-ups and get an inkling of what your future is really worth. Your ambitions are such that you will want to increase your earning power or plan on making a change. Your lucky number is 8.

Tuesday, April 22 (Moon in Libra to Scorpio 11:19 a.m.) Today's full moon illuminates social programs and plans, your friendship and group activities, and the roles you are playing in church and clubs. Scorpio and a Cancer are urging you to make more of an impact in a charitable and humanitarian way. You want your leisure time to really count. Hot combination numbers: 1 and 7.

Wednesday, April 23 (Moon in Scorpio) A Taurus and a Pisces can make a difference. Good trends exist in socializing on the grand scale, dressing to the hilt, and making a lasting impression on others. Spending time with a kindred spirit gives you peace of mind and soul. But be wary of a social acquaintance who tries to sell you things. The lighter blues are your colors. Lucky lottery: 3, 12, 21, 30, 39, 48.

Thursday, April 24 (Moon in Scorpio to Sagittarius 7:32 p.m.) It's another excellent day for socializing, enjoying the advance of spring, having a sidewalk luncheon, or spending a little time on a park bench. You want to feel the warmer weather in your bones. Contact friends you have been wondering about lately. Lemon is your color. Hot combination numbers: 5 and 2.

Friday, April 25 (Moon in Sagittarius) Today is excellent for dealing with the past, memories, and the possibility of cashing in on past experiences. What isn't entirely visible is pestering you, and there are mysteries that you want to get a handle on. It's one of those days when your sixth sense is functioning. Canary is your color; your number is 7.

Saturday, April 26 (Moon in Sagittarius)   Sagittarius is in the wings. Outdoor activities are beckoning to you. The day calls for great tact and diplomacy and it's fine for completions, epilogues, presenting work for approval, and filing papers away. Routines and schedules have a boring dimension. This evening offers you a break. Lucky lottery: 9, 18, 27, 36, 45, 6.

Sunday, April 27 (Moon in Sagittarius to Capricorn 1:32 a.m.)   Today is fine for gaining control over events that impact your career and your life in general. You are in your lunar-cycle high, when you can maneuver and shift the emphasis successfully. You can even turn your life in a different direction. Your winning color is antique white; your lucky number is 2.

Monday, April 28 (Moon in Capricorn)   Hold the initiative and take the lead for best results. Keep with the system that you are part of, with the program that you have helped put together. This is not a day for holding back. Speak up, air your aspirations and ambitions, and be ready to accept challenges. Dove gray is your color; your number is 6.

Tuesday, April 29 (Moon in Capricorn to Aquarius 5:50 a.m.)   Aquarius will have the answers you need. Push earning power and income advantages and opportunities. Excellent trends exist in selling and buying, and in uncovering a possible new source of income. Discuss job opportunities with those who will be looking for employment this summer. Hot combination numbers: 8 and 1.

Wednesday, April 30 (Moon in Aquarius)   This can become a wonderful day in wealth production if you will keep your nose to the grindstone. A Gemini and a Libra have key roles. Express yourself in such a way that nothing is left to the imagination of another. Be sure you are not trusting too much in a garrulous person. Lucky lottery: 1, 10, 19, 28, 37, 46.

MAY 1997

Thursday, May 1 (Moon in Aquarius to Pisces 8:50 a.m.) Push financial and business interests, uncovering some money that is earmarked for you. You can sell for profit today and find interesting items at auctions and special sales. An Aquarius and a Libra are on your side. Good trends exist in accounting and bookkeeping matters. Azure is your color; your lucky number is 1.

Friday, May 2 (Moon in Pisces) Excellent trends exist in learning, studying, and gaining new information. Today is fine for research, studies, asking questions, and registering for a seminar or special course connected with new work responsibilities. A Pisces and a Scorpio have key roles. Cerise is your color. Hot combination numbers: 3 and 9.

Saturday, May 3 (Moon in Pisces to Aries 10:59 a.m.) Take care of immediate and pressing duties for best results. Watch those interruptions that diminish your effort and the cooperation you expect from youngsters. Good deals can be found at garage sales. The emphasis is on your own neighborhood, siblings, and former neighbors. Strawberry is your color. Lucky lottery: 5, 14, 23, 32, 41, 50.

Sunday, May 4 (Moon in Aries) Let Aries present his or her ideas. You are receiving good directions now, but you may, at the last minute, decide to go your own way. The family may have some grievance to air. You could hear that some neighbors are moving away. Changes are the order of the day in your community. Your number is 7.

Monday, May 5 (Moon in Aries to Taurus 1:04 p.m.) Aries-ruled matters are strongly represented. In your horoscope, this includes domestic, residential, property, ownership, and community matters. Today is fine for getting estimates about spring cleaning you want done. Send valuable carpets and rugs off to a professional cleaner. Maroon is your color; your number is 2.

Tuesday, May 6 (Moon in Taurus) The new moon in your fifth house illuminates your love life. Romance, courtship, and encountering your future mate can all be part of this exciting picture. Today is fine for giving a party or attending a fabulous entertainment. Socialize to your heart's content. Hot combination numbers: 4 and 3.

Wednesday, May 7 (Moon in Taurus to Gemini 4:21 p.m.) Give quality time to your beloved and to your children. There is a strong sense of unity permeating all family matters. Your children will respond well to your objections and suggestions. Taurus and Virgo have key roles. Winning colors are turquoise and lavender. Lucky lottery: 6, 15, 24, 33, 42, 51.

Thursday, May 8 (Moon in Gemini) Gemini has a word for it, or perhaps an entire page. You will feel better after a good conversation about health and work. Don't waste money on expensive diets and exercise programs. You alone can get your weight to the numbers you want. One way is to cut all meals in half. Hot combination numbers: 8 and 1.

Friday, May 9 (Moon in Gemini to Cancer 10:13 p.m.) Domestic matters are speeded up as Mercury resumes direct movement in Aries. Health and work get a boost and contribute to your higher morale. An assignment that you have wanted can be moving more into your purview. Your winning colors are primrose and marigold; your lucky number is 1.

Saturday, May 10 (Moon in Cancer) A Cancer and a Pisces have key roles. Your marital state, business partnerships, and workable cooperation are all accented. This is a fine day for a final discussion and look-around before making a definite decision. Evening favors closer bonding with your mate. Azure is your color. Lucky lottery: 3, 12, 21, 30, 39, 48.

Sunday, May 11 (Moon in Cancer)   Sharing and joint endeavors get top billing. If you work together with your beloved, the results will be noteworthy. Be more understanding of your in-laws and happiness will show up in the eyes of your partner. The allowances you are making today will be returned to you tomorrow. Your lucky number is 5.

Monday, May 12 (Moon in Cancer to Leo 7:33 a.m.)   Leo lights up your sky and the day takes on greater promise. Fine trends exist for increasing your security. The changes you inaugurate today are going to last. What you do now can make the rest of the month go better. Consider a new financial investment. Orange is your color; your number is 9.

Tuesday, May 13 (Moon in Leo)   Save a little bit more money today than you did yesterday. The accent is on increasing your overall financial security. War on waste within your home, in the refrigerator, and around the stove. Acquire new, more adventurous and exciting ideas of using yesterday's leftovers. Peach is your color; your number is 2.

Wednesday, May 14 (Moon in Leo to Virgo 7:43 p.m.)   Talks with your broker, after you have run down all information about investments in which you are interested, can produce good results. The accent is on insurance, tax shelter, and budgeting matters. You could encounter considerable worry about the future of the economy. Lucky lottery: 4, 13, 22, 31, 40, 49.

Thursday, May 15 (Moon in Virgo)   Virgo shows dogged determination. You are fascinated with the advance of spring and the blossoms you see on so many beautiful trees. Your favorite pastels—lemons, limes, or-anges—are evident everywhere. News is arriving on time. What you have perking for yourself at a distance can show more potential. Your lucky number is 6.

Friday, May 16 (Moon in Virgo)   Travel gets good marks and green lights. Business and pleasure can be combined while away from home. But the time will speed by all too quickly and you may not achieve all that you set out to do. Taurus and another Capricorn can show up on time. Cerulean blue is your color; your number is 8.

Saturday, May 17 (Moon in Virgo to Libra 8:27 a.m.) You will keep busy today, whether you are at home or far away. There is exposure to hope, promise, and bright scenes. The people you meet are anxious to know you better. This is a good day for looking forward and making plans for the rest of the month. Lucky lottery: 1, 10, 19, 28, 37, 46.

Sunday, May 18 (Moon in Libra) Career concerns and demands will call you back to reality. You are anxious to get going on an important assignment and will do some of the groundwork today. A phone call to an assistant or competitor may be wise. Knowing the lay of the land is a big asset tomorrow. Titian gold is your color; your lucky number is 3.

Monday, May 19 (Moon in Libra to Scorpio 7:12 p.m.) Libra has a good picture of what is expected of you. Cooperation is necessary, even if you have questions in the back of your mind about some people. There's a sense of fairness in the wind upon which you can depend if things get out of hand. Your winning color is fuchsia; your lucky number is 7.

Tuesday, May 20 (Moon in Scorpio) It's a day for socializing, for smiling, for demonstrating how charming and charismatic you can be, and for seeing kindred spirits and letting your hair down. Have lunch with somebody who keeps you laughing. Pastels are your colors. Spending time in the great outdoors is relaxing. Hot combination numbers: 9 and 3.

Wednesday, May 21 (Moon in Scorpio) The sun moves into Gemini and you automatically feel vital. You will notice that others are feeling better about themselves and their coworkers. As a result, the day can accent progress and production-line miracles. Celebrate

255

family special days that occur this month. Lucky lottery: 2, 11, 20, 29, 38, 47.

Thursday, May 22 (Moon in Scorpio to Sagittarius 2:51 a.m.) The full moon illuminates epilogues, completions, and what you may be able to extract from situations and events you have considered closed and finished. The past is a valuable possession and you will have reason to appreciate this fact as the day progresses. Tangerine is your color; your lucky number is 4.

Friday, May 23 (Moon in Sagittarius) Finish up odd chores which could get in the way of a more promising future. Know when to discard a no-win project. Today is fine for evaluations, critiques, estimations, and follow-up studies. A Sagittarius and an Aries are in the picture. You will enjoy seeing former neighbors and coworkers. Your lucky number is 6.

Saturday, May 24 (Moon in Sagittarius to Capricorn 7:51 a.m.) Today, tomorrow, and the next day constitute your most powerful cycle for making personal progress. This is your lunar-cycle high, when you can change your life for the better. Be enthusiastic about all opportunities, literally pouncing on them and sticking with them until victory is yours. Lucky lottery: 8, 17, 26, 35, 44, 2.

Sunday, May 25 (Moon in Capricorn) Continue yesterday's winning program. Stand tall, let the world see you at your best—wise, patient, persevering—and you will turn this day to good account. Be enthusiastic and optimistic about the positions you have taken on urgent and cogent matters. Venetian gold is your color; your number is 1.

Monday, May 26 (Moon in Capricorn to Aquarius 10:20 a.m.) You're still in the lead. Don't budge from your catbird seat. Talk things over only with another Capricorn. What is taking place in business and in government circles can rebound to your benefit. This evening may find you a little tired, but more and more sure of yourself. Your lucky number is 5.

Tuesday, May 27 (Moon in Aquarius) Push earning power and income matters. An Aquarius knows what you are doing. Possessions are increasing in value. You can secure funding for projects dear to your heart by the explanations you put forth and the belief that others can read in your eyes and hear behind your words. Your lucky number is 7.

Wednesday, May 28 (Moon in Aquarius to Pisces 2:18 p.m.) It's a good money day, fine for sales, purchases, and keeping a good flow of cash. As summer moves closer and closer, it would be a good idea to get job leads for younger people. Some of the higher tuition payments will have to be footed by summer employment. Lucky lottery: 9, 18, 27, 36, 45, 6.

Thursday, May 29 (Moon in Pisces) Pisces and a Cancer have front seats. You achieve by sticking to minor, everyday, usual, and familiar matters. Studies, hobbies, communications, and transportation interests are favorably aspected. Your winning colors are indigo and earth. Hot combination numbers: 2 and 6.

Friday, May 30 (Moon in Pisces to Aries 5:18 p.m.) Siblings and neighbors are in the picture. You will enjoy looking back on old times. Get in touch with a former schoolmate or somebody you knew in the military for the sake of *auld lange syne*. You look back in pleasure under these trends. A Cancer and a Scorpio will prove helpful. Your lucky number is 4.

Saturday, May 31 (Moon in Aries) Listen to what Aries is saying about your community and the value of local real estate. You cater services well to your family under these trends. Your family spirit is particularly strong now, so get started on some shared project that augurs well for the future. Lucky lottery: 6, 15, 24, 33, 42, 51.

JUNE 1997

Sunday, June 1 (Moon in Aries to Taurus 8:39 p.m.) Excellent trends exist in domestic, real estate, property, ownership, and community interests. Aries and Sagittarius cooperate well. Inter-family talks, plans, and programming of upcoming events will produce good results. There can be some drop-ins, but the day goes on schedule. Cherry is your color; your number is 5.

Monday, June 2 (Moon in Taurus)   Your emotions are stimulated favorably. Love, romance, adventure, and spontaneous socializing are emphasized. Taurus and Virgo complete the picture. Fine trends exist for making love, discussing intimate and private matters with your beloved. Children have something to tell you. Your lucky number is 9.

Tuesday, June 3 (Moon in Taurus)   Today is fine for socializing on the grand scale, giving a party to celebrate a loved one's special day. Entertainments will go well. You impress others as a warm-hearted person now. Your winning colors are magenta and ecru. Order what you need by phone or mail. Hot combination numbers: 2 and 4.

Wednesday, June 4 (Moon in Taurus to Gemini 12:55 a.m.)   It's a rare June day that the poet sang about. You can improve your attitude and your approach to work that must be done now. Gemini and Aquarius have strong feelings about what you are and are not doing. Watch what you eat, for best results in health and work matters. Lily white is your color. Lucky lottery: 4, 13, 22, 31, 40, 49.

Thursday, June 5 (Moon in Gemini)   The new moon is born in your sixth house and illuminates health and employment matters. Gemini and Libra figure prominently. A new assignment that you believe you are about to receive can prove stimulating. People are terribly conscious of their aches and pains. Champagne is your color; your lucky number is 6.

Friday, June 6 (Moon in Gemini to Cancer 7:02 a.m.) Consult business partners and your mate before making any vital decision involving them. You can improve sharing and cooperating under prevailing aspects. A Cancer and another Capricorn have important roles. Make the most of the leisure time you spend with loved ones. Sage green is your color; your lucky number is 8.

Saturday, June 7 (Moon in Cancer)   Your marital state and other partnerships continue to top your agenda. Scorpio and Scorpio-ruled matters get full acceptance. Conferences can help you make up your mind on an important decision. Keep in close touch with relatives at a distance. Your winning colors are claret and olive. Lucky lottery: 1, 10, 19, 28, 37, 46.

Sunday, June 8 (Moon in Cancer to Leo 3:58 p.m.)   You can bond more closely with your beloved. Relations with your in-laws and with the friends of your mate can be improved. Your affections are easily stirred today when you are with family. Pisces and Cancer-ruled matters get much acceptance. Old rose is your color; your lucky number is 3.

Monday, June 9 (Moon in Leo)   Today is favorable for working on accumulations of money, energy, and time. See how you can increase your sense of security by improving savings, insurance, and investments. Buy items that help you perform chores better. Strawberry is your color; your number is 7.

Tuesday, June 10 (Moon in Leo)   Leo is empowered to help you decide on changes, improvements, and corrections. Mull these over in your mind and then discuss them before taking definite action. It's a good day for planning annual field days or sports competitions, and for introducing children to libraries. Hot combination numbers: 9 and 3.

Wednesday, June 11 (Moon in Leo to Virgo 3:43 a.m.)   Virgo-ruled matters are there for you to deal with: travel, what you have been perking for yourself at a distance, all long-range matters, as well as imported items you may wish to acquire. You can bring a lot of self-discipline into these situations. Your color is reddish-orange. Lucky lottery: 2, 11, 20, 29, 38, 47.

Thursday, June 12 (Moon in Virgo)   Keep on the go today. A long drive into a rural area would help clear away that sense of being surrounded and hemmed in. A change of pace and pattern, and some new scenes and new people will do you a world of good at this time of year. Your winning colors are maroon and violet. Hot combination numbers: 4 and 3.

Friday, June 13 (Moon in Virgo to Libra 4:35 p.m.) You can be somewhat dissatisfied with the local scene. It may be difficult to identify with the ideas of local people. Your mind can be far away, traveling in unusual and fascinating places. You handle long-range and long-distance interests well under these aspects. Azure is your color; your lucky number is 6.

Saturday, June 14 (Moon in Libra) Libra takes a strong stand in career matters. There is a bridge to be traveled between domestic requirements and the demands of your career. Seeing people with whom you work on a day such as this could be a mistake. Your personality is crying out for new ideas and new faces. Lucky lottery: 8, 17, 26, 35, 44, 2.

Sunday, June 15 (Moon in Libra) Career concerns can win out over any other interest under prevailing aspects. Gather your wits about you and the things you will require to do your work well tomorrow. By warming up to your career and place of business, you will be in a better frame of mind for pleasing your employer. Your lucky number is 1.

Monday, June 16 (Moon in Libra to Scorpio 3:51 a.m.) This is the day you have been waiting for. You can relax, see people, move about, and appreciate the advance of summer's aromas and scenes. Fine for rushing the season a bit and getting in a swim. Scorpio and Pisces are in your corner. Your winning colors are ecru and olive; your lucky number is 5.

Tuesday, June 17 (Moon in Scorpio) Friendships make your day. Group activities, church/club membership and participation, and opportunities to really express your personality and character assets are emphasized by the existing aspects. Today is fine for issuing and accepting social invitations. Your lucky colors are saffron and titian gold; your lucky number is 7.

Wednesday, June 18 (Moon in Scorpio to Sagittarius 11:39 a.m.)   Today is fine for relaxation, beach and water activities, and spending quality time with your children and senior citizen relatives. It's a day for expressing your true feelings with those you love, respect, and need. There is a sense of wanting to be better permeating your being. Lucky lottery: 9, 18, 27, 36, 45, 6.

Thursday, June 19 (Moon in Sagittarius)   Sagittarius has the fascinating ideas at this time and is full of encouragement and inspiration for you. You complete projects well today and deal in epilogues and follow-up chores. Today is fine for filing papers where they belong and can be found easily when you need them. Pinks are in. Hot combination numbers: 2 and 6.

Friday, June 20 (Moon in Sagittarius to Capricorn 4:02 p.m.)   Today's full moon illuminates the past and ways in which you might extract additional gains and profits from matters you ordinarily would consider finished and closed. Keep in touch with people you have been thinking about lately. You can regenerate old ties and ideals. Silver is your color; your lucky number is 4.

Saturday, June 21 (Moon in Capricorn)   Today and tomorrow constitute a power period. They bring you to your monthly lunar-cycle high, when you can figure out ways to get what you want. Success is always within your grasp on these powerful days. If you remain cheerful and self-confident, you can win big. Lucky lottery: 6, 15, 24, 33, 42, 51.

Sunday, June 22 (Moon in Capricorn to Aquarius 6:21 p.m.)   Continue yesterday's big drive forward. You are strongly aware of your full potential now and will impress others with your self-reliance and strength of purpose. Push your natural wisdom, patience, perseverance, and endurance and the world will accept you for the strong force you are. Your lucky number is 8.

Monday, June 23 (Moon in Aquarius)   You can have your way in money matters now. Your earning power is high and what you own is increasing in value. You can drive hard financial bargains. An Aquarius and a Gemini are on the scene. Financial discussions and business decisions are represented. Your number is 3.

Tuesday, June 24 (Moon in Aquarius to Pisces 8:09 p.m.)   Joint efforts and investments can be speeded up. Talks with your banker and broker will put you in a better bargaining position. It is often yourself with whom you are bargaining under this sky spectacle. Don't let organizational matters get in the way of your purposes. Hot combination numbers: 5 and 2.

Wednesday, June 25 (Moon in Pisces)   Pisces is nearby and can be depended on in everyday routines and schedules. Siblings and neighbors are ready to help you. Studies, hobbies, communications, and transportation matters are on the table. You narrow your sights now and zero in on split-second opportunities. Sky blue is your color. Lucky lottery: 7, 16, 25, 34, 43, 3.

Thursday, June 26 (Moon in Pisces to Aries 10:38 p.m.)   Attend to immediate and pressing matters. Your learning processes are strongly stimulated. You are more aware than most people of what you don't know and this is the kind of day when you take steps to acquire this knowledge. Register for a course of study, or perhaps take one via TV. Your lucky number is 9.

Friday, June 27 (Moon in Aries)   Aries may believe that you should be doing more and different things. Ambitious ideas and projects are dangled before you, but in the end, you are going to stick to your own convictions. Do this without putting out any of this Aries fiery enthusiasm for breaking new ground, however risky. Your lucky number is 2.

Saturday, June 28 (Moon in Aries)   Suggestions and recommendations abound as you discuss family and residential matters with a fire sign (Aries, Leo, and/or Sagittarius). It's the time of the year when people like Earth's vegetables and flowers are pressing forward and upward. Dining out this evening will help. Crimson is your color. Lucky lottery: 4, 13, 22, 31, 40, 49.

Sunday, June 29 (Moon in Aries to Taurus 2:23 a.m.) You can bond more closely with your beloved and with your children. You are in the mood to be loved and to love passionately in return. There is an aura of romance all about you and you gain in the eyes of others who see you in this happy mood. Spread goodwill far and wide. Your number is 6.

Monday, June 30 (Moon in Taurus) Taurus and Leo are on the scene. You are warming up to the idea of some improved savings plan and wiser investments. You feel in the pink, pleased with yourself and with your love life. You are very earthy in the clutches now. The evening is excellent for enjoying happy talk. Wear peach accessories. Your number is 1.

JULY 1997

Tuesday, July 1 (Moon in Taurus to Gemini 7:35 a.m.) Gemini and Aquarius will impact your day. Get adequate rest and relaxation at a time when fatigue can set in early. Less fat, less sodium, and less sugar is the new All-American theme. The work that must be done today can have a way of slipping out of control. Your winning colors are olive and emerald; your lucky number is 1.

Wednesday, July 2 (Moon in Gemini) Conversation should be as meaningful as possible under these aspects. Choose your words carefully, so that coworkers don't get the wrong impression. Work done amid distractions of any kind can prove of small avail now. Libra comes front and center. Your color is kelly green. Lucky lottery: 3, 12, 21, 30, 39, 48.

Thursday, July 3 (Moon in Gemini to Cancer 2:33 p.m.) Know what a child, not in sight, is doing. Take pains that dangerous firecrackers aren't falling into the hands of the very young. Some say that you are taking your obligations to your employer too seriously. Protect your knees at work and play. Hot combination numbers: 5 and 2.

Friday, July 4 (Moon in Cancer)   The new moon is born in your seventh house and illuminates marriage and other partnerships, the fine art of sharing and of cooperating, and all joint endeavors and joint investments. There is enlightenment for you in pleasing your peers. Your winning color is silver. Trust a Cancer and another Capricorn. Your number is 7.

Saturday, July 5 (Moon in Cancer to Leo 11:45 p.m.)   There's a strong sense of unity characterizing today. The desire to get along permeates you and those sharing some of these hours. Marriage and other partnerships can make demands, but in no way overwhelm you. A Scorpio and a Pisces are in the picture. Lucky lottery: 9, 18, 27, 36, 45, 3.

Sunday, July 6 (Moon in Leo)   Let Leo tell the story. There are good trends in learning from listening, permitting another to encourage and inspire you, and finding more acceptance for self-centered types. Read your financial pages for pointers on how the economy may be slowing down. Your color is red; your lucky number is 2.

Monday, July 7 (Moon in Leo)   Lavender and orchid are your colors. It's a favorable day for pushing budgeting, warring on waste, increasing savings, and discussing new investments with your broker. Aries and Sagittarius may be consulted. Generosity will be rewarded as your experiences are recycled. Your lucky number is 6.

Tuesday, July 8 (Moon in Leo to Virgo 11:22 a.m.)   Accumulated energies, money, and free time are all going to pay off under the prevailing aspects. You can give extra thought to decisions that have to be made. Duties, responsibilities, and obligations can be evaluated. A wise old person has much to tell you, but you must ask. Hot combination numbers: 8 and 2.

Wednesday, July 9 (Moon in Virgo)   Trust Virgo to know where to go. Fine trends exist in traveling together, getting in some unusual shopping and dining ventures, and enjoying the feeling of having gotten away. Push long-range and long-distance interests. Changes are being speeded up in your horoscope. Beige is your color. Lucky lottery: 1, 10, 19, 28, 37, 46.

Thursday, July 10 (Moon in Virgo)   Keep on the go, seeing people, taking in the changing scene, and enjoying the feeling that you are in control. Nothing about the day will bore you. You are full of get-up-and-go. Buy some attractive wardrobe accessories that at another time you would consider too expensive. Hot combination numbers: 3 and 6.

Friday, July 11 (Moon in Virgo to Libra 12:21 a.m.) Libra and Gemini are in the picture. Your career can make some burdensome demands on you, but you take it all in stride. You are careful to meet all duties, responsibilities, and obligations in the best Capricorn–Saturn manner. Coral and flame red are winning colors; your lucky number is 5.

Saturday, July 12 (Moon in Libra)   Away from your job, you are still going to think a lot about it. You are conscious of additional responsibilities due to the absence of a coworker. Also, it's like you to consider non-employment ways in which you can help the vacationing ones out. Blueberry is your color. Lucky lottery: 7, 16, 25, 34, 43, 3.

Sunday, July 13 (Moon in Libra to Scorpio 12:20 p.m.)   While taking it easy, your thoughts will turn to the week ahead and ways you can advance your career. By being honest in your judgments and evaluation of coworkers, you will win praise from your employer and others in power positions. Your color is white; your lucky number is 9.

Monday, July 14 (Moon in Scorpio)   It's summer and you want to enjoy some summer activities. Beach and water will beckon to you under prevailing aspects. The water signs (Scorpio, Pisces, and Cancer) dominate. Invite a friend and his/her youngsters to accompany you.

Dining at a resort restaurant imparts the proper atmosphere for a talkfest. Your lucky number is 4.

Tuesday, July 15 (Moon in Scorpio to Sagittarius 9:02 p.m.) Friendships, group activities, and spending time with somebody who shares your hobby interests are all represented. You want to really let your back hair down today and to be with people who understand the inner or secret you. Summer is singing a special song to you. Hot combination numbers: 6 and 4.

Wednesday, July 16 (Moon in Sagittarius) Sagittarius shows up. Fine trends exist for completing a job that you haven't enjoyed doing. There is emphasis on revelations, surprises, mysteries, and glamorous people who hope you are noticing them. Orange and tangerine are your colors. Buy trinkets that appeal to you. Lucky lottery: 8, 17, 26, 35, 44, 2.

Thursday, July 17 (Moon in Sagittarius) What is happening behind the scenes will impact the day. You dislike conspiracies of any kind, especially those in government and big-business circles. You are shocked by some revelations that are developing now. It's one of those "secret cabinets of history" days. Pastels are your colors; your lucky number is 1.

Friday, July 18 (Moon in Sagittarius to Capricorn 1:45 a.m.) Today and tomorrow constitute your lunar high cycle, when things will respond to the attention you give them. Seize and hold the initiative, be optimistic and positive, and demonstrate the highest in self-confidence and self-reliance. Lead, speak, and look like a winner. Hot combination numbers: 3 and 6.

Saturday, July 19 (Moon in Capricorn) Keep pushing forward in your own interests. Speak up, air your aspirations, and let others know that you mean to make progress. Be persistent and somewhat aggressive, and stick by your guns for best results. Another Capricorn and a Virgo can understand and help. Lucky lottery: 5, 14, 23, 32, 41, 50.

Sunday, July 20 (Moon in Capricorn to Aquarius 3:29 a.m.) This can be a good money day. Aquarius knows where the money happens to be. Fine trends exist in earning power, income, special sales, and extracting self-confidence and ego from what you own. You can be more independent in your spending than usual. Burgundy and white go well together; your number is 7.

Monday, July 21 (Moon in Aquarius) Bargain hunting goes well and you can realize some minor savings that will help with your summer budget. Experienced shoppers have come to believe that if one had more shopping time, and could wander from store to store, they'd see that Peter is lower on this item and Paul on that item; your lucky number is 2.

Tuesday, July 22 (Moon in Aquarius to Pisces 4 a.m.) Take care of immediate and pressing matters first. Pisces and Virgo will differ on how you should approach your work—the former more laid back, the latter more determined and persistent. You can't go both ways; it's up to you to make the decision on everyday routines. Your lucky number is 4.

Wednesday, July 23 (Moon in Pisces) The sun makes its Leo ingress and sets up support for you in savings, investments, insurance, inheritance, and tax shelter matters. Hobbies, studies, communications, and transportation matters get strong stimulation. You will enjoy moving about your neighborhood. Lucky lottery: 6, 15, 24, 33, 42, 51.

Thursday, July 24 (Moon in Pisces to Aries 5:03 a.m.) You are warming up to travel and to the idea of getting away for a while. Yet family responsibilities can take precedence. A relative may get the drop on you by announcing an upcoming visit in your area. What you can do with impunity is buy yourself something unique. Pink is your color; your number is 8.

Friday, July 25 (Moon in Aries) Today is fine for taking steps to make a room lighter and brighter; this might be done by creating some walls of mirror. The cost of living may be inching up. You can be more daring in the way you decorate your home under the direction or suggestion of an Aries. Mauve and buff are your colors; your lucky number is 1.

Saturday, July 26 (Moon in Aries to Taurus 7:53 a.m.)   You could be seen as overly possessive in love, courtship, and romance, and in the way you devote so much time to one person at a party. One child can see you giving preferential treatment to another. What you say and how you say it is ultra-important today. Lapis is your color. Lucky lottery: 3, 12, 21, 30, 39, 48.

Sunday, July 27 (Moon in Taurus)   Make love. Write affectionate letters to a dear one at a distance. Give a party and let the children invite whomever they choose. This is a good day for entertaining newcomers in your neighborhood and for demonstrating approval, appreciation, and affection. Cherry is your color; your lucky number is 5.

Monday, July 28 (Moon in Taurus to Gemini 1:04 p.m.)   You feel pretty good about what your loved ones are doing. You want to see your mate and children occupied with projects that instruct as well as make them happy. You spread such a lot of goodwill today that at least one critic is becoming more friendly and could end up admiring you very much. Your lucky number is 9.

Tuesday, July 29 (Moon in Gemini)   Gemini and Libra are in the scenario. Schedule any minor surgery children may require before school begins. It's a day that calls for different types of food, different meals. You will enjoy shopping for food items in unusual stores—Asian, Middle Eastern, American Indian. Your winning colors are pinks and lemons. Hot combination numbers: 2 and 6.

Wednesday, July 30 (Moon in Gemini to Cancer 8:38 p.m.)   Pay attention to the health needs of senior citizens. You may feel that assistants aren't doing much work under these aspects. There are many rumors making the round of your work place. Some good bargains can be found in rather fashionable stores. Lucky lottery: 4, 13, 22, 31, 40, 49.

Thursday, July 31 (Moon in Cancer)   Today is the perfect day for joint endeavors and investments with your beloved. You can improve relationships with your in-laws under the prevailing aspects. The friends of your spouse may wish you would give them a greater feeling of acceptance. Your winning colors are seaweed, forest, and okra; your lucky number is 6.

AUGUST 1997

Friday, August 1 (Moon in Cancer)   Spend quality time with your beloved. Know what business partners have in mind even if it's necessary to ask embarrassing questions. You could feel somewhat angry over the poor performances of a partner or other coworker. Don't make plans that concern another without a full discussion. Your lucky number is 5.

Saturday, August 2 (Moon in Cancer to Leo 6:27 a.m.)   Leo makes a dramatic entrance and things seem lighter and brighter. Fine trends exist in security matters and for financial discussions that can result in more savings or a more effective war on waste and improved budgeting. You can develop wiser investments today. Mocha and white are your colors. Lucky lottery: 7, 16, 25, 34, 43, 3.

Sunday, August 3 (Moon in Leo)   The new moon will illuminate your earning power and how to increase your savings. The changes, improvements, and corrections you have been considering can be implemented under the existing aspects. Aries and Sagittarius would love to hear from you now, preferably with an invitation to visit. Your number is 9.

Monday, August 4 (Moon in Leo to Virgo 6:15 p.m.)   Some are lucky in love and others in gambling under these Mars, Jupiter, and Saturn trends. But gambling isn't for you today. Avoid all get-rich-quick schemes and make certain that other adults are not encouraging children to gamble by chatter about winning streaks. Check things out with Aquarius.

Tuesday, August 5 (Moon in Virgo)   Travel and a strong yen to get away can characterize the day. You may yearn to see some kindred spirits at a distance, knowing full well they can inspire, encourage, and guide you well. A Virgo and another Capricorn have roles to play. Long-range thinking will pay handsome dividends. Your lucky number is 6.

Wednesday, August 6 (Moon in Virgo)   If you aren't able to get away, you always can recycle an earlier trip in your memory. It's a good day for making the choice to be cheerful, bright-eyed, and pleasant. You can win over people who in the past have been critical of you. You are aware of new dimensions in some of your friendships. Lucky lottery: 8, 17, 26, 35, 44, 1.

Thursday, August 7 (Moon in Virgo to Libra 7:17 a.m.) Libra has the capacity to cheer you up. There are aspects now that suggest career advancement and personality enhancement. Talks with executives can give you a better sense of job security. Run down information on what people in your chosen field do to achieve success. Your number is 1.

Friday, August 8 (Moon in Libra)   Today is fine for pinch-hitting for a worker who is away on leave. You can please your employer a lot by getting along with difficult coworkers. Be professional at all times and don't speak sharply to an underling in front of others, for this can cause a great deal of embarrassment. Ruby and crimson are your colors; your number is 3.

Saturday, August 9 (Moon in Libra to Scorpio 7:50 p.m.)   Weekday chores can spill over into today. There can be an impression of trying to catch up, but in truth you can let things slide a bit and enjoy available friendships and joint endeavors. Relaxing at poolside or reading a book under a shade tree will help you feel that summer belongs to you. Lucky lottery: 5, 14, 23, 32, 41, 50.

Sunday, August 10 (Moon in Scorpio)   Scorpio offers you an in-depth friendship. Phone, write, and show appreciation of social opportunities and advantages. You are at home in a group or in a church or club setting; you're anxious to respond to kindness and to feel a part of the big panorama. White and gold are winning colors; your lucky number is 7.

Monday, August 11 (Moon in Scorpio)   Work will get done, but just barely, because you feel a need to socialize, to be with people who are out to enjoy themselves. Have lunch in a different restaurant and enjoy bubbling conversation. A brief walk with a friend can rid you of any sense of aloneness. Azure blue is your color; your lucky number is 2.

Tuesday, August 12 (Moon in Scorpio to Sagittarius 5:45 a.m.)   Sagittarius and Aries and all matters ruled by these signs can impact your day. You finish one job so that you can begin another, with a sense of freedom and the ability to make choices. The past and the future come together in the present. You can use your talents and skills that you wanted to demonstrate much earlier. Hot combination numbers: 4 and 7.

Wednesday, August 13 (Moon in Sagittarius)   The past isn't going away. Former experiences, failures as well as victories, impact your present thinking and future planning. Secrets, confidential matters, and the mysterious and invisible are represented today. You have strong support for completing projects. Lapis blue and turquoise are your colors. Lucky lottery: 6, 15, 24, 33, 42, 51.

Thursday, August 14 (Moon in Sagittarius to Capricorn 11:42 a.m.)   Excellent trends exist for figuring out just what is in the minds of those in charge. Fine trends exist for coping with what you aren't told. Directions may not be to the point or even accurate. This is a fine make-do day for Capricorn. Browns are your colors. Hot combination numbers: 8 and 1.

Friday, August 15 (Moon in Capricorn)   Today and tomorrow find you in your powerful lunar-cycle high when you can take charge, stand tall, and hold to your own ideas about how things should be done to result in progress. Bring things together. Hold the initiative, give direction, and zero in to any area where you see deterioration. Your lucky number is 1.

Saturday, August 16 (Moon in Capricorn to Aquarius 1:58 p.m.) Push the interests that make most sense to you at this time. Put your strong personality and character traits to work—your endurance, patience, and perseverance—and you will win big. Don't waste time talking on the phone or listening to pointless chatter. Lucky lottery: 3, 12, 21, 30, 39, 48.

Sunday, August 17 (Moon in Aquarius) Study the financial pages and any magazines you have about money and investments. You can grasp some good ideas and suggestions with big dollar signs on them under the prevailing aspects. What you learn today you can put to good use over the week ahead. Tyrian purple is your color; your lucky number is 5.

Monday, August 18 (Moon in Aquarius to Pisces 2:01 p.m.) The full moon illuminates earning power, income, and possible new sources of capital and enlightens you on cost of living matters This is a wonderful day for holding a special sale, bartering, and buying items you know you can resell later at a better price. There's always money to be made and, with the secret channels of your mind ruled by mighty Jupiter, you understand this truth. Your number is 9.

Tuesday, August 19 (Moon in Pisces) Pisces can narrow things down for you and point out what is of immediate and pressing importance. Studies, hobbies, your basic learning processes, communications, and transportation interests are all emphasized over this good day. Shop for teaching books, texts, and brochures. Your lucky number is 2.

Wednesday, August 20 (Moon in Pisces to Aries 1:45 p.m.) Write letters, make phone calls, and keep in touch with those who expect to hear from you. Siblings and neighbors will remember it all. A Scorpio and a Cancer have roles to play. Educational matters get green lights. Do what you can so that children warm up to the idea of returning to school. Orange-red is your color. Lucky lottery: 4, 13, 22, 31, 40, 49.

Thursday, August 21 (Moon in Aries)   The accent is on community interests and involvements. Your family is strongly represented, along with property and ownership matters. Good family decisions can be made in conference. Property held by more than one member of the family can be put on the market. Silvery white is your color; your lucky number is 6.

Friday, August 22 (Moon in Aries to Taurus 2:57 p.m.)   Aries and Sagittarius figure prominently. Household maintenance is accented, and the day favors getting several estimates on needed repairs. Family decisions can be made concerning the health needs of an older relative. Pinks and blues give you a choice. Write to distant relatives who would want to know what's going on. Hot combination numbers: 8 and 2.

Saturday, August 23 (Moon in Taurus)   The sun moves into Virgo and you feel more free to travel and plan a vacation. Also, you can take a long-range view of your career, professional, and allied obligations. This is a fine day for enjoying fresh, recently picked vegetables, grapes, and strawberries. Lucky lottery: 1, 10, 19, 28, 37, 46.

Sunday, August 24 (Moon in Taurus to Gemini 6:56 p.m.)   Taurus and Virgo share their earthiness with you. Your emotions are strongly stirred by this lunar transit. Approval, appreciation, and affection permeate your relationships. Winning colors are tawny and buff. Keeping in touch with loved ones at a distance brings much pleasure. Your lucky number is 3.

Monday, August 25 (Moon in Gemini)   Today is fine for health improvements, and for discussing a possible diet and exercise program with your doctor. Your work may not give your body as much exercise as it gives your brain. Walking is one of the best exercises for Capricorn, but always choose your shoes and socks carefully before walking long distances. Your number is 7.

Tuesday, August 26 (Moon in Gemini)   Talking with the right person could be helpful. A Pisces or a Scorpio is interested in what you have to say and can respond well to your suggestions and questions. A Gemini leaves you with the feeling that only a doctor should discuss health and surgery this way. Azure blue is your color; your lucky number is 9.

Wednesday, August 27 (Moon in Gemini to Cancer 4:11 a.m.) The emphasis falls on your marital state, business partnerships, joint endeavors, sharing, and the fine art of cooperating fully in important matters. A Cancer and a Virgo deliver stability and steadiness. The family may wonder why you aren't confiding your travel plans. Lucky lottery: 2, 11, 20, 29, 38, 47.

Thursday, August 28 (Moon in Cancer) You and your spouse could work out a promising joint investment under this sky spectacle. Scorpio and Pisces are impacting your day. You and a Cancer relative could buy a more expensive gift for somebody you love if you pool resources. Blueberry is your color. Hot combination numbers: 4 and 7.

Friday, August 29 (Moon in Cancer to Leo 12:19 p.m.) Your marital state, business partnerships, cooperation, sharing, and joint efforts and investments are all in the big picture. Conversations with your beloved can produce good results and help you decide a personal issue. Domestic interests get a big boost. Yellowish greens are right for you; your lucky number is 6.

Saturday, August 30 (Moon in Leo) Leo has good investment ideas under these aspects. Your color is goldenrod. It's a fine day for bringing about financial improvements, shopping in out-of-the-way places for genuine bargains, and increasing the sense of security of much older loved ones. Lucky lottery: 8, 17, 26, 35, 44, 2.

Sunday, August 31 (Moon in Leo) Aries and Sagittarius have key roles. Today is fine for discussing household maintenance and renovation with your beloved. Schedule the attainment of estimates in the week ahead. Change is a big word now and you would like to alter everything for the better—more space, more light, more comfort. Your number is 1.